OTTO THE MAGNIFICENT

OTHER BOOKS BY
John Kobler

·

THE TRIAL OF RUTH SNYDER AND JUDD GRAY

SOME LIKE IT GORY

AFTERNOON IN THE ATTIC
(illustrations by Chas. Addams)

THE RELUCTANT SURGEON:
A BIOGRAPHY OF JOHN HUNTER

LUCE: HIS TIME, LIFE AND FORTUNE

CAPONE: THE LIFE AND WORLD OF AL CAPONE

ARDENT SPIRITS: THE RISE AND FALL
OF PROHIBITION

DAMNED IN PARADISE: THE LIFE
OF JOHN BARRYMORE

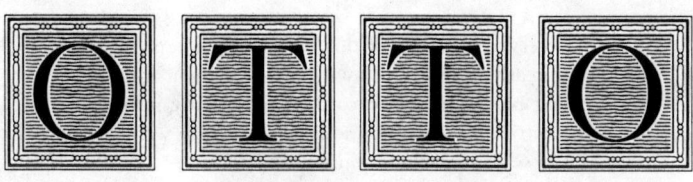

OTTO THE *M*AGNIFICENT

·

THE LIFE OF
OTTO KAHN

by

John Kobler

·

CHARLES SCRIBNER'S SONS · NEW YORK

Copyright © 1988 by Rita Stein Kobler

All rights reserved. No part of this book may be reproduced or transmitted in any form or by any means, electronic or mechanical, including photocopying, recording, or by any information storage and retrieval system, without permission in writing from the Publisher.

Charles Scribner's Sons
Macmillan Publishing Company
866 Third Avenue, New York, NY 10022
Collier Macmillan Canada, Inc.

Permissions acknowledgments appear on pages 231–32.

Library of Congress Cataloging-in-Publication Data
Kobler, John.
Otto, the magnificent: the life of Otto Kahn/by John Kobler.
p. cm.
Bibliography: p.
Includes index.
ISBN 0-684-19033-8
1. Kahn, Otto Hermann, 1867–1934. 2. Philanthropists—United
States—Biography. 3. Capitalists and financiers—United States—
Biography. 4. Kahn, Otto Hermann, 1867–1934—Art patronage.
I. Title.
HV28.K32K63 1989
361.7'4'0924—dc19
[B]
88-28243
CIP

Macmillan books are available at special discounts for bulk purchases for sales promotions, premiums, fund-raising, or educational use. For details, contact:

Special Sales Director
Macmillan Publishing Company
866 Third Avenue
New York, NY 10022

Book design by Debby Jay

10 9 8 7 6 5 4 3 2 1

Printed in the United States of America

FOR RITA,
my collaborator, my love

Ot·to (ot′ō; Ger. ôt′ō), *n.* a male given name; from a Germanic word meaning "rich."
The Random House Dictionary of the English Language

Contents

Acknowledgments	*xi*
1. The Strategist	3
2. The Kahns of Mannheim	6
3. America	15
4. A "Two-Dollar Broker"	23
5. Banking and the "Art Job"	29
6. Cedar Court	35
7. Harriman Triumphant	44
8. The Diamond Horseshoe	51
9. Ballet	63
10. Kahn vs. Hammerstein	70
11. England Beckons	77
12. War	86
13. European Mission	104
14. Oheka	111
15. St. Peter's, St. Bartholomew's, St. John's	120

16. Adventures in Theater	*127*
17. Paul Robeson	*136*
18. *The Miracle*	*140*
19. Of Parties, Premieres, and Grand Tours	*146*
20. Patronage	*160*
21. Women	*166*
22. Mussolini, Harding, and Hoover	*175*
23. From Conquest to Crash	*185*
24. Depression	*194*
25. Finale	*199*
26. "I Shall Die a Jew"	*206*
Source Notes	*213*
Bibliography	*223*
Index	*233*

Acknowledgments

From 1910 to the end of his life Otto Hermann Kahn preserved copies of virtually every letter he wrote and every letter written to him, along with enough newspaper and magazine clippings about his activities and himself to fill ten volumes. After his death, his son Gilbert gave the Kahn Papers (KP, as they are identified in my source notes) to the William Seymour Theatre Collection, Princeton University. I am deeply indebted to the curator of the collection, Mary Ann Jensen, and to her assistant, Andros Thomson, for their endless patience in guiding me through that research forest.

I am equally grateful to Margaret Ryan (Mrs. John Barry Ryan), Kahn's last surviving child, who shared with me memories of her father.

I thank Robert Tuggle, director of the Archives of the Metropolitan Opera, for access to correspondence of the Otto Kahn regime.

The aid and constructive suggestions that I received from my literary agent, Julian Bach, cannot be measured in material terms alone, and I bow to him. My editor, Edward T. Chase, merits my gratitude for his encouragement and support. I am also deeply indebted to his assistant, Charles Flowers, for his unfailing patience.

I wish to thank Louis Miller for his translations from the German of letters and miscellaneous literature.

The Mannheim Stadtarchiv under the curatorship of Friedrich Teutsch provided me with detailed information on the Kahn family background.

I owe a particular debt to my wife, Rita, for the invaluable help she rendered in correcting my manuscript and, generally, saving me from errors of fact and expression.

Finally, I am greatly indebted to the following people who helped me in innumerable ways: Benjamin J. Buttenwieser, Matilda ("Goldie") Clough, Lorraine Conroy, Helen Dartt, Lois Densky, Christof Eberstadt, Rowena Rutherford Farrar, Edith Friedlander, Mrs. Charles Gleaves, Earl Goodman, Sidney Gruson, Guy Gurney, William Hammerstein, Ursula Heil, Alfred Hubay, Edward Jablonski, Robert S. Johnson, Mrs. Gilbert Kahn, Burkhard Laugwitz, Ezra G. Levin, Ranald Lorimer, Irving Mariash, Abraham J. Peck, Ellen Pollock, Percy Preston, George Punton, Priscilla Roberts, Paul Robeson, Jr., Cecil Russell, John Barry Ryan III, Dorothy Schiff, Professor Ernst Schulin, Elizabeth Wansbrough, Edward M. M. Warburg, Elvira Williams, Elisabeth Woods.

OTTO THE MAGNIFICENT

The Strategist

The situation had elements of a Feydeau farce. The scene was the senior partners' room of Kuhn, Loeb & Co., the nation's second most powerful private bankers after J. P. Morgan. Some sixty feet long and forty feet wide, the room took up nearly all of the second floor of the firm's twenty-two-story headquarters on the corner of William and Pine streets. Each of the four senior partners received his clients at a desk in a corner of the oblong expanse, out in the open, visible to everybody in the room, with a small office behind for negotiations requiring greater privacy. The southwest corner belonged to Jerome Hanauer, the northwest to Mortimer Schiff, the southeast to Felix Warburg, and the northeast to the commander in chief of the firm, Otto Hermann Kahn, who had prepared the master coup that would excite Wall Street and the entire railroad industry.

By Kahn's choice it took place on a Saturday morning in April of 1928. Saturday, *Shabbas* (the Jewish Sabbath), was then a half working day, but while the senior partners were all Jewish, none was Orthodox, and each could therefore work or play as he chose. According to a house rule, however, at least one senior partner had to be on hand throughout the morning, and they took turns. The arrangement perfectly suited Kahn's stratagem, for Saturday was the quietest, least crowded time of the workweek, and so he opted for a Saturday convenient to the principals in his scheme.

The challenge Otto Kahn faced was to conciliate two warring railroad magnates, Leonor Fresnel Loree and William Wallace Atterbury, presidents, respectively, of the Delaware & Hudson and the Pennsylvania, both burly six-footers in their sixties. Loree's nose was disfigured by a skin disease.

At the time there existed four major Eastern railroad systems running between New York and Chicago—the Pennsylvania, the New York Central, the Baltimore & Ohio, and the New York, Chicago & St. Louis. Loree, whom ill-informed Wall Streeters dismissed as "a big man with a jerkwater road," proposed to create a fifth system in competition with the four. To that end he added to his holdings enough shares of the Lehigh Valley, the Wabash, the Western Maryland, and the Chicago & St. Louis to obtain control of those lines. Atterbury vigorously opposed the five-system plan. He threatened to file a protest with the Interstate Commerce Commission and to take other dire measures against the interloper. What distressed Kuhn, Loeb was that both adversaries were long-standing clients. They could not allow themselves to side against either. Otto Kahn, his colleagues agreed, had the technical and economic ken, the diplomacy, the knack for mediation, and the personal charm to restore peace between the two railroad titans.

Shortly before ten A.M., the hour fixed by Kahn, Loree went from his headquarters at 32 Nassau Street to Kuhn, Loeb, only a few steps away. Kahn, welcoming him warmly, walked him into his oak-paneled little office, asked him to wait a few minutes, and left, closing the door behind him. Shortly after ten, again in accordance with Kahn's design, Atterbury arrived from the Pennsylvania Station building and was shown into Mortimer Schiff's office. Neither Loree nor Atterbury was as yet aware of the other's presence. Kahn, a David between two Goliaths, now began moving from one to the other and back again, feeling each man out for any signs of a concession, striving to persuade each to yield a little, and in the end to renounce a destructive competition in favor of a lucrative alliance.

Kahn cut an appealing figure. Small, light-brown-eyed and ruddy-cheeked, his normal expression a gentle smile, he walked with a springy step, his spine erect, his stride soldierly, a carriage that he himself ascribed to his training as a young cavalryman in his native Germany. A slight Germanic accent lingered in his speech, mingled with the broad vowels and clipped consonants of upper-class England, where he had lived for three years. His hair was silvery white, and his mustache waxed to fine points. He wore pearl-gray spats, and the vests beneath his impeccably tailored jackets were trimmed with white piping. Spruce as a Savile Row dandy, a fresh rose in his lapel, he was one of New York's best-dressed men. Lewis Strauss, a later Kuhn,

Loeb partner and chairman of the Atomic Energy Commission, described Kahn as "the Lorenzo de Medici of his day . . . with an air of detachment from anything as plebeian as money."

The Loree-Atterbury conflict was not Kahn's only concern that Saturday morning. In Jerome Hanauer's office smoldering like Vesuvius, the Metropolitan Opera's bulky, irascible general manager, Giulio Gatti-Casazza, waited to confront Kahn, the president and chairman of the board of the Met, with a repetition of complaints. The stage was too short and shallow, the scenery warehouse too far from the theater. There were no rehearsal rooms for ballet, chorus, and orchestra, and too many seats in the side sections provided only a partial view. Felix Warburg's office was fragrant with the presence of a soprano whose identity and purpose the discretion of Kahn's colleagues has obscured. Thus, pulled in four directions, Kahn exercised his wizardry as a conciliator, a mediator, and an expositor of crystalline lucidity.

Gatti-Casazza left placated by the renewal of Kahn's promise to build him a new opera house. The smile illuminating the face of the departing soprano indicated that whatever she wanted she got.

There remained the contending railroad tycoons. At a moment when Kahn considered the psychological climate propitious, he brought them together. The three men now reexamined every facet of the issue. Was there to be the five-system network that Loree's ambition hankered for, or Atterbury's four systems? Toward one P.M., three hours after they had entered Kuhn, Loeb, a spectacular solution seemed likely. Subject to the agreement of his board, Atterbury offered to buy Loree's holdings for $102 million. There would be no fifth system. Diplomacy had prevailed. It was one of Otto Kahn's greatest achievements.

The Kahns of Mannheim

"God be praised that I am back again in my beloved Mannheim!" Mozart wrote to his father on November 12, 1778. ". . . Since I came here I have not been able to lunch home once, as there is a regular scramble to have me. In a word, Mannheim loves me as much as I love Mannheim."

During the four months he spent in the city with his mother, seeking to obtain a court appointment from the music-loving Elector Karl Theodor of the Palatinate, Mozart found the Mannheim orchestra "excellent and very strong. . . . They can produce fine music."

Under the auspices of Karl Theodor, himself a skilled musician who played several instruments, the Mannheim orchestra became one of the largest and most accomplished in Europe. A group of German composers affiliated with it, the "Mannheim School," figured among the precursors of classical symphonic and chamber music. In 1778 Mozart began a series of six sonatas for piano and violin (K. 301–306), the "Mannheim Sonatas," dedicated to the Elector's wife, but they failed to win him a court appointment. Some of his greatest operas were performed in Mannheim's celebrated National Theater not long after he wrote them. Johann Christian Bach, son of Johann Sebastian Bach, also visited Mannheim and wrote two operas for the court, *Temistocles* in 1772 and *Lucio Silla* in 1776.

Karl Theodor did not confine his patronage to music, though music predominated. It embraced all the arts, science, industry, and commerce. In or near the town that Goethe described as "friendly, cheerful, and fair,"* nestling between the Neckar and the Rhine, twelve miles southeast of Heidelberg, he laid out gardens modeled after those of Versailles, built imposing official structures, a winter and a summer palace, theaters, and the finest Baroque church in the Palatinate. Goethe was enthralled by the Hall of Antiquities in the Mannheim Academy of Art, famous throughout Europe for its reproductions of Greco-Roman statuary, and stood for hours gazing at the Apollo Belvedere, the Dying Gladiator, Castor and Pollux, and the Laocoön. "I did not yet know," he wrote in his autobiography, "how impossible it is to give at once an account of a sight so full of pleasure."

In January 1782, Schiller, then serving as a surgeon to a regiment garrisoned in Stuttgart, went AWOL to attend the premiere of his first play, *Die Räuber*, at the National Theater. After a second flight from the army he remained in Mannheim for two years, employed as a writer by the theater, which produced his next two plays, *Fiesco* and *Kabale und Liebe*.

Along with its cultural expansion, Mannheim achieved prominence in the worlds of banking, merchandising, and manufacturing. In 1816 Baron Karl Drais von Sauerbronn, the chief forester of Baden-Württemberg, devised the first bicycle in order to speed up his tours of inspection. Variously called the "draisine," the "hobbyhorse," and the "dandy horse," it lacked pedals and had to be propelled by the rider's feet thrusting against the ground until he came to a declivity and could simply let it roll. Different versions of the contraption enjoyed popularity among the young blades of England and America, hence "dandy horse."

From 1859 on, the Heinrich Lanz Company of Mannheim manufactured and exported agricultural machinery, and in 1916 one of its engineers, Fritz Huber, built the first "Lanz Bulldog," better known outside Germany as the bulldozer.

In 1885 another Mannheimer, Karl Benz, invented the automobile, a three-wheeler with an electric ignition, differential gears, a four-stroke gasoline engine, and a maximum speed of ten miles per hour.

Thus, Mannheim acquired a dual character as a major center of both commerce and culture. The career opportunities that its rapidly increasing industrialization offered attracted a myriad of new residents. The population in 1870 was 40,000; by the turn of the century it had reached 100,000.

---

* In his epic poem, *Hermann und Dorothea*.

Among the Jewish families who settled in Mannheim toward the middle of the nineteenth century were the Kahns, and, in the local tradition, they combined to a marked degree financial acumen with a love for the arts. The family fortune got a modest start in 1826 in Stebbach, a farming village thirty-seven miles southeast of Mannheim. There, Otto Kahn's paternal grandparents, Michael Benedikt and Franziska Kahn, converted part of their small house into a workroom for the processing of bed feathers; that is, they collected, sorted, and cleaned goose feathers with which to stuff the quilts that Germans slept under—and still do—in preference to a top sheet and blankets.

Four sons were born to the Kahns in Stebbach: Bernhard in 1827, Hermann two years after, Emil in 1832, and Leopold in 1841. As the feather business prospered, Michael built a factory close to home, then, in 1854, moved with his family to Mannheim, where he enlarged his operations still further. The streets at the center of the city were laid out on a grid pattern somewhat like those of mid-Manhattan, each block designated by a number and a letter. The Kahns occupied house No. 9, S1, transferring later to more opulent quarters near the National Theater.*

In 1848, drastic crop failures, together with the suppression of liberals and nationalists, precipitated uprisings all over Europe, none more violent than those in Germany. Like many young Palatine liberal activists, twenty-one-year-old Bernhard and his brother Emil, a firebrand though only sixteen, fled the police and were sentenced to death in absentia. They managed to reach America, where they established business contacts that would later prove valuable. Bernhard worked as a bank clerk, and in 1854 in Albany, New York, he became a naturalized citizen. The records do not indicate how Emil fared, but probably their father had given both brothers money before they left Germany. They came home twelve years later, following the Baden amnesty—Bernhard as the representative of an American bank—and swore allegiance to the new government.

Among other prominent members of Mannheim's Jewish community were Ferdinand Eberstadt, a merchant originally from the nearby city of Worms, and his wife, Sara Zelie Seligmann. They had three daughters, each a striking beauty: Emma Stephanie, the firstborn, then Elizabeth, and lastly Maria Johanna. On October 17, 1860, a fortnight before her twentieth birthday, Bernhard Kahn married

---

* In 1945 a series of bombing raids reduced both houses, along with most of Mannheim, to ruins.

Emma Eberstadt. They made an odd couple: Emma progressive to a degree that shocked her milieu, pert, vivacious, quick-witted; Bernhard sobersided, upright, dry. Of the eight children they produced within the next sixteen years at the rate of one every two years, a waggish kinsman quipped: "Only every other child was Bernhard's."

When Michael Kahn died six months after the marriage, Bernhard and Emil assumed the management of the feather factory, applying what they had learned about American industrial and commercial methods. On August 12, 1867, they undertook a new project. The *Neue Badische Landeszeitung* announced the opening of M. Kahn & Sons' Bank at Theaterstrasse 5, 82, 11. Two years later the brothers Hermann and Leopold launched a branch bank in Frankfurt. A third bank followed in Mannheim in 1873 under the partnership of Bernhard and Emil.

As Mannheim expanded, the liberal Bernhard Kahn exerted a marked influence on its political life, and for twenty-six years he remained a prestigious member of the city council. Philanthropist and humanitarian, he was the champion of numerous civic causes. These were pursuits that, together with banking and generous donations to the performing arts, his fourth child, Otto, would follow on a monumental scale.

The Kahns exemplified the duality of their city, devoting themselves with equal ardor to both finance and the arts. The paintings, the sculpture, the rows upon rows of books that filled their home reflected cultivated tastes, and the friends they entertained numbered many accomplished musicians, painters, poets, and playwrights. They held *conversaziones* at which participants would learnedly debate the merits of the world's greatest artists. There were private piano and violin recitals. Both the Kahns and the Eberstadts belonged to the Brahms Club, gathering frequently to study and perform the master's works.

Music was the Kahns' chief delight. They seldom missed a concert or an opera at the National Theater. The children, educated chiefly by private tutors, were exposed to music early. Otto could play the piano, the violin, and the cello before he was eleven. Years later, as chairman of New York's Metropolitan Opera Company, he often quoted lines from a minor German poet, Johann Gottfried Seume (1763–1810):

> *Wo man singt, da lass dich ruhig nieder;*
> *Böse Menschen haben keine Lieder.*
> (Where someone sings, there you can lie back in peace,
> For evil men have no songs.)

Felix Paul ("Uncle Fe"), Otto's youngest brother and the only sibling for whom he retained a profound affection, played the violin so well that he might have won success on the concert stage. Robert August, the third child, did become a composer and pianist, of whom Clara Schumann would write in her diary for October 5, 1887 (Robert was then twenty-two): "I played with Koning [Johan Naret-Koning, a Dutch violinist] a violin sonata by Kahn that gave me great pleasure as nothing by younger composers in a long time. There is a passion, warmth, loveliness; excellent work. All in all a piece that one would gladly play again. . . ."

Emma Kahn loved most her firstborn child, Franz Michael, who would distinguish himself as a lawyer and writer on jurisprudence. Her favoritism may have been one of the several reasons why Otto Hermann, craving supremacy as he did in everything, grew to dislike his siblings with the exception of Felix Paul. Emma's second child, plain-faced Clara Maria, incurred stinging sarcasms from her prideful mother because of her physical imperfections. When, as she dressed for her social debut, the family cook cried, "Isn't she beautiful!" Emma exasperatedly muttered: "Yes—from behind."

Franziska Elisabeth ("Lili") and Hedwig, children numbers five and eight, were as attractive and intelligent as any parent could wish. Hedwig married a Swiss-Italian financier, Raymond Pollack. They lived in London and adopted a girl who, as Ellen Pollock, became an illustrious actress and director, a friend of George Bernard Shaw, and a professor at the Royal Academy of Dramatic Art. *Who's Who in the Theatre* devoted four columns to her career.

Lili, an ethereally lovely creature, whose portrait Edward Burne-Jones drew, married Felix Deutsch, an executive of the mighty Allgemeine Elektrizitäts-Gesellschaft (General Electricity Company), and became intimately associated with Walter Rathenau, its president as well as a social philosopher, whom right-wing, anti-Semitic fanatics assassinated.

Paul Friedrich, the sixth child, was a born loser. He studied a diversity of subjects but could not bring himself to choose any one profession. Through his brother-in-law Felix Deutsch he got his first job at the age of twenty-nine, that of a minor executive in A.E.G.'s Berlin headquarters. He left after two years to become secretary to the playwright Gerhart Hauptmann and lived in Hauptmann's home in Silesia. While visiting Athens as a tourist in 1907 he met an attractive woman named Euphrosyne. They married the following year and had three children, Elsa, Gertrude, and Nora, but since his wife did not wish to live in Germany, Paul became—again through the intercession of Felix Deutsch—the manager of the A.E.G. Athens branch. But employed or unemployed, Paul Kahn always found himself in financial trouble.

The Kahns were nonpracticing Jews. They rarely set foot in a synagogue; nor did they observe the prescribed rituals; and they ignored the high holy days. "An intelligent man," said Bernhard Kahn, "can be neither Jewish, Catholic, nor Protestant." When Robert Kahn was admitted to the Prussian Academy of Arts as a professor of music, he was required to state his religion on a personnel form. He wrote: "None." Many German Jews expediently converted outright to Christianity, for despite the passage of the so-called Emancipation Act of 1871, which decreed economic and political equality for Jews, it was never fully implemented. While rich, educated Jews like the Kahns owned banks, department stores, and factories, and could enter professions formerly barred to them, social equality was another matter. No enactment could abolish bigotry.

Otto Kahn professed in later life to regret the absence of religious training during his boyhood. "It had the natural and irreparable effect," he declared in that orotund vein characteristic of his voluminous writings and speeches, "of preventing me from feeling that personal concern and taking that serious interest in Jewish affairs which I might as a matter of course be assumed to possess."

Otto Hermann was born on February 21, 1867. His early formal schooling was sketchy. He did not complete the Gymnasium (grammar school) and never got a university degree. Private tutoring, which his parents preferred, filled some of the lacunae. An incessant reader and writer, he poured forth, in addition to essays, poems, and stories, two five-act dramas in blank verse. His mother urged him to burn them. When Otto was sixteen, his father, having resolved that he join the family banking affairs, found him an apprenticeship in a small Karlsruhe bank. His principal duties consisted of fetching beer and sausages for his superiors, cleaning inkwells, and stamping letters. "Let me tell you," he recounted toward the end of his career, "how and why I got my first promotion in business: The firm . . . used to send out hundreds of circulars daily. In the somewhat primitive circumstances of that day and place sponges for the wetting of stamps were an unknown luxury. The process employed was the natural one of licking. From a sheet of one hundred stamps you tore off a row of ten, passed your tongue over the back of the row and then, by a deft manipulation, dispatched ten envelopes.

"Those of us sitting in a line were engaged for a certain period each day in that proceeding. By dint of strenuous application, I soon became an adept at the job and accomplished the triumph of holding the office record for speed in licking stamps, while yet observing the requirements of neatness and accuracy in placing each stamp straight and square in its proper place in the upper-right-hand corner of the envelope.

"Two or three times I noticed our 'boss' standing near the place where we worked, but I had no idea that the—to me—great man would deign to observe our humble activity. After a while, he called me before him and imparted to me the joyous news that I was promoted out of my turn, in recognition of the zeal, energy and accurateness with which I had accomplished the functions of stamp-licker.

"This little episode was, and has remained, a valuable lesson to me. . . ."

He told Bertie Charles Forbes, founder of *Forbes* magazine: "It was a useful, salutary training for it taught discipline and order. One must learn to obey before being fit to command. It instilled a proper sense of place and emphasized that the most humble of duties must be performed conscientiously and without any loss of self-respect. . . ."

Thus spoke his father's son. The paternal inheritance manifested itself, too, when he accompanied a millionaire banker to a performance of *Tristan und Isolde* at the Karlsruhe opera house. "I hate the arrogance of wealth," he declared years later. "I hate the man who has a feeling of superiority over others because he is richer than they. But there was one time when I felt like a plutocrat and while I have been a fairly successful man, I never felt so rich as I did that day. . . . It gave me something that lasted me always but the feeling of superiority came from my sense of superiority over my companion. . . . Instead of listening to the beautiful music, he immediately fell asleep, and even snored. My youthful scorn for that contemptible creature at my side can only be imagined."

As he approached his twentieth year and the compulsory draft, he decided to volunteer. He enrolled in the Mainz Hussars, headquartered near Mannheim, committing himself to one year's service. The experience left him with contradictory traits: a stiff, straight-backed carriage and an abhorrence of militarism.

Upon his discharge, eager to know something of the non-German world, and having embraced banking as a career, he asked his Karlsruhe employer to recommend him to a London bank. He left Mannheim forever in 1890 and within a year had succeeded to the vice-managership of the Deutsche Bank's London branch.

He was an attractive young man with brown hair and a hussar's mustache, later shortened, the points upstanding and waxed, sartorially impeccable in silk high hat and cutaway. He never entirely lost his German accent, but soon combined it with a clipped British one. His speech, his manner, were subdued, reserved, courtly. He smiled more readily than he laughed. He shared lodgings with Paul M. Warburg, Felix Warburg's brother and grandson of Moritz Warburg, who headed M. M. Warburg of Hamburg, a private banking house dating from the early eighteenth century. Through a fascinating family connection the doors to the brightest, most artistic, most bohemian circles of London opened to Kahn. The connection was his beautiful aunt Elizabeth Lewis, née Eberstadt (later Lady George Lewis).

Of Sir George Henry Lewis, a Sephardic Jew, the leading solicitor of the Victorian and Edwardian eras, Oscar Wilde observed: "Brilliant. Formidable. Concerned in every case in England. Oh—he knows all about us, and he forgives us all."

And according to the rakish Edward VII, whose friend and adviser in matters involving the royal mistresses Lewis became: "He is the one man in England who should write his memoirs, but of course he never can." Sir George never could without exposing the scandalous secrets, to which he was privy, of literary and theatrical celebrities, millionaires and aristocrats, and the luminaries of the court itself.

Elizabeth Lewis happily welcomed her personable nephew from Mannheim, and at 88 Portland Place, the mansion where she presided over a glittering salon, he was a frequent guest, mingling with such notable figures as Oscar Wilde, William S. Gilbert and Sir Arthur Sullivan, Lillie Langtry, Edward Burne-Jones, James McNeill Whistler, John Singer Sargent (who painted portraits of both Elizabeth and Sir George), Ellen Terry, Ignace Jan Paderewski (who gave his first private recital at the Lewises').

After his aunt's stimulating salons there was the joy of the theaters, more of them than in any other city except perhaps Paris, some hundred music halls, a good many of them clustered around Leicester Square, including the Empire, "queen of the music halls" and the mecca of fast livers. Kahn's love of music found abundant satisfaction in Queen's Hall, seating 3,000 people; in Royal Albert Hall next to it, inaugurated by Queen Victoria in 1871; in the smaller St. George's

Hall; and Piccadilly's St. James Hall, the last two ideal for piano, violin, and chamber music recitals.

But while Kahn rejoiced in these pleasures, he allowed nothing to divert him from his duties at the Deutsche Bank. His ready grasp of financial arcana, his attention to detail, his calm, soothing comportment aroused the admiration of both his fellow employees and his employers. His assimilation, save for a lingering German accent, was soon complete. In dress, manner, and attitude he was the very model of a modern Englishman, and he became Her Majesty's naturalized subject with every intention of making England his permanent home.

In 1893, however, Kahn's abilities were drawn to the notice of Edgar (later Sir Edgar) Speyer, a partner in the ancient German-Jewish international banking house of Speyer & Co. Speyer offered him a position as an arbitrage* clerk in the firm's New York office. Reluctant to leave his beloved England, to which he promised himself he would return in any event, yet open to new experiences, he accepted, and in the summer or 1893, at the age of twenty-six, he set sail for New York.

---

* The simultaneous buying and selling of the same securities, merchandise, or foreign currency in different markets to profit from the different prices.

America

He arrived amid one of the most devastating panics in American economic history. Fueled by a complexity of evils—frantic stock gambling, agricultural depression, reckless trust and railway financing, Wall Street greed—it had begun with President Grover Cleveland's second term and would last for four years. Unemployment reached a million. Food prices soared; wages plummeted. A glut of agricultural products ruined farmers by the thousands. Nearly six hundred banks and loan companies and a fourth of all railroad companies failed. At the same time the biggest investment houses emerged from the chaos bigger than ever after gobbling up cheaply the smaller houses facing bankruptcy.

Labor strife plagued the nation. The worst strike hit Chicago when Pullman Car Company workers protested wage cuts. Sympathy strikes by Eugene V. Debs's American Railway Union spread through twenty-seven states. As Chicago mobs burned and looted Pullman cars, President Cleveland dispatched federal troops, with consequent further violence.

An ethnic slur, which though it bore no relevance to the financial crisis, created a divisiveness among Wall Street firms at a time when their cooperation was desperately needed. The exclusive Union League Club blackballed Theodore Seligman, scion of one of New York's most respected banking families. A member who voted against him openly explained:

> . . . I think that a majority of the men who frequent the club habitually are opposed to the admission of Hebrews. Their opposition is not based

upon any dislike of particular individuals, but upon the general belief that men of the Jewish race and religion do not readily affiliate in any social way with persons not of their own persuasion. We know that there are a great many Hebrews in New York who are cultivated, public-spirited, and of high business standing. We respect them and do not dislike to meet them publicly; but practical experience seems to have proved that they are more contented and successful socially among themselves than when thrown individually among other associations.

Two of the most renowned Union Leaguers, Elihu Root, the president of the club and future secretary of war under Presidents William McKinley and Theodore Roosevelt, and J. P. Morgan, uttered not a word of protest. Theodore Seligman's father, Jesse, a founder of the club, resigned in a fury along with other Jewish members. *The New York Times* deplored the incident, coinciding as it did with the panic, when the country needed the united leadership of its best financial brains. On Wall Street a good many colleagues no longer spoke to each other.

The panic did not touch Otto Kahn personally. His job at Speyer's was secure, and he possessed a comfortable amount of money, partly earned in London, partly bestowed by his father. He rented an apartment at 26 West Thirty-fourth Street, just off Fifth Avenue. It was a congenial part of town for a man of his predilections. The Metropolitan Opera House stood barely seven blocks distant on Thirty-ninth Street and Broadway. Opened in 1883 and ravaged by a fire nine years later, its grand reopening took place on November 27, 1893, three months after Kahn reported for work at Speyer's on Wall Street. *Faust* introduced the season with Emma Eames as Marguerite, Jean de Reszke as Faust, and Edouard de Reszke as Mephistopheles.

For concertgoers, New York offered a feast. Carnegie Hall, on Fifty-seventh Street and Seventh Avenue, little more than a mile north of Kahn's bachelor quarters, had become the home of the New York Philharmonic Orchestra in 1892. Its first conductor there was Anton Seidl. (Two years before, Tchaikovsky, a guest artist of the Symphony Society, had conducted a program of his own works at Carnegie Hall. The two orchestras much later merged into the Philharmonic.) The Oratorio Society, organized in 1873 by Walter Damrosch, confined itself chiefly to sacred music; the Musurgia, to part songs for male voices; the Manuscript Society to performances of unpublished works by American composers; and half a dozen groups to German music.

As to the stage, Moses King, in his *Handbook of New York City, 1893*, wrote:

> New York stands first in the strength and scope of its interest in the drama. There is good reason, too, for claiming first position in the world, for aside from its purely local enterprises, New York is distinctly a metropolis in the dramatic field. It is the great clearing-house and outfitting depot for the theatrical enterprises of the entire continent. In this respect it is a city of greater importance than London, Paris, Berlin or Vienna. . . . Occasionally, four, five and even six new plays are put on at different theaters on a single Monday night. . . .

The heart of the theater district lay between Herald Square and Times Square, a few minutes' stroll from Kahn's door. Of the city's thirty-four theaters, the most prestigious was Palmer's at Broadway and Thirty-fourth Street, which opened in 1882 with Sheridan's *School for Scandal*, followed by Lillie Langtry's American debut in *An Unequal Match*. The Italian tragedian Tommaso Salvini transfixed audiences with his Shakespearean portrayals, though he declaimed in his native tongue. Richard Mansfield triumphed as Richard III. The new Abbey's Theatre at Broadway and Thirty-eighth presented Henry Irving and Ellen Terry in a repertory that included *The Merchant of Venice, Henry VIII*, and *Much Ado About Nothing*. The Star Theatre, on Thirteenth Street, far from the main theatrical artery, revived *Rip Van Winkle* with Joseph Jefferson, who created the role. Maurice Barrymore, father of John, Ethel, and Lionel, appeared in Oscar Wilde's *A Woman of No Importance* at the Fifth Avenue Theatre on Twenty-eighth Street. At the same theater Modjeska portrayed Hermann Sudermann's *Magda*. The impresario Charles Frohman staged the first New York production of *Charley's Aunt* at the Standard Theatre, at Third Avenue and Thirty-second Street, and Lillian Russell ravished the eye, if nothing else, in a foolish operetta, *Princess Nicotine*. For Germanophiles, Heinrich Conried introduced a series of German plays at the Irving Place Theatre.

To Kahn's joy, there was no dearth of opera. In addition to the Metropolitan Opera Company, the flamboyant Oscar Hammerstein staged both operas and plays at his Harlem Opera House. The former included *Il Trovatore* with his friend and supporter, Lilli Lehmann, singing Leonora. At his Columbus Theatre, also in Harlem, he ventured a startling innovation: operas sung in English, among them *Faust, Mignon*, and *Carmen*, and in 1906, barely seven blocks away from the Met, at Thirty-fourth Street near Eighth Avenue, he erected the archrival Manhattan Opera House, which imported such superstars as Mary Garden, Nellie Melba, Luisa Tetrazzini, and Lina Cavalieri, and such operas new to the American public as *Louise* and *Pelléas et Mélisande*. Money to finance opera, the only medium Hammerstein deeply cared for, flowed at the rate of $4,000 a week from his Victoria Theatre of Varieties, featuring the world's foremost vaudevillians. In several other theaters Heinrich Conried also put on operas as well as operettas like *The Gypsy Baron*.

Kahn worked as hard as he played. By day he could be found at 11 Broad Street, the New York office of Speyer & Co., where he acquired an impressive reputation for diligence. According to Mary Jane Matz's adulatory biography, *The Many Lives of Otto Kahn*, so energetic was his drive that he once slogged downtown to Broad Street through one of winter's heaviest snowstorms only to find that no other member of the firm had cared to battle the elements.

Speyer ranked high among international bankers, but not high enough to satisfy Kahn's ambition. At the top of the heap reigned J. P. Morgan, with Kuhn, Loeb a close second. The House of Morgan was a dubious goal for Kahn, considering the anti-Semitism of its master. Kahn cast his eyes instead upon Kuhn, Loeb.

Abraham Kuhn and Solomon Loeb, distantly related cousins, were, at the beginning of their partnership, cloak-and-suiters. Loeb, a round-face, pursy man with muttonchop whiskers, came from the Rhenish city of Worms, one of fifteen children born to an impecunious vintner and his strong-willed wife, Rosina. The adolescent Loeb, his body carrying no hint of the well-upholstered adult, was frail and nervous, with sad blue eyes. Kuhn, already settled in Cincinnati, was prospering there. Having started out as a street peddler, gone on to operate a dry-goods store, and then to manufacture men's trousers in his own plant, he had accumulated enough profit to send for his parents, his brothers and sisters, and a slew of cousins. Kuhn at forty, also stout and heavily whiskered, somewhat resembled Loeb, who was ten years younger. The ruler of the Loeb family, Rosina, decreed that her son Solomon should try his luck in Cincinnati. The year was 1849.

Kuhn, meanwhile, wanted to establish an outlet in New York for the pants he manufactured in Cincinnati, and when Loeb turned up he took him on as an assistant, first to set up the New York store, then to commute between Cincinnati and New York, laden with pants. Loeb fared well, and shortly he, too, brought over his family, most of whom went to work for what would be named Kuhn, Loeb & Co. Eventually the two groups of immigrants, numbering thirteen in all, moved together into a single capacious house. Solomon Loeb married Abraham Kuhn's sister Fanny, and Abraham Kuhn married Solomon Loeb's sister Regina. They thereby instituted a practice that became a dynastic Kuhn, Loeb tradition: nearly every partner, before or soon after he entered the firm, married the daughter of another partner.

Regina Loeb bore a daughter, Therese. Then tragedy disrupted the busy household. In a second childbirth both Regina and the baby died. The widower returned to his native land, seeking as a new wife the kind of solid housekeeper, cook, and stepmother for Therese that he felt only the German-Jewish community of his youth could provide. In Mannheim he found Betty Gallenberg and brought her to Cincinnati.

Betty, however, detested Cincinnati and railed against it until Solomon agreed to move to New York. Kuhn chose to stay put for the moment. In any event, both brothers-in-law had wearied of the clothing business, and both had built up a fortune substantial enough to ensure their comfort in retirement. The mood did not last.

On February 1, 1867, at 31 Nassau Street, Abraham Kuhn and Solomon Loeb founded a private banking house with a capital of $500,000. In their original announcement they proclaimed: "We employ no salesmen. . . . We do not chase after business. . . . We do business with people who come to us. . . . If I am known to be a pretty good doctor, I am liable to keep my practice. If not, and if for any reason it is possible to think somebody is coming up who is better, the patient will quit me . . . cold." The same simile was used, somewhat more elegantly, sixty-six years later by Otto Kahn.

From then until 1911, every partner was related by blood or marriage to either Kuhn or Loeb. Among the first, who entered the firm on January 1, 1875, was a young stockbroker who had emigrated from Frankfurt-am-Main ten years before and would prove to have one of the most astute minds in the annals of investment banking. At sixteen Jacob Henry Schiff had entered the business under his father's tutelage. Two years later, in New York, he headed his own small brokerage firm. A short man, standing five feet two inches tall, broad-browed, with large blue eyes, he had command presence. An observant Jew, he attended Temple Emanu-El, a Reform congregation, though he committed himself neither to Reform Judaism nor strict Orthodoxy, respecting both forms. He termed himself a "faith Jew," rather than a "race Jew."

He became a naturalized citizen in 1870, dissolved his brokerage firm when one of his two partners decided to live abroad, and left New York to pay his parents a visit. While lingering in Frankfurt for a year, his father having died, leaving his mother alone, Schiff met Kuhn, who was visiting relatives. The forceful personality of the youth—Schiff was then twenty-seven—so impressed itself upon the older man that he suggested he return to New York and join Kuhn, Loeb. Schiff hesitated to leave his widowed mother, but she urged him to grasp the opportunity. "You are made for America," she said.

Neither Kuhn nor Loeb was exceptionally enterprising. Homesick both, they were content to pass the leadership of the firm to this tireless, aggressive newcomer, and almost from the start Schiff influenced the major decisions. After 1885, when the original partners retired, they left Jacob Schiff to reign supreme. During his first stay in New York he had come to know Therese, Loeb's daughter by his first marriage. (The second marriage to Betty Gallenberg produced two sons and two daughters.) He wrote to his mother in 1874: "I know you haven't any clear conception of what an American girl is like. You may think she is rather uncultured and even a feminist—but don't imagine that of the girl I've selected. She might have been brought up in the best of German families." Five months after entering the firm, of which he had become a full partner, he married Therese Loeb.

Another early partner was Abraham Wolff, a widower with two daughters, Clara and Addie.* In the Kuhn, Loeb tradition Otto Kahn married into the firm. His bride was Addie Wolff, the younger daughter, a small, birdlike girl of twenty with a strong, well-furnished mind. The wedding took place on January 10, 1896, in Wolff's house at 33 West Fifty-seventh Street, which he had bought from Jacob Schiff.† The honeymoon, combined with business, lasted a year, most of it in England, where the groom renewed old acquaintances in the West End, Bloomsbury, and Mayfair, and the bride fell in love with English ways.

When they returned to America a staggering surprise awaited them. Wolff had built in Morristown, New Jersey, at a cost of half a million

---

* Various writers have mistaken Addie as a nickname for Adelaide. Not so. Addie was her full given name at birth.

† The year before, Felix M. Warburg, who was admitted to partnership in 1897, had married Schiff's daughter Frieda, and the year before that, two members of Solomon Loeb's family, his son James and a nephew, Louis Heinsheimer, became partners. By 1921 two of the eleven partners were great-great grandsons of Solomon Loeb, and a third was a grandson. To unravel the skeins of intermarriages and divorces was a genealogist's nightmare.

dollars, twin three-story houses, one for each daughter. Designed in the style of an Italian Renaissance villa, they were placed at right angles to each other and connected by an archway. Wolff bestowed the north structure upon Otto and Addie. The name of the estate, Cedar Court, derived from the two cedar trees flanking the entrance to a huge courtyard. Wolff himself shared the Kahns' villa on weekends and holidays and spent weekdays at his New York house.

He had also wanted to buy for each daughter a million-dollar life insurance policy, but the insurance company, in that day of high childbirth mortality, rejected Addie. Clara, on the other hand, who married a Henri Wertheim, proved incapable of childbearing and so was insurable. Ironically, Clara died two years later of pneumonia, whereas Addie lived to be seventy-three. (A stroke carried off Wolff in 1900, and Kahn acquired ownership of the entire property.)

On April 26, 1896, Jacob Schiff had written to Ernest (later Sir Ernest) Cassel—his close, perhaps closest, friend, Kuhn, Loeb's foreign agent, the Prince of Wales's playmate, and one of the richest men in the world:

> As conditions now stand I probably must follow Wolff's wishes and agree that his son-in-law, Mr. Kahn, shall enter into our firm, unpleasant as it may be to me. I do not want to have Wolff feel badly about it as he has always been a very good friend to me. He told me he would be very unhappy if his eldest son-in-law should not become his successor. As soon as Morti [Jacob's nineteen-year-old son Mortimer] will be a few years older I hope to be able to retire from active work and than [sic] I also hope that Morti will get the whole business into his hands. He is fortunately developing a keen understanding and interest in his training in the various departments of the Great Northern Company. We must send him to Europe next fall so that he may acquire another point of view for practical business. We shall start at Warburg's in Hamburg, who conduct quite an extensive banking business besides their note arbitrage. After that I hope you will assist me in the spring of 1897 to find a place for Morti in London (for about a year) where he may get a thorough knowledge of English business conditions. . . .

Schiff's antipathy to Kahn is not surprising. It arose from the great disparity of their values and life-styles: Schiff a practicing Jew, Kahn never attending a synagogue, preferring the esthetics, if not the spiritual beliefs, of Catholicism; Schiff austere, patriarchal, wholeheartedly committed to investment banking; Kahn amiable, charming, playful, as interested in the performing arts as he was in the arcana of high finance, a protean figure, fond of all sorts of games and sports, world travel, sociability.

What *is* surprising is Schiff's profound affection for Ernest Cassel, who embodied many of the same predilections that Schiff deplored in Kahn. Cassel, too, loved parties, entertainments, the theater, horses, and horse racing. Stout and thick-bearded, he resembled the Prince of Wales, whom he served as unofficial financial adviser, making millions for him, as he did for himself. He was also the fun-loving prince's companion in frolics all over the world. Curiously, his mistress for years, Ella Joshua, was a cousin of Otto Kahn's. Worse, this Jew from Cologne, heeding the pleas of his tubercular Catholic wife, Annette, converted to her faith. Not long after she gave birth to a daughter, Maud, she died. Maud grew up to marry the extreme-right-wing Wilfred William Ashley (later Lord Mount Temple). A child born to them in 1901, the year Edward VII mounted the throne, they named in his honor Edwina. She became Countess Mountbatten of Burma. At seventeen, her mother dead and her father remarried, she gratefully accepted Cassel's invitation to live with him and act as his hostess at his palatial Brook House.

For forty years the American banker and the British financier corresponded, apprising each other not only of business developments but also of domestic and personal matters. Schiff thought so highly of Cassel that he loaned him money without security. From 1879, the year they first met, to Schiff's last days in 1920, he wrote about fifteen hundred letters to Cassel. When the United States and England together loaned money to Mexico with Mexico's customs revenue as collateral, Schiff cabled: IF THEY DON'T PAY WHO WILL COLLECT THE CUSTOMS. Cassel replied: YOUR MARINES AND OURS.

4

A "Two-Dollar Broker"

Kahn's arrival at Kuhn, Loeb coincided with the boldest exploit the firm had ever ventured upon—the purchase and reorganization of the Union Pacific Railroad. In 1862 an act of Congress created the Union Pacific and the Central Pacific Railroad companies in order to connect the West Coast with the Eastern states by the nation's first transcontinental line. The government granted to the companies 25,000 square miles in alternate sections along the designated route and a subsidy of bonds with which to raise construction capital. The Union Pacific started laying track westward from Omaha, Nebraska, the Central Pacific eastward from Sacramento, California. On May 10, 1869, Leland Stanford, former governor of California and president of the Central Pacific, drove a gold spike that joined the two lines at Promontory, Utah. Disaster soon followed. A multitude of evils—profiteering, the rapacity of robber barons like Jay Gould, general mismanagement—threw the Union Pacific into bankruptcy. It owed the government $45 million. More than half its trackage had become unusable. "A draggled creature of the market-place that every philandering speculator had his will of," wrote a pair of biographical collaborators, quoting an unidentified source and adding: "In the degradation to which it had sunk few were willing to make an honest railroad out of it." To J. P. Morgan, who had abandoned an attempt to salvage the wreck, the Union Pacific was "two streaks of iron rust across the plains."

Jacob Schiff, whom Morgan contemptuously referred to as "that foreigner," thought differently. With the immense migratory movement westward and the fast-growing need for transport to convey building materials and goods of every description into virgin territory, the benighted railroad, Schiff concluded, could be revived at a great profit, given congressional support and capital to acquire bonds. No investment house, however, would attempt such a venture without first satisfying itself that the mighty Morgan had no designs of his own upon the Union Pacific. Who would compete against the country's most powerful banker? Schiff suspected the hand of Morgan behind a series of mysterious impediments. There were inexplicable congressional postponements, an unfriendly press, foreign clients who shrank from ratifying contracts already agreed upon. Was Morgan behind it all? Schiff would have confronted him in any event before proceeding. Now it was imperative, and he betook himself to Morgan's Wall Street sanctum.

The old colossus, seated at his rolltop desk before a blazing coal fire, chomping on a huge black Havana cigar, dismissed Schiff's suspicions. He wanted no part of the dilapidated railroad, he assured him, but added: "It's that little fellow Harriman, and you want to look out for him."

Edward Henry Harriman, a "two-dollar broker," as Morgan described him, was not a personable figure. Spindly, pallid, and stooped, prey to a succession of diseases, his eyes rheumy, his nose leaky, he wore a soupstrainer mustache that added no charm to his appearance. In business dealings, as in personal relations, he was cold, ruthless, ill-mannered. His gruff, growly voice was so low that it obliged the listener to lean closer. But behind the repellent exterior was a mind quick, sharp, and prescient.

Descended from English immigrants, the son of a New Jersey Episcopal clergyman, he quit Trinity School in New York City at the age of fourteen to work as a Wall Street office boy. By his twenty-first year his nose for money had won him enough to buy a seat on the stock exchange for $3,000. In 1879 he married Mary Williamson Averell, the daughter of a banker who headed a small railroad company. They had a son, William Averell Harriman, future ambassador to the U.S.S.R. and to Great Britain, governor of New York, and President John F. Kennedy's special roving emissary. Through his father-in-law, E. H. Harriman acquired a lifelong passion for railroading. In 1883 he became vice president of the prospering Illinois Central, and the dominant voice in its management.

Schiff summoned "that little fellow" and said, "Mr. Harriman, my associates and I, as you doubtless know, are trying to reorganize the Union Pacific. For a long time we have been making good progress;

but now we are meeting everywhere with opposition, and I understand that this opposition is being directed by you. What have you to say about it?"

"I am the man," Harriman admitted.

"But why are you doing it?"

"Because I intend to reorganize the Union Pacific myself."

Schiff smiled skeptically. "How do you propose to do it, Mr. Harriman? Most of the securities of the company are in our possession. What means have you of reorganizing the Union Pacific?"

"The Illinois Central ought to have that road," Harriman insisted, "and we are going to take charge of the reorganization. We have the best credit in the country. I am going to issue one million dollars in three per cent bonds of the Illinois Central Railroad Company and I am going to get close to par for them. You, at the best, can't get money for less than four and a half per cent. In that respect I am stronger than you are."

Flabbergasted by such arrogance, Schiff replied dryly, "You'll have a good time doing it, Mr. Harriman, but meanwhile, what is your price?"

"There is no price. I am determined to get possession of the road."

Were there no conditions on which they could base a collaborative effort?

"If you'll make me chairman of the executive committee of the reorganized road, I'll consider the expediency of joining forces with you."

Out of the question, said Schiff. The chairman had already been chosen.

"Very well, Mr. Schiff," said Harriman. "Go ahead and see what you can do. Good day."

The obstructions resumed until Schiff came up with an alternative offer. "If you will cooperate with us," he promised Harriman, "I'll see that you are made a director of the reorganized company and a member of the executive committee. Then, if you prove to be the strongest man in that committee, you'll probably get the chairmanship in the end."

"All right," said Harriman, who had no doubt that he would prove the strongest. "I'm with you."

Before the year ended Harriman was voted chairman. No sooner elected than he set forth on an inspection tour of the entire Union Pacific line. Riding an observation car by daylight, he scrutinized every mile of track, noting rusty ties, eroded rails, loose bolts. In subsequent tours he stopped at every major depot to interrogate officials (whom he astounded with his technical knowledge), to interview shippers, to assess the characters of the men in charge.

Delays en route irritated him. When he asked the reason for them, a division superintendent explained: "Engine taking water, sir."

"Why not make the feed pipe bigger?" Harriman barked.

"Can't be done, sir. The engine wouldn't take any larger feed pipe."

"Then we'll get some bigger engines."

He did not hesitate to direct such improvements on his own responsibility. Without waiting for the executive committee's approbation, he ordered the sides and roofs of old boxcars removed so as to use what remained for flat cars. As one of many economizing measures, he resolved to withdraw most of the light rolling stock and to put a ceiling of $10 each on the cost of repairing any of those remaining. Toward the end of his first inspection tour he telegraphed the committee in New York demanding authority to purchase some $25 million worth of new equipment. He got it.

Kahn followed Harriman's operations with awe and admiration. Unaffected by the railroader's disagreeable personality, he respected his intellect and approached him as an eager student approaches an inspirational teacher. They became friends as well as investment collaborators.

Harriman could not resist a dare, and, puny though he was, he once put on boxing gloves for a friendly bout with an ex-prizefighter, thereby incurring some painful punishment. Horse racing was among his favorite spectator sports. One autumn day he set out for the trotting races at Goshen, New York. He missed the local Erie Railroad that stopped there, and with no other train available to get him to the races on time except the Chicago express, he telephoned the Erie administrative office and asked if, as a professional courtesy, the express could let him off at Goshen. This was not an unusual request among railroad executives, but he received a brusque refusal. The Chicago express, however, would stop at Goshen if any passengers there intended to journey to some point west of Buffalo. Harriman wired a colleague in Goshen, instructing him to buy a single ticket for Chicago. When the express reached Goshen, a signal flag halted it to let aboard whoever purchased the ticket to Chicago. No such passenger appeared, of course, but the stop allowed Harriman to step off the train and proceed to the races.

With Kuhn, Loeb as his bankers, Harriman achieved the prodigious feat of wresting control of the Northern Pacific Railroad from under the noses of J. P. Morgan and his ferocious associate, James Hill. Harriman's blow was an act of retaliation against Hill, because Hill had refused to let him participate in the control of the Burlington line, which would form an essential part of the Great Northern Pacific system. Otto Kahn, moving molelike, acquired for the account of his mentor $65 million worth of Northern Pacific shares at $200 a share, thereby establishing a corner. The stock soared to $1,000 before Morgan and Hill realized what had happened. "A promising chap," the National City Bank's James Stillman had once observed of Kahn, who was collecting a lot of fine paintings, "if only he will forget that art nonsense."

The young Kahn's considerable revenue flowed from two main sources. Every December, Kuhn, Loeb, which had outgrown its 27 Pine Street offices and in 1903 erected a twenty-two-story building on the corner of Pine and William streets, distributed the annual profits among the partners. What percentage each partner received depended on seniority, the volume of business he had engendered, and other considerations. Kahn eventually got 14 percent. Railroad reorganizations in the Harriman mode and railroad securities yielded the fattest returns. When Kuhn, Loeb assembled and managed a security-purchase syndicate, it customarily charged a fee of one percent. During their first nine years the securities they underwrote totaled approximately $821 million. Kahn's second major source of capital was Wall Street, where, as an astute investor, he repeatedly realized a killing. Thus, his means, together with Addie Kahn's inheritance, enabled the couple to live grandly. But he was never, as the press persistently misreported, "one of the richest men in America." It is difficult to estimate how much his fortune amounted to at any given period because he spent money as fast as he made it, sometimes faster. "I must atone for my wealth," he said on several occasions. "I will reward the country of my adoption for the great benefits I have gathered." In all probability his liquid assets never topped $50 million, a paltry sum in those halcyon days before federal taxation when compared to the royal wealth of a Rockefeller, a Carnegie, or a Morgan. It was more than enough, however, to maintain a town house just off Fifth Avenue at 8 East Sixty-eighth Street.

On February 5, 1905, while the Kahn family was at the New York house, a faulty flue and an overheated furnace started a fire near Mrs. Kahn's boudoir at Cedar Court. The caretaker, who occupied a cottage half a mile distant, saw the flames shooting through the roof, called the Morristown fire department, and with the rest of the domestic staff formed a bucket brigade. By the time the fire engines pulled up, the villa had been gutted, though the adjoining dwelling remained untouched. The blaze engulfed art objects, paintings, and an Egyptian rug woven at a cost of $100,000 to cover a living room seventy-five feet square. The total damage came to $750,000.

On the site of the incinerated house Kahn built a Palladian villa harmonizing with the architecture of the surviving structure, and he further embellished the grounds.* Together with what his father-in-law had laid out there were now horse trails, an eighteen-hole golf course, a squash court, a croquet court, a tennis court, greenhouses, sunken gardens, a pond on which swans floated amid exotic water plants, a forty-acre deer park, and a wooden roller-skating rink that meandered through woods where the deer grazed. The estate, according to one of the gardeners, "showed people what God could have done if he'd had the money."

Meanwhile, in March 1905, Otto's father died in Heidelberg, where he had acquired the majestic Villa Hassig perched on a rise above Heidelberg Castle. He bequeathed his entire fortune to his wife, stipulating that she provide assistance to the needy of Mannheim. The will noted that years earlier he had given Otto 40,000 marks (equivalent to about $10,000) and 200,000 marks ($50,000) to each of two sons-in-law, Lili's husband, Felix Deutsch, and Clara's husband, Paul Jonas. His widow, following his further instructions, established the Bernhard Kahn Reading Room, precursor of Mannheim's public library. Otto dutifully contributed to its maintenance and remitted small amounts of money to those of his brothers and sisters who asked for it, though it irritated him to do so. He cared little for his relatives and maintained no regular communication with them. He disliked the *Weltanschauung* of the German-Jewish intellectual that they typified. In fact, he had come to dislike most things German, with a particular detestation of Prussianism.

"Thank God," he wrote to his aged mother, who died soon after her husband, in 1906, "the sensitivity for the beautiful in nature and art, and for the great, runs in our blood, and I intend—to the extent that it is possible under the horrid conditions of life of a New York businessman—to see to it that I don't lose this precious heritage."

---

* Sold in 1920 to a diabetic clinic, it is now the site of Allied Signal Corporation, formerly Allied Chemical.

5

Banking and the "Art Job"

James Hazen Hyde was a sybaritic, megamillionaire opera buff who sat on the board of some fifty corporations, among them the Metropolitan Opera and Real Estate Company. The last was a shareholding corporation that rented its theater to impresarios who chose the seasonal schedule of operas and hired the cast.* Despite the aura of anti-Semitism that then pervaded the institution, Hyde, in 1903, invited his banker, Jacob Schiff, to join the directorate. Schiff declined, but suggested that such an appointment would perhaps interest Otto Kahn.

Kahn, whose love of opera dated from adolescence, was indeed interested. Men in Kahn's business milieu tended to regard the opera world as effete, no place for a serious financier. Colleagues warned him against involving himself in operatic or theatrical activities lest he alienate people important to his business. No reputable banker, they insisted, should associate himself with such frivolous doings.

He consulted Harriman, who, to his amazement, told him: "You just go ahead and do your art job, but don't dabble in it. Make it one of your serious occupations. As long as you do not let it interfere with

---

*Today, Lincoln Center for the Performing Arts, Inc., a nonprofit institution, owns the Metropolitan Opera building, while the City of New York owns the ground beneath it. The building is leased to the Metropolitan Opera Association, Inc., consisting of thirty-five directors who manage the opera. In the event that the opera should end a season with a profit, the funds would go to the association for the directors to decide how best to use them.

your other work, with your business duties and ambitions and thoughts, it will do you no harm. On the contrary, it will exercise your imagination and diversify your activities. It ought to make a better businessman out of you."

Kahn needed no further encouragement, and he presented himself at the next board meeting, which included Clarence Mackay, Robert Goelet, Alfred G. Vanderbilt, and other luminaries from New York's social heights. His participation began just as the Met's "golden age" was dimming. Under the tenancy of Maurice Grau's company (1893–1903) the opera house had been unsurpassed in its abundance of superb interpreters, its innovations, and the quality of its conductors and orchestra. Grau introduced to New York the unabridged *Der Ring des Nibelungen* with Ernestine Schumann-Heink, Emma Eames, Lilli Lehmann, the de Reszkes, and imported many other peerless performers. He produced the Met's first Puccini operas, beginning with *La Bohème* and followed by *Tosca*. Nellie Melba sang Mimi in the former, Antonio Scotti sang Scarpia in the latter. All three of Mozart's greatest operas—*Don Giovanni, The Marriage of Figaro,* and *The Magic Flute*— made their American debut under Grau's aegis. The singers included Lillian Nordica, Marcella Sembrich, Pol Plançon, and Johanna Gadski. When Grau retired in 1903, he left not only a splendid record as an opera impresario, but substantial profits in the Met till.

As the succeeding lessee, the board chose Heinrich Conried, born Cohn in Austria, who had been staging German dramas at the Irving Place Theatre. He styled his company the Conried Metropolitan Opera Company. A penny-pincher, he had invented in his younger days a metal clasp for pocketbooks. Two momentous events distinguished his first Met season. On November 23, 1903, he presented a *Rigoletto* with the role of the Duke of Mantua sung by an Italian tenor already renowned abroad but little known in America. This was Enrico Caruso, whose contract Conried had inherited from Grau. Extremely nervous during his initial appearance, Caruso failed to impress the audience. The critics, moreover, deplored his exaggeratedly melodramatic Italian gestures. But by the end of the season, during which he astounded the audience as Nemorino in Donizetti's *L'Elisir d'Amore*, an opera urged upon Conried by Otto Kahn, he secured his pedestal as tenor nonpareil. For the next sixteen years the leading star on opening night was traditionally Caruso. He and Kahn became devoted friends. Caruso spoke of Kahn as "Il Grande Signore" or "Il Ottokan." On Christmas Eve of 1903, Conried produced the

American premiere of Wagner's *Parsifal*—again at Kahn's suggestion—to the plaudits of both critics and public.

Conried's regime continued to prove profitable, especially to himself. His salary was $20,000 a year, and in addition to his dividends as a major stockholder, he retained half the profits after expenses. The board also allowed him to keep the proceeds from an annual benefit concert at which the artists performed without fee. Altogether, his income came close to $400,000. (Yet he paid the members of the chorus only $15 a week.) But too many of Conried's productions lacked originality and vitality. More theatrical showman than operatic impresario, he knew little about opera. He was so biased against French composers that he failed to buy the rights, when the opportunity arose, to the proven successes of Massenet, Charpentier, and Debussy. Also, his health was beginning to fail.

Upon joining the Met board, Otto Kahn bought two hundred shares of stock. James Hazen Hyde owned three hundred, and when he left New York to live in Paris, Kahn bought them. When Henry Morgenthau retired, Kahn bought his three hundred shares. Eventually he amassed 2,750 shares, and for all practical purposes owned the Metropolitan Opera.

On January 22, 1907, Conried daringly presented Richard Strauss's *Salome* with Olive Fremstad as the psychotic princess who demands from Herod the head of John the Baptist. A large part of the audience walked out. The *Tribune*'s music critic, Henry Krehbiel, wrote: "The reviewer should be an embodied conscience stung into righteous fury by the moral stench with which *Salome* fills the nostrils of humanity," and Walter Pritchard Eaton reported in the same newspaper: "Many voices were hushed as the crowd passed into the night, many faces were white as those at the rail of a ship, many women were silent and men spoke as if a bad dream were upon them."

Salome split the board into two factions, one in favor headed by Kahn, the other against headed by J. P. Morgan. The latter won. *Salome* was banned from the Met.

As Kuhn, Loeb clients passed Kahn's desk, they were sometimes bemused to glimpse an opera score lying open beside a stock exchange report. Among his own visitors, sober-faced investors frequently alternated with some gesticulating foreign musician, a stage director, a voluble prima donna. Such incongruities tended to rouse in his fellow bankers, observing him from across the partners' room, puzzlement and scorn. How could any serious financier serve with equal devotion both Hermes and Euterpe? What particularly irritated Jacob Schiff was Kahn's habit of singing an aria while he worked. But Kahn proved faithful to the precepts of Ned Harriman.

In the litigation, investigations, and hearings that arose from investment banking practices, Kahn proved a valuable asset to his firm as a witness—cool, methodical, fluent, and frequently entertaining. No attorney, however astute, could daunt him. The reorganizations of the Denver & Rio Grande Railroad, for example, produced a spate of lawsuits, in one of which Kahn faced the formidable lawyer, Samuel Untermyer. A passage of the dialogue between them became embedded in the Kahn legend.

A group of former shareholders filed a $200 million claim against the bankrupt Denver & Rio Grande, charging that the company's transactions had wrecked it. In reality, it had foundered some fifteen years before the alleged offenses, and though Kuhn, Loeb had been its bankers, Kahn could not recollect certain details.

"Mr. Kahn," Untermyer observed, "I understand that you are reputed to have a very good memory."

Kahn: "Yes, some people pay me that compliment."

Untermyer: "I understand also that when you're in a transaction, you know all about it?"

Kahn: "Yes, I make a studied practice that when I'm in a transaction I try to know all about it. I just don't rely on my associates."

Untermyer: "Well, how do you account for the fact that you handled this transaction fifteen years ago and now you don't seem to recall anything about it?"

Kahn: "That's exactly right, counsel."

Untermyer: "Well, how do you account for that?"

Kahn: "I'll tell you how. I reiterate, while I'm handling a transaction, I make it a studied practice to know as much about it as possible. Then, as soon as it's over, I similarly try my best to purge my memory of every bit of knowledge about it, so as to be ready for the next one."

Untermyer, turning to the presiding federal court judge, Martin Manton: "Your honor, I'll refresh Mr. Kahn's memory."

Kahn: "I'm sorry, Mr. Untermyer, if I have no recollection, you can't refresh it."

A Dickensian atmosphere pervaded the Kuhn, Loeb premises. The company's pride and self-confidence were reflected in its letterhead, which bore no identification other than the unnumbered address, "William and Pine Streets." Every business communication was signed by either a partner or an employee who had power of attorney. Instead of carbon paper the clerks resorted to a kind of letterpress to copy the typewritten original. Between the tissue-paper pages of a heavily bound book they would place the letter, dampen it with a wet cloth, and squeeze the book in a press, thus reproducing the text on the tissue paper and establishing a permanent record of the date the letter was written and, from the letters bound in the book before and after, when it went out—vital evidence should the letter ever figure in a lawsuit. The result, however, as Lewis Strauss, a member of the firm from 1919 to 1946, and later chairman of the Atomic Energy Commission, recalled: ". . . the outgoing mail was generally a watery affair, looking as though it had been retrieved by deep-sea divers from a shipwreck. The firm rather prided itself on this and other archaic business procedures."

Each executive had a buzzer on his desk. When he pressed it, a corresponding light flashed on a panel of lights at the rear of the floor, summoning a clerk to the proper office.

Kahn used the letterpress system for his personal correspondence, keeping the copies in a book with a lock. To put the originals through the letterpress, he often assigned either Charles Ascher (later a well-known urban planner) or Leo Mielziner, Jr. (under the stage name, in his mature years, of Kenneth McKenna, an actor and director), who wore a pince-nez attached to a long black ribbon. ". . . I remember one of the things that outraged me so," Ascher said long after, "was . . . that he was quite content to have these two young men see his most personal correspondence, on the principle that we were part of the office machinery. We weren't human beings, we were just like a typewriter, what difference did it make if we saw letters to some of the ladies in his life? And the gossip was rife. Many of the opera prima donnas were ladies in his life. . . ."

According to Ascher, Kahn could be impatient and irritable; often he would keep his finger on the buzzer, indicating an irate mood. The two youngsters would toss a coin to decide who should face the terror. One day, when Ascher had lost, he found, as he entered, that Kahn was still pressing the buzzer. "No, no, not you—," Kahn cried, "the other boy, the one with the string on his glasses."

Among the bookkeepers was a hunchback named Woog, who stood writing all day at a high desk. As lunchtime approached, he would shout to the clerk: "Call up Max [the proprietor of his favorite restaurant]. Ask Max if he has a good meat soup today, not what he calls a good meat soup, what I call a good meat soup."

Kuhn, Loeb's single most lucrative operation was to purchase the depreciated shares of a distressed railroad, which then, once they reorganized it, rose steeply. As a railroad reorganizer second only to Harriman, Kahn took in hand such systems as the Baltimore & Ohio, the Missouri Pacific, the Wabash. "Reorganizations," he observed, "embody a certain element of romance; they call for constructive imagination. To take a broken-down property, a few streaks of rails, and aid in working a transformation which will bring into being a transportation system to serve the country and, incidentally, to rehabilitate the owners, is a species of creative work that fascinates me. It yields the joy of creation."

Kahn played a dominant role in the delicate game that opened the Paris Bourse to American securities. Kuhn, Loeb placed the first such security there in 1906—a $50 million Pennsylvania Railroad bond issue. Kahn was also instrumental, during World War I, in Kuhn, Loeb's issue of $50 million in City of Paris bonds and of $60 million of Bordeaux, Lyon, and Marseille bonds.

At about the same time a $50 million conglomerate holding company, the American International Corporation, was established with the support of Kuhn, Loeb, the Rockefellers, and numerous other companies and individuals. Within two years the United States was involved in industrial construction, machine manufacture, public utilities, shipping and shipbuilding, and tea exports in seventeen countries.

Kahn was a vital presence in the formation and management of the A.I.C. He moved through its dense financial thickets with a gentle smile, speaking softly in his Anglo-German accent, seldom raising his voice, calm, deliberate, lucid. "I don't know what we would have done without the counsel and practical assistance of Mr. Kahn," said Charles Stone, the A.I.C. president. "He is a wonder. His understanding of international affairs is amazing."

6

Cedar Court

The Normandy Heights section of Morristown was an enclave of conspicuous consumption. Here, some thirty miles east of New York, men of wealth and social prestige established country seats, which many of them used chiefly as an escape from the searing summer heat of the city. The hinges and doors of the Great Hall in Valley View, the pleasance of Jesse Leeds Eddy, an anthracite magnate, were wrought in solid silver. Over the marble hearth was inscribed a line from Walter Scott's *Lochinvar:* "Heap on more wood!—the wind is chill." Peter Frelinghuysen, a Columbia Law School classmate of Franklin Delano Roosevelt, who was an usher at his wedding, raised prize-winning Jersey cattle on his 150-acre Twin Oaks Farm. Eugene V. Brewster, author, editor, and publisher, acquired as a love nest for his mistress, a Southern stunner named Corliss Palmer, Cherrycroft, comprising six acres of gardens, terraces, fountains, and pergolas.

Altogether, Morristown, with a population of 12,000 at the time the Kahns settled there, had one of the nation's highest per capita incomes. It numbered seventy-six millionaires with a combined wealth of $289 million.

To accommodate those potentates, who commuted between Morristown and New York, the Delaware, Lackawanna and Western Railroad added to its "Royal Blood" train three sumptuous club cars. Drawn by its Engine 100, the Centennial, it left Morristown every weekday at 8:25 A.M., stopping only at Madison en route to Hoboken, and left Hoboken at 4:15 P.M. The run was thirty-one miles and took about an hour. At Hoboken the passengers boarded one of the ferries that eased into a New York slip.

To ride the "Millionaire's Express," as the train became popularly known, cost $6 besides the regular fare and required the majority approval of the club-car membership. Acceptance was a mark of social distinction. Hours before the "Millionaire's Express" pulled in, bell clanging, engine snorting, the estates of the commuting swells were abustle with preparations as liveried chauffeurs dusted and warmed up the Packards, the Pierce-Arrows, the Marmons, the Daimlers, the Rolls-Royces, and grooms, coachmen, and footmen in gleaming boots and high hats curried and harnessed horses for those who preferred to proceed to the depot by four-in-hand or carriage. Kahn, a fair equestrian, often chose a saddle horse. If any club-car member was tardy, the train waited for him, to the annoyance of the common ruck.

The interior of the club cars, each of which could seat forty-two passengers in white wicker chairs with green cushions, was wood-paneled and thickly carpeted. There were six tables for card players and two sofas for those who wished to lounge. Each rider had his own chair, and if he failed to show up it remained empty. Near the entrance of each car a porter stood in attendance, ready to serve coffee and rolls (and in dire circumstances Bromo Seltzer) on the trip out and cocktails on the trip back. As the train approached its terminal, he dusted every gentleman's suit.

Another duty remained. According to a circular from the general superintendent to the porters:

> You are instructed to be more circumspect in opening doors of toilets in your cars after leaving terminal and at local stations where stop is made, to make sure that they are not occupied by unscrupulous persons beating their way over the road. If you should find a door bolted, a trainman should be stationed there to keep watch and designate the passenger to you as soon thereafter as practicable.
>
> Reports have reached this office which indicate that more care on your part in this respect is necessary.

For Addie and the children, Cedar Court was a year-round residence, while Kahn, happily overladen with his functions at Kuhn, Loeb and at the Met, in addition to multifarious artistic and social pursuits, lived in the Sixty-eighth Street town house during the week. He delighted in the company of beautiful young women, and from time to time spent an evening with one. Like many another bon vivant, he seldom missed an opening night at the Ziegfeld Follies. A sizable percentage of the backing that Florenz Ziegfeld needed for his lavish extravaganzas came from wealthy men around town enamored of some showgirl. Ziegfeld's personal secretary, among other insiders, could usually sense when such a romance was brewing. Having banked a large sum of money from an angel, Ziegfeld would tell her to expect a certain young dancer for an interview and to show her directly into his office. (As for the donor, "Give him anything he wants.") Presently, the dancer would present herself, talk briefly with Ziegfeld, get an audition, and win a small part in the next edition of the Follies. The secretary and her fellow Ziegfelders surmised that among such backers was Otto Kahn.

One evening the Follies' switchboard operator, Alice Poole, notorious along Broadway for her rough tongue, received a call from Kahn asking her to deliver a message to a certain chorine, whom he wanted to meet him for supper after the show. "Ask her yourself," Alice retorted. "What do you think I am—a pimp?"

During the first eleven years of their marriage, the Kahns produced four children. Maud Emily (nicknamed "Momo") came first, on July 23, 1897; then Margaret Dorothy ("Nin") on Independence Day, 1901; next Gilbert Sherburne ("Gil" or "Gilly") on July 18, 1903; and lastly, Roger Wolff ("Pips") on October 19, 1907.

Addie Kahn ruled her progeny with an iron hand. From the moment they opened their eyes in the morning until they closed them at night they were subjected to a multitude of rules and regulations designed to discipline their minds and bodies. Addie herself, impelled by a driving sense of duty, would often perform an action distasteful to her. "For mother," her younger daughter, Margaret, recalled, "much of life was a painful duty." Addie's tiny, delicate frame—she stood five feet two inches tall—belied her grand-marshal personality. High-principled, strong-willed, cultivated, and demanding, she was a constant presence under whose supervision a platoon of preceptors strove to instill in the four children good manners, self-control, and culture. The pupils worked long hours every day. Praise was sparing, punishments abundant.

In infancy the children were tended by two black-uniformed English nannies. As they approached adolescence, an English tutor, Ponsonby by name, was employed for the two boys and a governess for each of the girls. The first governess at Cedar Court, from whom they learned German, was Fräulein Tippe, who insisted that her charges sit at the dinner table with their pinkies resting on the edge, the way, according to her, German officers sat at mess. Her successor, Fräulein Braun, was called by Margaret behind her back "The Educator." Another governess, Mademoiselle Bleyfus, taught them French. Later, when the family moved to New York, the boys went to the fashionable St. Bernard's School, and the girls attended private classes run by a Mrs. McIver. "The Kaiser's Court," observed German governess No. 1, "was no more solidly founded on tradition than the Kahn household."

Twice a week a fencing master, Monsieur Gouspie, arrived to teach the sport to the children. A riding master, Martin Sykes, trained them in horsemanship. The Kahns at first preferred horses to automobiles, and the stables abounded in carriages, sleighs, four-in-hands, and saddle horses. (Rolls-Royces eventually became the conveyances of choice, and Kahn employed three chauffeurs.) Each child owned a pony and later a full-size mount. On Christmas Eve a huge sleigh, drawn by a team of holly-decked horses, would sweep up the long drive to the courtyard, and James Fraser, the estate superintendent, in the guise of Santa Claus, would descend and unload a mountain of gifts as he bellowed, "Ho, ho, ho!"

Kahn's homecoming on Friday evenings was the signal for a disruption of discipline. Addie could only shake her head despairingly while the paterfamilias, playful and prankish, undermined the week's lessons in decorum and deportment. At dinner, served by a butler and a maid, he might roll some bread into pellets and flick them across the table at his giggling offspring, fashion miniature paper boats to float in the finger bowls, or stick toothpicks in the butter.

Writing to his children in one of his mischievous humors, he occasionally enclosed mildly scatological doggerel. For example:

> A lady did in Jersey dwell
> There is not much of her to tell
> But she was fond of high-spiced food
> And her digestion none too good.
> Elizabeth, that was her name,
> Lived in a town that's called the same.
> One day when walking near the station
> Immersed in gentle meditation
> She felt a sudden strong requirement.
> "Ah," she exclaimed, "Oh, mamma mia,
> I fear I must have diarrhea!"
> Perplexed she stood, the need was great,
> She rushed within the station gate.

> She flew with anxious, eager face
> Until she found the welcome place.
> "For ladies,"—oh, relief so sweet!!!
> The poet turns away discreet.
> And while she lingered fondly dreaming
> A train arrived thund'ring and steaming,
> "Elizabeth," with sounding shout
> The station's name was given out.
> The call aroused the musing maid.
> " 'Tis surely Harry's voice," she said,
> "He's looking for me, the dear boy!"
> And in a voice of tender joy
> And yet with earnest striving in it,
> She answered back "Yes—in—a—minute."

With Nin, or "Niggie," as he also called Margaret, Kahn's bond was stronger than with that of any of his other children. They golfed together, rode together, swam together, chaffed each other, went to the opera together, and when apart, corresponded frequently. Another jingle of his own composition that Kahn enclosed in a letter to Nin ran:

> The gent you see depicted here
> Is well known as a financier.
> The men who our papers edit
> Give him considerable credit:
> He's hailed a speaker of renown,
> He wears the late Maecenas' crown,
> His general knowledge does enrage,
> His English style commands much praise,
> In movements for the public weal
> His are a leader's skill & zeal.
> Besides the competence stated
> Others might be enumerated.
> But let that be! What I have writ
> Is more déjà than he'd permit
> For, being shy & reticent
> These things are irksome to our gent.
> He spurns the tawdriness of fame
> He shuns publicity's acclaim.
> Far sweeter than the flattering din
> Counts he the term "Father to Nin."

In appreciation of a poem she had sent to him while he was in Germany, he proclaimed in a postcard:

> All hail, O poetess sublime
> I greatly hail your noble rhyme:
> You are indeed your father's heir;
> How you like this "Schloss am meer?"
>
>   love,
>   Fathie.

Few parents in that era ventured to explain the "facts of life" to their young, and the Kahns were no exception. Nin could not remember ever hearing the word *sex* uttered in her home. Addie, indeed, seemed not to have heard of its existence, for far from issuing any words of caution to her immensely alluring daughters as they entered adolescence, she took not the slightest notice if they chose to closet themselves with a caller for hours.

Kahn's brother Felix, the only other Kahn to have crossed the Atlantic since the flight of Bernhard and Emil in 1848, also lived at Cedar Court and eventually became an American citizen. Handsome, witty, and endearing, he greatly enlivened the household. He was an excellent violinist, always ready to entertain his kinsmen and their guests, or give an impromptu recital with his brother, who still played the cello. Felix performed frequently with various amateur chamber music groups but did little by way of gainful employment, relying upon the largesse of Otto, who promised him $750 quarterly. Otto once wrote to his sister Hedwig, whom he also supported for a while: "You will have to learn to adjust your way of living to match your income."

Because of the profusion of Kahn's business involvements and recreational diversions, he lived by the clock, assigning to virtually each moment some specific objective. If he had an appointment at, say, 9:30 A.M., and the others showed up at 9:35, they would find him immersed in work and not to be distracted, or gone altogether. At home, before dinner, he might announce: "It is now six-forty. I am going to lie down until seven-ten," and at seven-ten sharp, having automatically awakened, he would spring to the floor, eager to begin the next activity.

This insistence on exact promptitude, on punctilio, was at times an odd little power game he liked to play. "Meet me at six-fifteen," he would command, and he meant six-fifteen to the minute. "He showed he could make people do as he wished," recalls Mrs. Charles Gleaves, the daughter of Edward Ziegler, the Metropolitan Opera's administrative secretary under Kahn. "He showed his power."

He doodled continually when engaged in serious discussion, and even his doodling had a certain geometrical exactitude. "It's not the swift work that wears you out," he said. "Action is a tonic that stimulates. It is having to sit still in board meetings and listen to long-winded reports and minutes. In short, it's inaction, not action, that kills."

He made it a rule to read for one hour before retiring. The books he ordered from Brentano's within a single month included a thirty-two-volume set of Napoleon's correspondence, Heinrich Heine's *Memoirs*, Madame de Sévigné's letters, de Tocqueville's *De la Démocratie en Amérique*, Joergensen's *Saint Francis*, *L'Art dans la Maison*.

He was as fastidious a dresser, and as vain of his person, as a matinee idol. His clothes closets contained, among a vast collection of ensembles, eight identical pinstripe business suits, and he would stand before them lost in contemplation before choosing the one he would wear to work that morning.

At musical or theatrical first nights, on or off Broadway, no matter how unpretentious the performance, he would emerge from one of his Rolls-Royces in full fig, a satin-lined cape draped over evening dress, wearing a silk top hat and swinging an ebony cane with a silver ball for a handle.

Saturday morning was devoted to golf on his own eighteen-hole course. From the age of fourteen, Nin, along with Martin Sykes, played with him. If he invited others to join him, the time customarily fixed was ten. Should they fail to appear within three minutes after the hour, he was likely to tee off without them. A bit of a duffer, who hated to lose at any game, he would, if he hit too often into a bunker, have it removed, and if he shot too wide of a green, he would order the green repositioned.

Years later, after moving to Long Island and installing a golf course on his estate there, he enjoyed his finest golfing moment, of which he treasured ever after a self-testimonial that read: "On June 10, 1928, playing on my own golf course at Cold Spring Harbor, I made the sixth hole (150 yards) in one, using a No. 3 iron. Witness_____." But somehow the witness, whoever it was, neglected to inscribe his name.

Such was his passion for the game that while vacationing briefly one summer at Isleboro, Maine, he instructed an attendant: "Please telephone to Morristown to tell them that I shall be there for luncheon on Sunday and to let my professional and the caddies know that I shall want to play golf at three o'clock in the afternoon."

It was falsely rumored that he cheated at golf. His caddies, however, sometimes saw to it that he got a good lie.

The rest of the weekend Kahn usually spent riding and hiking with the children around Cedar Court, which embraced almost 150 acres. He liked to pile them all into a four-in-hand and tear across the property—a perilous diversion from which Addie shrank, because his control of the horses was unsure. As the four-in-hand whisked around the corner of a wall or building, the wheels were apt to nick a chunk off the masonry. Afterward, as a special treat, one of the governesses would conduct the brood by sleigh or carriage, season depending, downtown to Smith's Drug Store, where Eddie, the soda jerk, let them concoct their own sundaes or ice cream sodas.

The interior of Cedar Court rapidly assumed a museumlike grandeur. In 1904 Kahn purchased from an English art dealer his first important painting, *St. John on Patmos* by the Flemish artist Joos van Cleve (1480–1540), a choice seconded by Addie, whose esthetic judgment was impeccable. Two years later he paid another English dealer $100,000 for *Three Children of Captain Little* by George Romney (1734–1802), one of the artist's finest works. In 1910 he bought Rembrandt's *Portrait of a Young Student* from a Leningrad collection for $150,000. The same year, at Christie's auction gallery in London, an agent of J. P. Morgan was authorized to go as high as $400,000 for *Family Group* (1648) by the Dutch master Frans Hals (1580?–1666). Through the Machiavellian art dealer Joseph Duveen, Kahn, heeding as always Addie's opinion in artistic matters, shut out the bidding at $500,000, thereby snatching the prize away from the voracious Morgan. During the next two decades he acquired such marvels as *Giuliano de Medici* by Botticelli (1444?–1510), considered among the greatest historical portraits; *Man in Armor* by Vittore Carpaccio (1450–1522), which, like the Hals, hung on loan exhibition at the Metropolitan Museum of Art; Giovanni Bellini's (1430?–1516) *Rest on the Flight to Egypt;* Andrea Mantegna's (1431–1506) *St. Jerome*—to list only a few among scores of masterpieces.*

Addie's artistic judgment, upon which her husband relied, was not limited to paintings. She acquired an authoritative knowledge of Chinese bronzes, assembled an important collection, and willed them to the Metropolitan Museum of Art. She was also an amateur sculptor.

---

* The Kahn art collection was widely dispersed among museums and individual purchasers by his heirs. *St. John on Patmos*, for example, hangs today in the University of Michigan's Museum of Art at Ann Arbor; the Rembrandt, which was sold at auction to raise money for Metropolitan Opera scenery, in the Cleveland Art Museum; the Hals in the Thyssen-Bornemisza Collection, Lugano, Switzerland.

Husband and wife respected each other but never grew close. They lived in separate worlds, Kahn loving beautiful women, high life, the theater, music, Addie being scholarly, reserved, and self-sufficient. In 1909, at a New York dinner party, she met the renowned art critic Bernard Berenson. Two years after, at a London luncheon, the acquaintance began to ripen into friendship. Eventually she became a frequent guest at Berenson's Florentine residence, the Villa I Tatti, and joined him on art expeditions. The relationship remained a strictly platonic one, though it aroused the jealousy of Berenson's mistress in residence, Nicky Mariano.

There was a worm in the Morristown apple. The worm was anti-Semitism. It pervaded the top echelons of the city's Brahmins, to which Kahn aspired. The Morris County Golf Club adjoined Cedar Court. Kahn hardly needed a second golf course, but membership in the club was the sine qua non of social supremacy. After Sunday services at nearby St. Peter's Episcopal Church, the gentry would drop in for a preprandial refresher. No Jews were accepted. Though a proud man in other respects, Kahn submitted his application. Two blackballs sufficed for exclusion, and at least two were cast against him. Kahn turned the other cheek. On Sundays, when the links were closed, he allowed its members to play golf on his course. He later tried again to gain admission and was again rejected. According to an apocryphal story, the second rejection was due to a member so hostile to Kahn that he stole into the clubhouse late at night and popped a blackball into the voting box.

Kahn was finally accepted in 1911 but was never permitted to run for a club office or to serve on a club committee. Addie enjoyed the privileges of an associate member, and their daughter Maud was voted a full membership. But the still snobbier Morristown Club, founded in 1884 by twelve millionaire burghers and limited to male members, never admitted Kahn.

7

Harriman Triumphant

To Big Business, which feared and hated Theodore Roosevelt as the Devil fears and hates holy water, an unexpected and odious turn in the soaring career of Otto Kahn was his amicable relationship with the twenty-sixth president. It seemed the more astounding since high on the presidential roster of "malefactors of great wealth" was Kahn's hero, Ned Harriman.

In 1902, within a year of President McKinley's assassination and Vice President Roosevelt's succession, the new president brought a suit through the attorney general to dissolve Northern Securities, a railroad holding company formed to circumvent the Sherman Antitrust Act.

Northern Securities, with a capitalization of $400 million, proposed to end competition among the railroad titans—J. P. Morgan and James Hill in one camp, Ned Harriman and William Rockefeller in the other—and thus create a peaceful climate in which all the former rivals might flourish. The upshot, of course, would be a monopoly and restraint of trade that could place the entire American railroad system under the domination of a single power. The U.S. Circuit Court ordered Northern Securities dissolved, and on appeal the Supreme Court sustained the decision.

On October 8, 1906, Roosevelt, in one of his trust-busting rampages, and further enraged by a report (probably untrue) that Harriman had bragged he could, if he so chose, buy the judiciary, the legislatures, and Congress, wrote to Republican congressman James Schoolcraft Sherman of New York:

It shows a cynicism and deep-seated corruption which make the man uttering such sentiments, and boasting, no matter how falsely, of his power to perform such crimes, at least as undesirable a citizen as Debs, or Moyer, or Haywood.* The wealthy corruptionist, and the demagogue who excites, in the press or on the stump, in office or out of office, class against class, and appeals to the basest passions of the human soul, are fundamentally alike and are equally enemies of the Republic.

The following April he wrote to Thomas MacDonald Patterson, Colorado's former Democratic senator: "The real trouble with Harriman and his associates is that they have found themselves absolutely powerless to control any action by the National Government. There is no form of mendacity or bribery or corruption that they will not resort to in the effort to take vengeance. . . ." And to Bryn Mawr's president David Scull: "That some trouble has been caused by the action I have taken against great and powerful malefactors, I have no doubt. . . ."

The action had brought on to the national scene the Interstate Commerce Commission, the nation's first government regulatory body, established in 1887 originally with jurisdiction over railroads only but gradually expanded to deal with all forms of transportation. The I.C.C. grew out of the public sense of outrage at the monopolistic depredations of the railroad robber barons. Harriman was in the forefront of these nabobs who drew the greatest obloquy, not only because of his unpleasant manner and demeanor, his rudeness and grim taciturnity, but because of his naked attempts to preempt the major railroad systems of the West.

But Kahn never wavered in his fidelity or his service to Harriman. "The Harriman Extermination League," as Kahn dubbed his idol's detractors, "played its trump-card by poisoning President Roosevelt's mind against Mr. Harriman, with whom he used to be on friendly terms, by gross misrepresentations, which caused him to see the embodiment of everything that his moral sense abhorred, and the archetype of a class whose exposure and destruction he looked upon as a solemn patriotic duty."

The cunning manipulations of Edward Harriman, who became president of the Union Pacific in 1904, extended its mileage from less

---

* Eugene V. Debs, Charles Moyer, and William D. ("Big Bill") Haywood were socialist labor leaders who organized the Industrial Workers of the World.

than 2,000 in 1898 to more than 6,000 in 1906. He also achieved control of the Southern Pacific system, which embraced 7,000 miles of trackage as well as steamships and steamship ports. The combination of the two systems restrained competition and created a virtual monopoly, in contravention of the 1890 Sherman Antitrust Act, the first congressional measure to proscribe trusts. The acquisitions of the controlling securities were realized through Kuhn, Loeb, with Otto Kahn frequently planning and handling the intricate negotiations. Each year brought an enormous increase of the Union Pacific's receipts. Within three years, from 1903 to 1906, they soared from around $55 million to more than $75 million. The surplus for 1906, after the payment of dividends, exceeded $12 million, more than double the surplus in 1903. By 1907, Harriman controlled, directly or indirectly, through the Union Pacific and Southern Pacific systems, ten major railroad lines, five navigation companies, the street railway systems of Los Angeles and Ogden, Utah, and substantial interests in coal, oil, land, town-site, and miscellaneous other corporations. In the empire of American railroads he was the emperor.

Roosevelt continued to view Harriman with a jaundiced eye. He believed him, as well as his Union Pacific associates, not only to have violated the antitrust law but to have traded insider information when the company directors voted to increase the dividend from 6 to 10 percent. At Roosevelt's instigation the Interstate Commerce Commission, in February 1907, began an investigation into "the matter of consolidation and combination of carriers, relations between such carriers, and community of interests therein, their rates, facilities and practices."

The witnesses included Harriman, Kahn, Jacob Schiff, and other Kuhn, Loeb directors. The faithful Kahn, however, felt that his mentor had committed a grievous blunder. "Whether long continued, nerve-racking, physical suffering had for once affected his otherwise unfailing judgment," Kahn said years later, ". . . whether the contemplation of the Union Pacific's dazzling prosperity overcame temporarily the hitherto so potent sobriety of his brain, . . . whether for once his vast and restless ambition had broken through his calm reasoning, or whether it was simply an unaccountable error of judgment . . . whatever be the cause or the explanation, he took action in that year which, it always seemed to me, was the one serious mistake of his management of Union Pacific affairs.

"I refer to the purchases of very large amounts of stocks of many other companies, which were made for the account, and placed in the treasury, of the Union Pacific. . . ."

On the witness stand Harriman made no bones about his passionate acquisitiveness. Like most of his fellow multimillionaire industrialists, he hardly took the antitrust act seriously, considering himself, in any event, above the law. (When, after the short but devastating stock exchange panic of May 1907, a reporter asked J. P. Morgan, whose maneuvers had contributed to it, whether he did not owe the public an explanation, the piratical Morgan growled: "I owe the public nothing.") After enumerating some of the companies Harriman had invaded, Interstate Commerce Commissioner Franklin K. Lane exclaimed, "Where is this thing going to stop?"

With sublime arrogance Harriman replied, "I would go with it, if I thought we could realize something more than we have got from those investments, I would go on and buy some more things."

"What about the Santa Fe Railroad?"

"If you will let us, I will go and take the Santa Fe tomorrow."

Lane repeated, "You would take it tomorrow?"

"Why certainly I would; I would not have any hesitation; it is a pretty good property."

"Then it is only the restriction of the law that keeps you from taking it?"

"I would go on as long as I lived."

"Then after you had gotten through with the Santa Fe and had taken it, you would also take the Northern Pacific and the Great Northern if you could get them?"

"If you would let me."

"And your power, which you have, would gradually increase, as you took one road after another, so that you might spread out not only over the Pacific coast, but spread out over the Atlantic coast?"

"Yes, but hasn't your organization increased its power?"

"It undoubtedly has. That is what I am coming to. Do you think the law itself should intervene there and restrict you in your power to use your money raised for railroad purposes, or should you be allowed to use it for the acquisition of other railroads?"

"I think we should be allowed to use it for the acquisition of other railroads, under proper regulation."

Kahn, who followed Harriman to the witness stand, also refused to answer key questions involving specific stock transactions, such as how many shares of Illinois Central were transferred to the Union Pacific and whether these securities were acquired by a syndicate or a pool (in a railroad pool, rival companies contract to unite their businesses from which the money received is divided among them in fixed percentages). Since 1887, pools had been illegal under I.C.C. rules.

"Let me state," said Kahn, "I will answer every question bearing upon our dealings with the Union Pacific freely and willingly, but I will not answer any questions bearing upon our relations to our clients."

His testimony was otherwise notable for its clarity, concision, and knowledge of railroading and railroad finance. Quietly smiling, soft-spoken, his Anglo-Teutonic mixture of accents soothing, sartorially exquisite, he recounted the minutiae of the Union Pacific reorganization, Kuhn, Loeb's role in it, and the purchase and sale of various companies, all mined from his memory without consulting a document. It was an astonishing performance, and it impressed his interrogators.

They insisted, however, on answers regarding specific transactions with the Illinois Central and other railroad companies, and they later instituted legal proceedings to compel Kahn and Harriman to respond. The following year the United States Supreme Court ruled that the commission was not entitled to press questions relative to private transactions. When a complaint is filed, the Court noted, that railroad officials have conspired to create illegal combinations or restrain trade, the case clearly calls for criminal prosecution. No such prosecution ever befell Harriman, Kahn, or any member of Kuhn, Loeb.

In June 1909, Harriman sailed to Europe, hoping to repair a state of health ravaged by worries and tension he had kept bottled up for years. Running into Kahn in Munich toward the end of the summer, he reviewed triumphantly their joint achievements. They had cause to rejoice. The first fiscal year after Harriman joined the Union Pacific board, the surplus earnings, when applied to $107 million of common stock, were $5.8 million. As the two men chatted, the surplus earnings (not counting Southern Pacific), applicable to $216 million of common stock, were $41.5 million. The company's free assets aggregated $210 million. "There is more before us during the next ten years," the ailing Harriman predicted, "than in the last ten." A few weeks later, on September 9, 1909, he died at the age of sixty-two. He left a personal fortune of $78 million.

Deaf to the slurs that had besmirched Harriman's memory, Kahn presented a lengthy encomium on January 25, 1911, at New York's Finance Forum. Like the innumerable addresses he gave on a wide variety of topics, it was rescued from pomposity by his patent sincerity and the charm of his delivery. "Not infrequently," he said, "he [Harriman] would come to meetings at which ten or twelve men sat around the table with him . . . a large majority of whom were opposed to the measures he would propose. Yet, I know of hardly an instance of any importance where his views did not prevail finally, and what is more, generally by unanimous vote. . . . He once said to me . . . : 'All the opportunity I ask is to be among fifteen men around a table.'. . .

"His genius was the genius of the conqueror, his dominion was based on rugged strength, iron will, irresistible determination, indomitable courage, tireless toil, amazing intellect and last but not least, upon those qualities of character which command men's trust and confidence. . . .

". . . The way to the heights of power leads always through the valleys of envy, jealousy and animosity; but in Mr. Harriman's case the opposition, the enmities, the hatreds, which dispute and contested his progress were bitter, violent and numerous, far beyond ordinary measure. Yet, by the irresistible force of his genius, he acquired in the space of but ten years a position in the railroad world such as no man had held before him and no man, I believe, will hold again.

"Though he was lacking in the faculty of attracting men in general . . . he did have the gift in a most marvelous degree of attracting power as the magnet attracts iron. . . .

"He had measured strength with all those who cared to cross swords with him, and out of every fight he had come, if not invariably victorious, invariably unscathed, bigger and stronger than before. The railroad properties in his charge had grown and prospered beyond all others. There were enemies left, but none that cared any longer to try conclusions with him. . . .

"His word was equally good to friend and foe, and it was truly as good as his bond. . . . Never did he break faith. . . . He was loyal to a fault. . . . I have known him to take upon himself the whole brunt of defense or attack, from a fine feeling born of chivalrous consideration for those on whom he might have unloaded part of the burden, and from a proud consciousness of his ability to cope with difficult situations single-handed and unaided. Never have I met any one more utterly free from vindictiveness and malice. Whether from religious sentiment (for he was deeply and genuinely religious), from principle, or simply because his nature happened to be constituted that way, vengeance, retribution were no concern of his. . . .

"His career was the embodiment of unfettered individualism. For better or for worse—and personally I believe for better unless we go too far and too fast— the people appear determined to put limits and restraints upon the exercise of economic power, just as in former days they put limits and restraints upon the absolutism of rulers. Therefore, I believe, there will be no successor to Mr. Harriman; there will be no other career like his."

In an obituary, the weekly *Living Age* commented: "Harriman will be remembered as an extremely successful and unscrupulous manipulator of Wall Street."

Otto Kahn hung a portrait of Harriman on the wall behind his office desk, and would sometimes turn toward it when discussing a security, especially a railroad security.

Roosevelt went on to assault powerful corporations for a variety of trade abuses. Kahn branded himself a maverick when he publicly upheld the necessity for government to regulate business. In his day he may have been the country's only progressive banker. "Mr. Kahn," said Roosevelt, "has his face set toward the light."

From time to time Roosevelt consulted Kahn on fiscal problems. In one of their extensive talks, Kahn reproached him, not for his assaults against questionable corporate practices, but for the violence with which he expressed his accusations. Roosevelt rejoined, as Kahn recalled: "If my actions were called for, as you are inclined generally to agree, my speeches were a necessary prerequisite or concomitant."

After Roosevelt's death in 1919, Kahn wrote a statement at the request of the Roosevelt Memorial Association:

". . . He saw that business had grown to exercise excessive and, in certain aspects, almost uncontrolled power, and he knew that such power, whenever, wherever, and by whomever exercised, breeds abuses, and is a menace to the State and in the unavoidably resulting ultimate consequences, a grave danger to the class that wields it.

"He determined to challenge that power, to impose reasonable restraints and regulations upon it. . . . It took courage at that time to challenge seriously the power of business, and to summon it to surrender certain prerogatives which it had gradually acquired and which it had come to regard as naturally and justly due it. . . . What afterward became 'business baiting' and harassing bureaucratic overregulation, was an act of bold and hazardous resolution at the time and under the circumstances when Roosevelt undertook it."

8

The Diamond Horseshoe

When Kahn first sat on the board of the Metropolitan Opera Company, fashion and social protocol took precedence over music. The "Diamond Horseshoe," comprising thirty-five parterre boxes, so dubbed because of the cascades of jewelry flashing upon the bosoms of the lady occupants, was a rendezvous of Vanity Fair. (Originally it was the "Golden Horseshoe," when, as Irving Kolodin notes in his *The Metropolitan Opera, 1883–1935*, "the first *Faust* in 1883 found the representatives of half a billion dollars in the boxes of the Metropolitan.") Each box, along with a thirty-fifth interest in the building and property, belonged to a shareholder who had subscribed, for the privilege, to three hundred shares at a par value of $100 a share. In addition, the shareholder bought $30,000 worth of a bond issue for the reconstruction of the opera house, begun in 1893 after a fire the previous year. He was further assessed $15 per share a year for the maintenance of the building. Beside the door of each box, which between operas was kept curtained and locked, the boxholder's name was engraved on a brass plaque, the ultimate symbol of social ascendance. A woman attendant unlocked the door, admitting the owner and his party to a tiny salon decorated in red and gold, the chairs gilded and upholstered in velvet. Some boxholders provided their own furnishings. The Grand Tier above contained nineteen additional boxes, which were leased for one or more days throughout the season.

The by-laws prohibited the transfer of shares, which was tantamount to the sale of a box, to anybody not approved by the board. The owner of the box, however, remained free to rent it for one or more days a week throughout the season. According to an unwritten law, of which J. P. Morgan was among the principal champions, no Jew could own a box. Kahn, though a member of the board, later the chairman, and finally the president, was not spared this humiliation. Why did he swallow it? Perhaps his love of opera, the opportunity to take an active hand in its production, stifled any impulse he may have had to resign. (His initials, O.H.K., it was suggested, stood for "Opera House Kahn.") Perhaps, too, he welcomed the prospect of fraternizing with the grandees of New York society. Some seasons he would rent a parterre box from the owner. At times he subscribed to two orchestra seats, one for his hat and coat.

Seventeen years after his election to the board, Kahn was allowed to buy Box 14. He is reputed to have said in a rare mood of bitterness—for he was not a bitter man: "A kike is a Jewish gentleman who has just left the room."

The predominant figure of New York society, queen of the Diamond Horseshoe, was Mrs. William Waldorf Astor, who wore a stomacher ablaze with diamonds. Her ballroom could comfortably contain no more than 400 guests, a limitation that inspired social arbiter Ward McAllister to decree 400 to be the number of socially acceptable persons. "If she invited you," it was said, "you were in; if she did not, you were out." Kahn was never invited.

Mrs. Astor set the style for opera-going as she did for most pursuits of the upper crust. She chose Monday nights to attend the Met because they were the opening nights, and so did her peers. She and they usually arrived after the overture—though sometimes the manager would hold the curtain for Mrs. Astor—and departed after the second intermission.

By 1907 the Metropolitan Opera and Real Estate Company wanted to rid itself of Conried. Not only was his poor health affecting his managerial ability, but his personality—crude, self-important, despotic—had long irked his associates. To buy his lease the board offered him $90,000, a figure based on his claim that the Conried Metropolitan Opera Company had $130,000 in the till. In reality, only $30,000 remained. The board announced his resignation on February 12, 1908. He died the following year.

Kahn's first major mission for the Met had been to find a new general manager. Conried's lease still had three years to run, but the Metropolitan Opera and Real Estate Company was determined to displace him by hook or crook.

As general manager of Milan's Teatro alla Scala, Giulio Gatti-Casazza occupied the most prestigious administrative position in the world of opera. A large, bearded, fiery-tempered man of aristocratic bearing, he had studied naval engineering; but when his father withdrew from the directorship of Ferrara's Municipal Theater, the son replaced him. So distinguished was Gatti's rule there that in 1898, at the age of twenty-nine, he was appointed general manager of La Scala. He indulged a satyrlike appetite, with a predilection for the singers he employed. During his first year at La Scala a Spanish soprano, Maria Barrientos, made her debut in the title role of Léo Delibes's *Lakmé* at the precocious age of fifteen, to which her proud mother drew attention by standing in the lobby flourishing the prodigy's passport. Maria eventually became Gatti's mistress, only to be supplanted by the New Zealand born soprano Frances Alda, who, after marrying him in 1910, had to share him with Rosina Galli, the prima ballerina of the Metropolitan Opera.

In June 1907, Gatti received a letter from "a very distinguished lady, a good friend of mine" (which is her only identification in his autobiography): "I am writing you on behalf of a very important person who, for the moment, does not wish to be named, and who, personally, does not know you. Here is the matter: if you have followed the affairs of the Metropolitan Opera in New York you have seen that on account of the illness that has overtaken the General Director, Heinrich Conried, they are thinking of finding a successor. Many names have been submitted and among these is yours. If on the whole you are disposed to enter into negotiations please let me know and I shall not fail to give you further news and developments."

Gatti was dining that evening with Arturo Toscanini, the chief conductor of La Scala since 1898, and he showed him the letter. "Look here, Gatti," said Toscanini, "you know that during the past year Conried asked me to come to the Metropolitan as conductor and you will also remember that I refused immediately. . . . You also know that I have not remained at La Scala very willingly for many reasons. If you care to consider the proposal that has been made to you and if you arrive at an agreement that is suitable to you, I will go to the Metropolitan willingly this time. We have known each other for twenty years, we have always been in agreement, we will continue to be in accord. After all, each of us knows his own métier and, when that is said, we can be certain of getting by honorably in every theatre."

It was early July, the time of year when Kahn, observing the seasonal fashion, went abroad with his family. Gatti visited him in Paris at an apartment he had rented on the Place des États-Unis. There Kahn asked him if he would accept the post of general manager of the Met. Gatti answered in a florid outpouring. "I thank you, Mr. Kahn, for the faith you have shown in me. I am well aware that you are besieged and importuned by a large number of persons who aspire to Conried's place. I certainly will not importune you in any way, the more so since I am very well situated in every respect. Nevertheless, if you and your colleagues believe that I am the person suited for the Metropolitan, please let me know and in that event I hope that we shall be able to come to an agreement. I should wish in that case that an offer should also be made to Maestro Toscanini, who has already been invited to come to the Metropolitan during the past season."

Toward mid-January of 1908, La Scala, still under Gatti's command, was performing Alberto Franchetti's *Cristoforo Colombo*, an opera composed to commemorate the four hundredth anniversary of the discovery of America. At the end of the second act, just as the ship-borne chorus hails the American landfall, a cablegram was delivered backstage to Gatti, affirming Kahn's original proposal.

Kahn had one reservation. On January 1 of that year Gustav Mahler made his debut at the Met conducting *Tristan und Isolde*. He scored a resounding success and was offered a contract to conduct not only the Met orchestra the following two seasons but the New York Philharmonic as well. Would Toscanini see eye to eye with the brilliant Viennese composer-conductor? Gatti put the question to him. "But of course I will have no difficulty at all," Toscanini replied. "There is room at the Metropolitan for several conductors and I am very happy to find myself with an artist of Mahler's worth. I hold Mahler in great esteem, and would infinitely prefer such a colleague to any mediocrity."

Two three-year contracts followed. As "First Orchestra Conductor for operas, concerts and oratorios to be performed in the Metropolitan Opera House in New York and in such other theatres or halls in the United States of America where the Company will give performances," Toscanini was to receive $7,000 a month, payable in advance, for each month from fall to spring, or about four and a half months, and "to have full authority in all matters of artistic consideration with reference to the performances directed by him." Gatti received about the same financial terms and the "authority to make contracts with artists, conductors, publishers, contractors of various supplies, orchestra, music bands, chorus, ballet personnel, employees, artisans and with whom else he may find it convenient to contract in the interest of the company. . . ." Both contracts were signed by Kahn in his capacity as "Chairman and Executive Director."

The agreements, for which Kahn was largely responsible, bore their first fruit on Monday, November 16, 1908, the opening night of that season. It was the gala of galas. For the first time Arturo Toscanini bowed to an American audience. The opera was *Aida* in a new scenic production designed by La Scala's Mario Sala and Angelo Parravicini. The Czech soprano Emmy Destinn made her American debut in the title role. Caruso sang Radames; Louise Homer, Amneris; and Antonio Scotti, Amonasro. Though the critics praised the singers, they reserved their highest accolade for Toscanini: ". . . in the best sense, an artist, an interpreter, a re-creator," declared the *Tribune*'s Henry Krehbiel.

Toscanini's second opera led to a romantic entanglement that would interrupt his American career. The beauteous Geraldine Farrar made her Met debut as Madama Butterfly. The highly susceptible Italian conductor and the queenly American soprano began a love affair. When, in 1915, toward the end of his second contract, she demanded that he choose between her and his wife and children back in Italy, he chose his family and sailed home.

No such emotional conflict perturbed Gatti, a bachelor, though an avid collector of attractive women. On April 3, 1910, he married Frances Alda, who had performed under his management at La Scala and made her Met debut in 1908 as Gilda in *Rigoletto*. Not long after the wedding the bride chanced to be watching a rehearsal from a box when she overheard in the adjoining box, separated from hers by a velvet curtain, her husband discussing the 1910–11 season with the impresario Henry Russell. "As the director's wife," Gatti was saying, "it is much better if Alda does not sing this season." Alda swept back the curtain, terrible in her wrath. "I suppose," she said, "it would be all right if I were his mistress instead of his wife. I resign right now." And she did not appear again on the Met stage for two years, until, in 1912, she relented and sang Desdemona in Verdi's *Otello*. She remained at the Met for the next two decades, one of the most brilliant jewels in the company's diadem.

Gatti's initial reaction to the opera house was dispiriting. He started out agreeable enough. "The auditorium . . . ," he told Kahn, "represents a rather happy compromise between the old opera house and the new," but then he changed his tone: ". . . first, the seats in the orchestra, the boxes, the dress circle, and the two balconies are too near the stage on the sides. Second, the close contact between the standees and the seatholders in the orchestra circle represents an unpleasant inconvenience. . . . As for the stage, although we are dealing with a theatre you have wanted to modernize, this modernization would have only partial and incomplete results. Moreover, the stage has the defect of being too short and too narrow. There is no modern equipment of any kind.

"The Metropolitan lacks, moreover, rehearsal rooms for the artists, the chorus and the ballet. The storehouses are too far away, and one must leave the scenery in the street for hours, often exposed to rain and snow.

"If one takes into consideration the length of the season and the richness of the repertoire, certainly the Metropolitan is an opera house that leaves much to be desired."

"Well, dear Mr. Gatti," Kahn replied sweetly, "what you say is perfectly true, and we have noticed these things before you. But don't worry about it and have patience. In two or three years a new Metropolitan Opera House will be built, answering all our needs. Make for the present what changes will be most useful. And have patience; you will be satisfied shortly."

Kahn strove, however, to meet Gatti's specifications. He had already backed Heinrich Conried to the extent of $50,000, as did each of his twenty-nine fellow Metropolitan board members, in a plan to erect the New Theatre on Central Park West between Sixty-second and Sixty-third streets. It was to be a national repertory theater, offering both plays and operas. A series of disasters, beginning with the Wall Street panic of 1907, and including structural defects of the vast, elaborate edifice, horrendously bad acoustics, and a hostile press that viewed it as a superfluous rich man's toy, ended the project. The New Theatre was eventually reborn as the Century Theatre, a house of spectacular showpieces.*

The cool-headed banker and the haughty, hot-headed opera manager collaborated with relatively little friction. Kahn, musically sophis-

---

* The site is now occupied by the Century Apartments.

ticated, with an acute ear for vocal superiority, listened to artists in Europe and America and recommended to Gatti those he deemed worthy to sing at the Met. Gatti, in turn, submitted his choices to Kahn, though his contract required no such consultation. During twenty-three years of their regime they produced the American premieres of fifty-two operas, among them Tchaikovsky's *Eugene Onegin* and Strauss's *Der Rosenkavalier*, new productions of Wagner's Ring cycle, and eighteen world premieres, including Puccini's *La Fanciulla del West*, Humperdinck's *Koenigskinder*, Granados's *Goyescas*, and ten American works.

Financially, their collaboration consistently kept the Met in the black for twenty seasons, due partly to the business acumen and the personal contributions of Kahn, who provided close to $2 million as needed. "It is no secret," wrote the music critic W. J. Henderson, "that the present sound condition of the Metropolitan Opera House is due chiefly to the combination of artistic enthusiasm with business sagacity."

At the outset of his board membership Kahn also organized a baseball team among the Met employees, supplying all their uniforms and equipment. On their jerseys was sewn the acronym MOH. A Boston Opera team challenged them in 1909, and Kahn dispatched his MOHs to the Massachusetts capital, all expenses paid. The Bostonians, to Kahn's fury when he found out, sneaked in a pro pitcher and soundly beat the visiting team. Kahn insisted on a return match at New York's Polo Grounds and quietly hired two pros of his own. The Bostonians never got to first base. Kahn then treated both teams to a banquet at the Met restaurant, followed by an all-day boat excursion to Coney Island. This was not the kind of bonhomie that appealed to Gatti, who tended to hold himself aloof.

Both Kahn and Gatti treasured Caruso as their star of stars, but with Kahn friendship transcended profit. He loved the man. Caruso had endeared himself to Kahn even further when, before the 1908–1909 season, Oscar Hammerstein had offered him $5,000 to quit the Met and sing for the Manhattan Opera Company. The tenor was then receiving $2,000 a performance in New York and $2,500 on the road. Kahn left the money line on Caruso's new contract blank for him to fill in with whatever sum he wished. "I don't think," said Caruso, "there is one singer in the world who can give in one performance more than twenty-five hundred dollars' worth of singing. If I ask you for one cent more than twenty-five hundred, the public will find out one way or another and want from me that cent more of singing, which I have not got." And he refused to accept any increase.

To forge closer links of friendship with Caruso, Kahn began studying conversational Italian. He persuaded the tenor's Italian secretary, Bruno Zirato, to ride downtown with him mornings to the Kuhn, Loeb offices so they might rehearse words and phrases en route. Often, after the opera, Il Ottokan would join Caruso and his jovial, boisterous cronies for a garlicky supper at Del Pezzo's on West Thirty-fourth Street, not far from the Met, the singer's favorite restaurant, and a game of *scopa* afterward.

On August 5, 1921, Kahn cabled Gatti, who was summering abroad: I AM INFINITELY SHOCKED AND GRIEVED ABOUT POOR CARUSO'S DEATH [on the 2nd in Naples] AND WITH YOU I MOURN PROFOUNDLY THE UNTIMELY TAKING OFF OF THIS ADMIRABLE MAN AND GLORIOUS ARTIST I KNOW HOW DEEP MUST BE YOUR SORROW ABOUT THE LOSS OF ONE WITH WHOM YOU HAVE COLLABORATED FOR SO MANY YEARS & TO WHOM YOU WERE ATTACHED IN WARM PERSONAL FRIENDSHIP PLEASE ACCEPT THE EXPRESSION OF THE HEARTFELT SYMPATHY OF YOUR SINCERE FRIEND OTTO KAHN.

As a self-appointed impresario for the Met, Kahn kept his eyes and ears open for promising talent wherever he traveled and transmitted his observations to Gatti. Thus, in 1918, he recognized the supremacy of Feodor Chaliapin. The Russian basso had already made his Met debut on November 20, 1907, at the age of twenty-four, in the title role of Boito's *Mefistofele*, but proved an abysmal failure. The critics condemned his interpretation as coarse, carnal, and vulgar. Kahn beheld a totally different artist eleven years later in the mature Chaliapin as Boris Godunov, and he urged Gatti to reengage him for that role at the Met. This time, on December 9, 1921, both critics and public cheered.

Also in 1918, Kahn first heard the Italian basso Virgilio Lazzari at the Chicago Opera and wrote about him enthusiastically to Gatti, but not for fifteen years was Lazzari free to make his debut at the Met as Don Pedro in Meyerbeer's *L'Africaine*.

The Italian baritone Mattia Battistini, an exemplar of bel canto singing and a notable Don Giovanni, who performed in England, Spain, and Russia, also captivated Kahn, but his terror of ocean travel was so intense that he could not bring himself to accept a Met engagement.

Nothing so irked Kahn as the popular notion that the Met, with its autocratic general manager and its multimillionaire president, snobbishly ignored American artists. ". . . I don't know of a single instance," he protested, "where there was even remote reason to suspect that the manager or any of the conductors favored the engagement of an artist or the production of a work of art because of the country they came from or that they were guilty of the folly and disloyalty of opposing or failing to do justice to American art and artists because they were American. . . .

"The policy of the Metropolitan Opera Company and the way in which it conceives its functions and its duty are . . . first, to make every effort to give opera in the best possible manner . . . ; second . . . to bring here the best available talent from everywhere; and third, to give preference, other things being equal, to American art and American artists over foreign art and foreign artists. The Metropolitan Opera does not believe itself called upon to lower its standards for the sake of proving its 'Americanism,' nor does it feel that by doing so it would best serve the cause of art in America or please its patrons or even be able to retain their patronage."

Furthermore, he maintained, "a potential music lover may be found in almost every home in America."

Unlike Gatti, an operatic conservative, Kahn was responsive to the original, the experimental, the avant-garde, and at times moved well ahead of the prevailing mode. Of the testimonials to his musical judgment, the most flattering came from Sergei Prokofiev, who was then living at 340 West Fifty-seventh Street. On May 6, 1919, he had submitted to Kahn the outline of his opera *The Gambler*, hoping for a production at the Met. Kahn had explained that the Met's 1920–21 schedule was already set. Prokofiev wrote again on January 18, 1920:

"Last spring you paid me the honor of expressing your interest in my opera 'Le Joueur' [The Gambler]. As it was the month of May, you told me that the repertory of the Metropolitan was already made up, but that in the future you would be interested in knowing the music from that work. My other opera 'L'Amour des trois Oranges' [The Love for Three Oranges] will not be given this season because of the death of Maestro Campanini [the chief conductor of the Chicago Opera, which had undertaken to produce the work], though [Boris] Anisfeld has already made the costumes. The Association of the Opera of Chicago is determined to produce it next season, but I do not think that they have the right to do so having breached the contract, according to which they were to have given it this year. At the moment I am trying to work on my third opera, 'L'Ange Flemboyant' [*sic;* The Flaming Angel], based on a romantic and dramatic subject.

"Knowing that you are a true connoisseur of modern art and remembering the interest that you have expressed toward my art, I am taking the liberty of asking your permission to see you to discuss these three operas and, if you wish, to play for you some excerpts. . . ."

Kahn replied three days later: ". . . I should have been delighted to hear extracts from your operas, but I am about to leave for Europe. . . .

"I spoke on the subject to Mr. Gatti-Casazza, and he asks me to say to you that if you wish to give him an opportunity to acquaint himself with the libretto and in due course with the score of your new work, 'L'Ange Flamboyant,' he will be pleased to give it careful and sympathetic consideration. Personally, I should be happy to see a work of yours produced at the Metropolitan Opera House."

But Prokofiev knew what to expect from the conservative general manager. "I wish to express to you my deep regret at your departure for Europe," he wrote to Kahn on the twenty-second, "as I doubt that Mr. Gatti-Casazza, with his eyes turned to the past, could see the possibilities of my opera as well as you would with your eyes turned to the future."

No Prokofiev opera was ever produced by the Met.

The German modernist Ernst Křenek's jazz opera, *Jonny Spielt Auf* (Johnny Strikes Up the Band), inspired by the rhythms of life in the age of technology, was performed all over Europe in eighteen different languages. Kahn saw it in Leipzig and badgered Gatti, whose dish of tea it decidedly was not, to mount it at the Met. The premiere was January 18, 1929, and the third performance was the last ever in that house.

The prospect of a jazz opera continued to intrigue Kahn. He encouraged Irving Berlin and Jerome Kern, among others, to compose one. Said Berlin: "I'd give my right arm to be able to do syncopated opera, but I don't feel I'm equipped for the work." Kern declined on the same grounds. George Antheil, the self-styled "Bad Boy of Music," composer of the sensational *Ballet Mécanique*, partly scored for sirens and motors, accepted a commission from Kahn to write, with John Erskine as librettist, an opera about Helen of Troy. The Met turned it down. The Juilliard School of Music gave a few performances, all of them failures.

In the lounge of an ocean liner, in July 1924, Kahn heard a young composer named Gershwin play an unfinished melody that charmed him. (When completed, it was entitled "The Man I Love," and George's brother, Ira, wrote the lyrics.)

Not long after, the Gershwins and the producer Alex Aarons began work on a new musical, *Black-eyed Susan* (later retitled *Lady, Be Good!*). They invited Kahn to invest in it. He refused on the somewhat quixotic grounds that he only backed shows bound to lose money; surefire hits didn't need his support. But when Gershwin played the melody, now completed, of which Kahn had heard only part while at sea, he immediately agreed to invest $10,000. *Lady, Be Good!* became one of the very rare shows that returned Kahn a profit.

In musical circles it was rumored that Gershwin, after reading DuBose Heyward's novel *Porgy* in 1926, hoped to compose an opera based on it. Kahn offered him a bonus of $5,000 if the Metropolitan Opera could stage the finished work. Gershwin refused because the Met could not guarantee more than half a dozen performances, and he therefore preferred a Broadway run. A Met premiere of *Porgy and Bess* did finally take place—on February 6, 1985.

After the debacle of *Jonny Spielt Auf*, Kahn came to feel that a jazz opera in the literal sense was perhaps a contradiction in terms. "But I do hope," he said, "that some of the young American composers who, at present, are devoting their talents to producing jazz music and jazz songs, will tackle more important and exacting tasks. I hope some of them will try their hand at opera and endeavor to express themselves in their own way—themselves and the spirit of the life which surrounds them—however unconventional that may be.

"Such an opera will probably contain some of the motives, rhythms, and characteristics of jazz, but whether it does or not is immaterial. The main question is: Has the work got musical merit? Does the composer have something to say, and does he say it in the manner which, to him, is the natural and spontaneous way of expressing himself? . . .

"There is a call for a new departure in opera. That does not mean that the old may be neglected, or looked at askance, or thrust aside. But while respectful of the accumulated treasures, achievements, and lessons of the past, and reverential of the masters, music should seek to express its day and even to anticipate. True art is eternal, but it is not stationary."

Kahn's interest in jazz was further stimulated by the musical precocity of his younger son Roger Wolfe Kahn, who was named for his grandfather Abraham Wolff but for reasons unknown substituted, in his teens, an *e* for the second *f*. At the age of ten he acquired a ukulele and an instruction book; by the age of fifteen he had managed to organize a dance band. To finance it, Roger extracted an advance of

$25,000 from his father, who wanted him to attend M.I.T. and pursue an engineering career, by threatening to borrow the money elsewhere. Within a short time he had returned every cent of the money. The band's first engagement was at the Knickerbocker Grill. Roger himself could play eleven instruments, all learned by ear, and as a crowd-pleaser would keep a set of them in a basket at his side, picking up first one, then another. A small, shy, jug-eared youth, he proceeded to assemble ten more bands that played under his name up and down the Atlantic coast in theaters, vaudeville houses, and resort hotels, eventually earning an average of $50,000 a year. The future jazz masters who performed under his aegis included Tommy Dorsey, Artie Shaw, Joe Venuti, and Claude Thornhill. Morton Downey and Gertrude Niesen sang with the bands. Roger composed a number of popular tunes himself, among them "Following You Around" and "Crazy Rhythm."

The youth's success melted the elder Kahn's resistance. After one of Roger's bands opened with éclat at New York's Hippodrome, while Roger himself was in London, his father cabled, on August 25, 1924: CONGRATULATIONS YOU HAVE $3000 IN BANK YOU WILL NEED ALL OF IT TO PAY YOUR LOSSES AT GOLF AS I HAVE RECOVERED MY TRUE FORM. He publicly announced his support when, the following year, the Dutch Treat Club, a theatrical and literary sodality, gave a luncheon in Roger's honor. Otto Kahn, embracing him, proclaimed, "I can underwrite him for all I've got."

Otto later went so far as to back Roger in establishing Le Perroquet de Paris on Fifty-seventh Street, one of the most opulent nightclubs jazz-age society ever patronized. It proved too opulent, and Roger closed it to devote himself to jazz as band leader and composer, as well as to his new interest, aviation.

9

Ballet

At the turn of the century classical ballet was so little known in America that when, in 1910, Anna Pavlova and Mikhail Mordkine danced at the Met, brought there by Otto Kahn, the nature of the art required elucidation. Some New York critics described it as "ocular ballet" and "visual ballet," terms that were used wherever they toured. Their unofficial American debut took place at a private soiree given in late February by Mrs. Harry Payne Whitney. Addie Kahn followed suit on March 4 with a dinner at Sherry's restaurant, after which Pavlova danced, the Spanish soprano Elvira de Hidalgo sang, and a one-act opera by Emmanuel Chabrier was performed. Between these glittering events Pavlova, Mordkine, and a pick-up company danced the first act of *Coppélia* at the Met, following the regularly scheduled opera, Massenet's *Werther*, which ended near midnight. They appeared in Boston and Baltimore and in the fall returned to New York to dance *Giselle* and embark on a cross-country tour.

Kahn had first seen the pair at the Paris premiere of Serge Diaghilev's Ballets Russes, the company's first public performance outside of Russia, at the Théâtre du Châtelet on May 18, 1909. The principal dancers included, in addition to Pavlova and Mordkine, the dazzling superstar Vaslav Nijinsky, Mikhail Fokine, and Tamara Karsavina, and the opening ballet was the dazzling *Le Pavillon d'Armide*, music by Nicolas Tcherepnine, costumes and decor by Alexandre Benois. Kahn was overwhelmed. Logistical obstacles, however, precluded an early American engagement. Instead, he booked Pavlova and Mordkine for the following year.

Hostile voices, among them Nijinsky's wife, Romola, whispered that Kahn sponsored ballet to acquire social distinction. There may have been a modicum of truth in this, but his desire to extend the cultural frontiers of his adopted countrymen was unquestionably sincere. "The lives of the vast majority of people are cast upon a background of sameness and routine," he said in an address at the annual dinner of the American Federation of Arts on May 16, 1924. "Perhaps this is unavoidable. The world's daily work has to be done. But all the more reason and needfulness for opening up, for making readily and widely accessible, and for cultivating, those pastures where beauty and inspiration may be gathered by all.

"We all, rich and poor alike, need to give our souls an airing once in a while. We need to exercise the muscles of our inner selves just as we exercise those of our bodies. We must have outlets for our emotions. Qualities and impulses of the right kind, when given due scope, enhance the zest and happiness of our lives; when thwarted, starved or denied, they are apt to turn to poison within us.

"Some of the unrest, the unruliness, the transgressions even, of the day, some of the seeking after sensations, some of the manifestations of extreme and subversive tendencies, arise in no small part, I believe, from an impulse of reaction against humdrumness and lack of inspirational opportunity of everyday existence. Much can be done by art to give satisfaction to that natural and legitimate impulse and to lead it into fruitful channels instead of letting it run a misguided, or even destructive course.

"Art is not the plaything of opulence. It is robust, red-blooded, deep-rooted and universal. It is true equality of opportunity.

"Art is the truest League of Nations, speaking a language and preaching a message understood by all people. . . ."

He bestowed upon Pavlova, in addition to her contractual pay of $1,000 per performance, the benefit of his financial judgment. When, during her cross-country tours, the box-office receipts fell steeply, he would send her rescue sums of from $5,000 to $10,000, and for many years after he served gratis as her investment adviser. At her death in 1931, the depth of the Great Depression, she left $377,000, thanks in part to Kahn's guidance.

During the summer of 1915, Gatti-Casazza, in Milan, at Kahn's request completed a mission distasteful to him. He reached an agreement with Diaghilev to bring the Ballets Russes to the Met the following season. Had Kahn foreseen the imbroglios this would entail he might have abandoned the project, but his determination to raise the American cultural level, mingled perhaps with a touch of social ambition, drove him on. Gatti, on the other hand, opposed the Russian invasion because it would cut deeply into the opera schedule, three weeks of it as it turned out. He also had personal reasons.

The personal reasons revolved around Rosina Galli, the Met's prima ballerina and ballet mistress. Gatti had known her since her preteen years as a member of La Scala's ballet troupe. From La Scala, at seventeen, she emigrated to the Chicago Opera Company, and thence, in 1914, to the Met, where, some half dozen years after Gatti's marriage to Frances Alda, she became his mistress. It is indicative of his discretion that he managed to maintain both relations for a decade without causing an emotional explosion. Alda finally divorced him in 1929, and the following year he married her rival—and remained with her for the rest of his life.

Even less than Gatti did Rosina Galli relish the advent of such formidable competitors as the Ballets Russes. But Kahn, the Met's majority shareholder, wielding greater power than all the other directors combined, could not be gainsaid.

Among the paramount conditions stipulated in the contract with Diaghilev was that the stars must include the legendary Nijinsky, for he was the one performer, Kahn knew, whom everybody would want to see, and Karsavina. Kahn, meanwhile, who planned to dispatch the Russians on a national tour, undertook the Herculean task of organizing it, raising the funds, and placating the opera patrons, who, like Gatti, resented the interruption of the regular opera schedule.

On January 12, 1916, the Ballets Russes, 125 dancers and musicians strong, with tons of scenery and costumes, disembarked in New York. To Kahn's chagrin, neither Nijinsky nor Karsavina was aboard. Nijinsky, his wife, and their daughter Kyra had been interned in Budapest almost since the outbreak of war, while Karsavina was stranded in St. Petersburg. Diaghilev was aware of this when he signed the contract, but, typically, hoped somehow to retrieve his two leading attractions. Kahn had no choice but to proceed as planned. So that the Met schedule not be disrupted, the premiere took place at the Century (formerly the New) Theatre on January 17 with *The Firebird, The Enchanted Princess, The Midnight Sun,* and *Schéhérazade.* After a third week at the Met itself, the company toured as far west as Kansas City. Kahn defrayed the deficit, which came to some $300,000.

The overriding dilemma now was Nijinsky's internment. No matter how stunningly the Ballets Russes performed, no matter how laudatory the critics, the hard fact remained that without Nijinsky, the ballet could not sustain public interest. Kahn pulled every string within his grasp. He appealed to Secretary of State Robert Lansing, seeking his intervention in behalf of the dancer. He sought help from Elisabeth, Comtesse Greffuhle, the enormously influential Paris *salonière* upon whom Proust modeled his Duchesse de Guermantes. It was probably the countess who persuaded Emperor Franz Josef to help free the Nijinskys. They were transported first to Vienna from Budapest, then permitted to go on to Switzerland.

But Kahn's troubles had scarcely begun. Nijinsky, fearing U-boat attacks, announced that he would not risk the crossing. Then, on the French border, Russian authorities stopped him as a potential draftee and threatened to return him to his native land, but in the end they allowed him to proceed.

On April 4, 1916, the French liner *Espagne* reached New York with the Nijinskys aboard. Amid the throng of reporters and Metropolitan Opera officials, Diaghilev was waiting dockside, a smile of greeting on his lips, flowers in hand. But it was the last amicable exchange between the impresario and the dancer, who had once been lovers. When Nijinsky had married, Diaghilev had brutally kicked him out of the company, and even now, despite the outward show of reconciliation, he had forbidden the members of the company to speak to him. Diaghilev, moreover, owed Nijinsky 500,000 gold francs, according to a court judgment, and though Nijinsky's Metropolitan Opera debut was set for the Wednesday matinee of April 12, he refused to appear until the debt was cleared. In addition, having no formal contract with Diaghilev, he demanded a salary of $3,000 a week as well as a share of the box-office receipts. But Diaghilev was, as usual, teetering on the verge of insolvency.

Nijinsky's demands for money, his frequent changes of plan, and his androgynous personality provoked mocking headlines. Was he going to dance or wasn't he? The general frustration moved the Met's administrative secretary, Edward Ziegler, to pen this doggerel:

> O Mr. Nijinsky
> Where have you binsky?
> And if you are here
> Why don't you appear
> And save the ballet from ruinsky?

The Nijinskys met Kahn for the first time in his Kuhn, Loeb lair. Immediately following the amenities, Nijinsky poured forth his grievances against Diaghilev, declaring that he would not appear at the Met until he received the money owed him. Kahn, outwardly calm, promised to see to it. Within a few days he handed Nijinsky the entire sum, transferred, in all probability, from his own pocket. To spare the dancer further entanglements with Diaghilev, he signed a private contract between Nijinsky and himself, whereby the dancer would give eleven performances at the Met.

Three days before the Met opening Nijinsky received a letter from the Russian consulate in New York asking when to expect his military enrollment. Frantic, Nijinsky sought advice from Kahn, who told him to postpone his reply. Having received no further word, Nijinsky, tremulous with anxiety, fulfilled his Met engagement.

The first program, on April 12, consisted of *Petrushka*, *Schéhérazade*, *Prince Igor*, and *Le Spectre de la Rose*, with Nijinsky's famous climactic leap through a window. While most critics commented on the extreme effeminacy of his personality, virtually all acclaimed him as a marvel without peer. The audience went wild.

Kahn resolved to sponsor a second season and tour in October, but the discord between Diaghilev and Nijinsky had proved so disruptive that Kahn would tolerate no more of it. He insisted that Diaghilev stay out of the country while Nijinsky replaced him as artistic director throughout the return engagement. Kahn would, in effect, lease the company from its founder. Diaghilev, his finances in disarray, had no choice but to accept.

Shortly a cable arrived from the Russian government ordering Nijinsky to return forthwith to Russia or risk the fate of a deserter. He turned again to Kahn, who assured him that nobody would seize him and urged him to keep going as planned.

Trouble preceded the second tour and worsened as it progressed. The Russian military authorities again notified Nijinsky that he was eligible for the draft. Kahn wrote in his behalf to the Russian ambassador in Washington, George Bakhmetieff:

". . . I am thoroughly convinced that one of the most effective ways to bring nations nearer to each other is to spread the knowledge and understanding for each other's art.

"The presentation of Russian art . . . is bound to be of use to the cause of Russia in this country, and the cancellation of that tournee, which would become necessary in case of Nijinsky's withdrawal almost at the last minute and after announcements and contracts have been made in a large number of cities, would lead to much dissatisfaction and disappointment on the part of many thousands of people who have been looking forward to the visit of that world-famous Russian organization.

"Perhaps I may also venture to hope that your Government may feel inclined to consider the Board of Directors of the Metropolitan Opera Company entitled to a certain measure of consideration, inasmuch as, solely because of their enthusiasm for the art of the Russian Ballet and from a desire to make that art known to the American public, they took it upon themselves, in the face of heavy financial loss [most of it absorbed by Kahn], which they knew beforehand was inevitable, to bring that organization to America for a limited tournee last season, and from the same altruistic motives (again in the face of certain loss) once more engaged the Russian Ballet this season for a more extended tournee.

"The French Government has sent Mr. [Pierre] Monteux direct from the trenches to conduct the orchestra for the Russian Ballet. With the termination of his engagement he will return to his military duty. [Actually, Monteux remained to conduct the Met orchestra.] May I not hope that your Government will not permit the question of a few months' delay in the arrival of a single soldier, Mr. Nijinsky (who, moreover, would still be a prisoner in Austria but for the efforts of the Metropolitan Opera Company last spring), to offset the considerations which I have taken the liberty of presenting in this letter. . . ."

Bakhmetieff replied: "I quite understand the situation and your anxiety about the matter and will do my best to assist you, although the orders to Nijinsky were very absolute. . . .

"I will let you know the moment I get an answer, but it will probably be some days, as the matter has to go before the Military authorities. . . ."

At length the Russians relented, and Nijinsky departed with the company.

But the ambiguity of Nijinsky's situation, his persistent fear of extradition, the crushing responsibilities of directorship, for which he was totally unqualified, further frayed his already worn nerves. He canceled bookings, confused schedules, sometimes failed to appear himself. The tour limped to a sorry end.

Nijinsky, who showed increasing signs of instability, never danced again in America. Nor did he dance much anywhere else. By 1919 he had lapsed into irreversible mental illness. He spent the rest of his life in sanitariums and died in 1950 at the age of sixty.

The second American tour cost Kahn more than half a million dollars. Yet he was not heard to complain. Perhaps he foresaw his reward. Lincoln Kirstein, founder and general director of the New York City Ballet, observed in 1959: "When we realize that the Bolshoi is sold out all over our nation in advance of its first appearance, every balletomane should burn a candle in his heart to the memory of the friendship, the understanding, the sense of cultural necessity that animated Otto Kahn and Serge Diaghilev."

Pierre Monteux, amused by Kahn's occasionally pragmatic means to an end, later recalled: "When I arrived at the Metropolitan Opera House [in 1917, to conduct *Faust*, his first opera there], the critics continued in their disapprobation of me, now saying that I was not an opera conductor, but a symphony and ballet conductor! Mr. Otto Kahn, obviously harassed by these articles which reached their apotheosis in a leading magazine having to do with music and artists in the concert and opera world, then told me, 'Don't worry, Monteux, I will stop this.' I wondered how he could educate a critic, but he did, by taking a five hundred dollar advertisement for me in that magazine. Would you believe it? The articles stopped!

"Mr. Gatti-Casazza then called me to his office and asked me to make him a list of all the operas I had conducted. I did, and the list filled two pages of typewritten paper. He roared with laughter and sent the whole list to the critics. . . ."

10

Kahn vs. Hammerstein

The sharpest thorn in the Met's side was the Manhattan Opera Company. The opening of the latter on December 3, 1906, had stirred the interest of the entire nation, for the moment putting the Met, which presented Flotow's *Marta* the same evening with Caruso, in the shade. The 3,100-seat theater had been sold out, standing room was tightly jammed, and outside, crowds surrounded the entrances and exits hoping to catch a glimpse of celebrities. But the countrywide enthusiasm revolved not so much around the opera itself—the American premiere of Bellini's *I Puritani*, then a relatively obscure work, with the tenor Alessandro Bonci making his first appearance in the United States—as around the career and personality of Oscar Hammerstein.

A German-Jewish immigrant from Berlin, the son of a struggling stockbroker, he came to New York in 1862. Marrying young, he fathered four children (of whom his son William became the father of the lyricist Oscar Hammerstein II). His first financial success, after a succession of profitless enterprises, was several inventions for the manufacture of cigars. But like Otto Kahn, he loved everything to do with the performing arts, especially opera. He produced vaudeville, plays, musical comedies, and he finally established the Manhattan Opera Company.

The Manhattan was no match for the social glitter of the Met, but its acoustics were superior, its productions opulent, and among the singers Hammerstein brought to America were some of the world's finest. As a national celebrity himself, he had few equals. His appearance—top hat, Prince Albert frock coat, black-and-white striped trousers, goatee and mustache, a homemade cigar protruding from his mouth—became, through newspaper stories, interviews, and cartoons, as familiar as Teddy Roosevelt's.

Hammerstein bore Kahn no warm affection, and he detested the Met, which he vowed to destroy. But Kahn admired Hammerstein despite their conflicting objectives. With Addie he attended several opening nights at the Manhattan Opera and applauded vigorously. When, in 1908, Hammerstein brashly built a second theater in Philadelphia, chiefly to outdo the Met, which included the city on its national tours, Kahn saw a production there of *Carmen*. "Mr. Hammerstein, you are a genius," Kahn said afterward. "For years I have been watching you, and every day that passes my admiration for you increases.

"The house is magnificent. No one but you could have built it in the incredibly short time. I doubted, at first, that you could do it. But then I knew that Oscar Hammerstein was back of the project, and I jotted down in a notebook that the Philadelphia Opera House would be completed on time.

"I think the house is one of the greatest in the world and I most heartily congratulate you. It is a great achievement in your wondrous career!"

But both men knew that New York could not support two competing major opera companies. As they strove to outshine each other, they both incurred enormous expenses. The 1907–1908 season, for example, ended for the Met with a loss of $84,039. Hammerstein's revenue from his first Manhattan Opera season showed a profit of $100,000, but after his second season, he commented philosophically: "My season was successful inasmuch as I lost only $50,000, whereas I expected to lose $75,000."

The rivalry between the Met and the Manhattan Opera grew fiercer, to the detriment of both. A prize they contended for was *Elektra*, Richard Strauss's next opera after *Salome*, and his first collaboration with the dynamic librettist Hugo von Hofmannsthal. Hammerstein got a head start. Soon after the Met's *Salome*, he journeyed to Berlin to ingratiate himself with the composer. He yearned not only to revive *Salome* but also to stage the American premiere of *Elektra*, which, as the musical world knew, Strauss had been composing since 1906. For the latter he guaranteed $10,000 for the American production rights and advance royalties of $18,000. Strauss, still smarting over *Salome*'s one-night stand at the Met, viewed the offer favorably. Kahn was dismayed. Desperate to secure *Elektra*, he initiated a correspondence with the composer. In an effort to place the blame for the ban where it belonged, he wrote to him on May 29, 1908:

". . . Your frank comments are most appreciated. I can understand completely your 'lust for revenge' against those responsible for the unfortunate *Salome* episode in New York. It is also quite understandable that you should regard 'Orestes' Hammerstein as a ready tool for atonement; but permit me to point out that you are looking for Clytemnestra and her paramour in the wrong place.

"The responsibility for the *Salome* veto must be shared by the clumsiness and the honestly-felt, but, in this case, totally inappropriate religiosity of Morgan. Conried tactlessly called the dress rehearsal for Sunday at eleven—the hour for church services—and invited 'tout New York,' thus attracting the attention and anger of churchmen, who stirred Morgan into action. . . . However, our own company, the Metropolitan Opera, is made up predominantly of 'rare birds,' who together with myself have campaigned most energetically for *Salome*.

"You ask me who is in charge here. Gatti-Casazza, an excellent man, who admires you very much, is General Manager, [Andreas] Dippel is Administrative Director. I am Chairman of the Board of Directors. . . .

"Whether or not we produce *Salome* . . . whether or not we produce *Elektra*, is of absolutely no concern to the wallet or emotions of Mr. Morgan and his company. Their protest, however, remains effective until, sooner or later, your hoped-for and inevitable retraction is coming. Ergo, since you aim your wrath at us you affect Mr. Morgan not at all; instead you harm *us* first of all and second, yourself, financially at least (for if you make punitive conditions for us but not for Hammerstein, the unavoidable result will be that your works will be done only by Hammerstein and not in both houses—not to mention the fact that our troupe tours a good portion of the country, while Hammerstein plays only in New York and Philadelphia). The only one who can profit is 'Orestes' Hammerstein, the 'tertius gaudens duobus litigantibus' [the third party who rejoices at the quarreling of the other two].

"So, you see the guilty ones are not in our house. You are on the wrong track, and I hope most sincerely that you will call a halt so that the 'horrible being of the night' [Elektra] will no longer haunt our guiltless steps.

"I was very happy to hear of the tremendous success of the Berlin Philharmonic under your direction. I should very much like to have the opportunity sometime to admire you as a concert conductor; perhaps that pleasure awaits me when I visit Europe next year. It is a shame that you are not coming here, but it is not surprising that you have no desire to do so. . . ."

Strauss was not to be placated. The world premiere of *Elektra*, with Anny Krull in the title role, took place at the Dresden Staatstheater on January 25, 1909, before a shocked but enthralled audience; the American premiere, under Hammerstein's banner, on February 1, 1910, with Mariette Mazarin in the title role, provoking an almost hysterical enthusiasm. As for *Salome*, Hammerstein had staged it nine times during the preceding season without offending moral sensibilities. The Met did not stage it again for twenty-five years.

But in the Met–Manhattan Opera fracas, the Met held the trump card. With its wealthy board members and a fair portion of New York bigwigs available for loans, it could withstand the siege longer than the besieger. Hammerstein had nobody but himself. Without taking any action at all, in fact, the Met could let the old gentleman bleed himself to death. But Kahn, moved by his devotion to opera and his admiration for the man who had done so much to promote it, had proposed a generous alternative. Why not buy him out?

In 1910, after almost two years of involuted negotiations, with Hammerstein's son Arthur acting under power of attorney, the figure reached was $1,250,000. Hammerstein at sixty-three, heartbroken, had no choice short of bankruptcy. Kahn paid the sum himself. In return, Arthur Hammerstein pledged that neither he nor his father would produce any opera for ten years in New York, Philadelphia, Chicago, or Boston. In addition, the Met absorbed the American rights held by Hammerstein to all the operas, scores, scenery, props, and costumes as well as contracts with his star singers, including John McCormack, Mary Garden, and Luisa Tetrazzini.

But Hammerstein could no more renounce opera than he could forgo cigars. In his monomania he determined to go to London and challenge the Royal Opera with his own London Opera House. When an English newspaperman, dropping by to view the new theater abuilding, asked him, "How's business?" Hammerstein replied, "Opera's no business. It's a disease."

Incurably afflicted, he opened his London Opera House on November 11, 1911, with an operatic treatment by one Jean Noguès of Henryk Sienkiewicz's novel of ancient Rome, *Quo Vadis?* His first season earned a modest profit. His second, lacking artists of any marked distinction, proved catastrophic. Returning to New York, still undaunted, he announced—in violation of his agreement with the Met—the launching of the Lexington Opera House. The Met obtained an injunction. Hammerstein then showed movies in the theater that had cost $1,225,000 to build. He was soon forced to sell it for $820,000 to pay his debts.

He now guilefully approached what he saw as the enemy camp, responsible for all his frustrations. On April 23, 1917, he wrote to Kahn:

"In the spring of 1913 during your journey in Europe I called upon Mr. Powell [i.e., Paul] Cravath, the attorney of the Metropolitan Opera Company.

"This is in substance what I told him:

" 'My contract with the Metropolitan Opera Company prevents me from giving opera in the city for ten years. I have respected the contract and intend to do so until its expiration, nevertheless, it will not prevent anybody else from becoming a competitor to your clients. To my positive knowledge various concerns are planning the erection of an opera house in the city. . . . I have a plan by which the Metropolitan Opera Company can remain without competitors, even after my own contract expires, and by which I can be of great value to your company, and of incalculable value to the musical element of this city if not to the country at large. Permit me to erect an opera house in this city far away from the location of the Metropolitan Opera House and in the poorer section of the city, and in which I could give grand opera, principally in English, at prices ranging from 25¢ to $1.50; it is obvious that such an enterprise cannot be made to yield any profit in the commercial sense, but the creation of such an institution solely devoted to grand opera is sure to gradually educate the masses to an appreciation and love for grand opera, and automatically become a feeder to the presentations of the Metropolitan Grand Opera Company; but above all, it will for all time discourage any attempt at competition to the Metropolitan Opera Company by others; the permission of the directors of the Metropolitan Opera Company to me to carry out this, what I can justly call a great philanthropic undertaking, can only result in praise of the press and the public.'

"Mr. Cravath complimented me in the highest terms; he declared himself in sympathy with my proposition and had no doubt that it would be gladly accepted by the directors of the company. . . .

"Unfortunately, within a few days after the interview with Mr. Cravath the city advertised an auction sale of the old children's hospital on Lexington Avenue between Fiftieth and Fifty-first Streets. The location appealed to me as an ideal one for my purpose, and without waiting for the permission of Mr. Kahn and Mr. [William K.] Vanderbilt, I secured the site, laid the foundation of the opera house, and made numerous contracts with singers. . . .

"When, suddenly, the Civic Club entered upon the project I intended to carry out, aided by Mr. Cravath, Mr. Kahn and Mr. Vanderbilt, I was already too heavily involved in contracts to retreat. To stop meant utter ruin for me. Driven almost to desperation, I undertook to contest the validity of my contract with the Metropolitan Opera Company. I was defeated, and had to devote the great structure, which I expected to be a source of pride, and a field for my natural abilities, to the cheapest kind of amusement; the result was financial calamity, the breaking down of my health, and confiscation of the opera house by the mortgagees in collusion with a certain attorney representing my interests, though taxes and interest had been paid. While this matter is before the Supreme Court now, it will shortly become a subject for the consideration of the Grand Jury.

"The incentive of this letter, my dear Mr. Kahn, is the report that Mr. [Cleofonte] Companini [*sic*, i.e., Campanini] has leased the Lexington Opera House for one year. . . .

"I cannot resist the impulse to point out to you the correctness of my predictions, and the honesty of my purpose at the time I first laid my proposition before Mr. Cravath. I would consider it no small favor if your co-directors in the Metropolitan Opera Company may, perchance, be allowed to peruse this communication; perhaps they will no longer look upon me as a chronic contract breaker, and an all around bad man.

"With a low and lowly bow, I remain
  "Yours truly, O. Hammerstein"

Kahn's courtly reply failed to appease Hammerstein. Finally, on June 10, 1919, he vented his frustration upon the Met attorneys. He posted a copy of the letter he wrote them to Kahn along with a note of defiance: ". . . I beg to state that even if I lose my property, owing to the pending conspiracy, Grand Opera will be given by me in the near future, to deter me, which seems to be the object of the present proceedings, will fail. . . ." His letter to the attorneys began without a salutation:

"See here you.

"Tomorrow, owing to your machinations, the stock of the Hammerstein Amusement Company is to be sold at auction. I am informed that you, or your agents, will be the buyers. Inasmuch as I am the owner of the stock which I cannot redeem on account of your having conspired in a certain document with my former attorney . . . the sale will relieve you and the Rialto Theatre Corporation of a claim of over $500,000.00. Owing to bad health and financial reverses, I have been unable to follow up the proceedings instituted sometime ago in Police Court before Magistrate Breen. But now that you brazenly and cunningly attempt to take away from me what you suppose is the last vestige of recourse against you, I am giving you notice that I shall publicly expose your conspiracy . . . in obtaining my Victoria Theatre without even paying a cent for the same. I will recite my case in pamphlet form in unmistakable terms and appellations, so as to force you to begin libel proceedings and bring the whole infamous affair to the attention of a Jury. . . .

"The Victoria Theatre, now being the Rialto, are public institutions. By the meanest devices, taking advantage of my almost deadly illness befitting, the lowest tombs sheister [sic], you and your confreres obtained control of my property, which was free and clear then and which yielded me and is now yielding your gang, hundreds of thousands of dollars a year.

"I am not goilg [sic] to let you get away with this. The chagrin of it is preventing me from regaining my health. . . ."

Kahn hastened to reassure the half-mad old battler:

". . . I am in no way either informed about, or concerned in, the proceedings, past or present, to which you refer, but I am quite certain that you are under a misapprehension as to the facts which you charge.

"I have not the slightest feeling on the subject of your giving opera as soon as your contract with the Metropolitan Opera Company permits you to do so. And I have done nothing, and shall do nothing, to put difficulties in your way. I had hoped that you knew me well enough to realize that even if I were opposed to your operatic plans, I would not resort to unfair methods in order to defeat your purpose. . . ."

Hammerstein died suddenly seven weeks later on August 1, 1919.

For all their widely disparate beginnings, education, and fortunes, the two adversaries were a good deal alike. Both faithfully served the same goddess, putting art before gain. Both sacrificed millions to opera.

11

England Beckons

For the coronation of George V, Kahn sailed with his family to England aboard the Cunard liner *Mauretania* on March 15, 1911. They occupied four suites and were attended by two maids, a valet, a stewardess, a governess, two nurses, a laundress, a chauffeur, and a butler with wife and child. Another Cunarder, the *Caronia*, transported three of Kahn's automobiles and four more servants. In England, Kahn leased the Countess of Essex's Cassiobury Park near London. The children were captivated by the local legend that the heart of Robert Devereux, Earl of Essex, whom Queen Elizabeth I loved and dispatched to the scaffold, was immured somewhere within the masonry of the estate.

Margaret, then nine years old, however, was less than enchanted by some of the distinguished guests. Her father normally spent no more than two weeks vacationing with his family before eagerness to renew his multiple activities overtook him and he left them to enjoy life by themselves. Of Mrs. Patrick Campbell, Margaret wrote to her father, who had returned to New York: "[She] came yesterday and of course she had to bring her rotten little dog Georgena and while she was having tea she fed Georgena with one of the tea table spoons. . . ."

Lili Deutsch was traveling in England at the time, and she visited Cassiobury Park for a reunion with relatives she had not seen for years. Neither England nor most of the relatives pleased her. In a letter to her perpetually needy, ineffectual brother Paul, when she returned to Germany, she wrote: "I had a strange time in England: I didn't like it at all and came back chauvinistically German. . . . I found the family quite unpleasant. I got along best, as strange as it seems, with Addie and also with Otto. . . . Generally, I wouldn't want all that money. I like my own way of living a thousand times better; one really doesn't need more. Otto is tortured by terrible ambition, but is generally much better than before and quite original, actually. Addie suffers from boredom and solemnity, but is quite intelligent and respectable. We put your matters in order with just a few words, so don't worry yourself. [Evidently Paul was in financial hot water again.] Otto was extremely nice, and it's not worth the trouble at all. Otto and we [Lili and her husband, Felix Deutsch] will share, then you'll have another 500 M., which should let you take a trip or whatnot each year. You shouldn't for a moment have a pressing feeling of gratitude; I wouldn't in your position. So that's the end of that—all right? . . ."

During that spring and summer Kahn saw a good deal of Sir William Maxwell Aitken (later Lord Beaverbrook), a young Canadian millionaire who amassed his fortune organizing industrial mergers. They had met in New York four years earlier through Paul Cravath, the Met's attorney, and taken a strong liking to each other, though on Aitken's side affection was perhaps slightly tainted by his intention to use Kahn. Aitken had moved to England to foster imperial free trade. Elected to Parliament as a Conservative member for the borough of Ashton-under-Lyne, he became private secretary to a fellow Canadian and future prime minister, Andrew Bonar Law, and proposed to help him secure the Conservative party leadership.

While Kahn had resided in America for eighteen years, he had yet to seek naturalization, and was thus eligible for political office as a British subject. Why had he abstained so long from American citizenship? Did he nurture the hope, as some mischievous tongues conjectured, of one day acquiring a baronetcy? Or was it the promise he gave Addie that they would eventually settle in the country she loved so much?

Aitken urged Kahn to stand for Parliament. As Kahn's constituency he had in mind the Lancashire borough of Gorton, comprising 19,000 voters and neighboring his own Ashton. Aitken also wanted him to buy the *Daily Express*, which could then serve as a powerful Conservative ally.

Not long after they got back to Morristown, on November 24, the Kahns had their three oldest children—Maud, fourteen; Margaret, ten; and Gilbert, eight—baptized in St. Peter's Episcopal Church. Roger, at the age of four, was christened there the following year. The parents expected thereby to spare their young the social abrasions of being Jewish, in general to make life easier for them, and on the whole they succeeded. They themselves had rarely entered a synagogue. Nor did they convert to Christianity, despite the canards circulated by the press and widely credited. They still persist.*

Kahn found Hebraic services unappealing—the cantorial chanting, the interdiction against musical instruments, the art that excludes the human form. Catholicism, on the other hand, strongly attracted him with its vibrant sacred depictions in stained glass and oils, the diapasons of the organs, the whole floral and candle panoply of its ceremonies. He liked now and then to attend a Catholic or Episcopal service for esthetic, if not spiritual, uplift, and one Easter he attended both. By a good many people, Kahn was unjustly deemed an anti-Semite. In reality, he was simply indifferent to Judaism. Yet, unlike the mighty banker August Belmont (born Schoenberg), among other Jewish apostates, he changed neither his name nor his ethnic identity.

Said George Whitney, a J. P. Morgan associate: "I never knew what Kahn was in terms of religion or anything else. [He was] a curious fellow."

Aitken pressed his plea. He felt confident, he assured Kahn on November 20, 1911, that if he agreed to run, arrangements could be made on his behalf, among them a safe constituency. Their personal relations, Aitken added, would be close, and they would accomplish a good deal of work together.

Kahn cabled on the nineteenth: MANY THANKS GREATLY INTERESTED BUT WOULD IT NOT BE POSSIBLE TO KEEP OFFER OPEN SAY FOR TWO WEEKS WITHIN WHICH TIME I EXPECT TO REACH DEFINITE CONCLUSION REGARDING FUTURE PLANS.

Ten days later Bonar Law himself declared that he would be happy to welcome Kahn as a member of the party.

Kahn fully endorsed Bonar Law's tariff reform policy and wrote to tell him so on December 1: ". . . I may have leave to say how gratifying and encouraging a circumstance I consider it that the choice of the Party has fallen upon a man who, on the vitally important

---

* Libbian Benedict in *The Reflex*, a Jewish monthly magazine published in Chicago, November 1927: ". . . Kahn is now on the list of parishioners at St. Bartholomew's Church [New York City]"; *New York Herald Tribune*, March 31, 1934: "Mrs. Kahn is a communicant of St. Bartholomew's Protestant Episcopal Church"; Ermaline Weiss, a Morristown freelancer, in *Morris County*, Spring 1984: ". . . the Kahn family joined St. Peter's Episcopal Church. . . ."

subject of tariff reform, has taken the determined and bold stand which is yours. To bring Great Britain's fiscal policy in line with the change which has taken place in the economic conditions, both of its own empire and of the world, from what they were at the time when Free Trade was adopted (and for many years thereafter), seems to me, amongst the tasks confronting British statesmanship, probably one of greatest urgency and of most far-reaching import. I believe that a wise and moderate, carefully and scientifically adjusted measure of protection, including Inter-Empire Preference, would prove an incalculable boon to the country, and more especially to its wage earners, cure the ills consequent upon superstitous adherence to superannuated economic doctrine, go a long way towards remedying many of the evils incident to all too long a regime of fatuous ultra-radicalism, and would usher in a chapter of splendid development all along the line. . . ."

And on December 11, Kahn informed Aitken: . . . HAVE PRACTICALLY CONCLUDED TO FOLLOW YOUR ADVICE AND EXAMPLE PLEASE KEEP THIS STRICTLY CONFIDENTIAL AS I PARTICULARLY DESIRE NOT TO HAVE ANYTHING KNOWN TILL I AM READY TO ANNOUNCE IT INTEND MAKING SHORT VISIT LONDON JANUARY WOULD MUCH LIKE DEFER UNTIL THEN DECISION AS TO PAPER [the *Daily Express*].

The next day he wrote to Bonar Law: ". . . I am looking forward to the privilege of putting whatever modest capacities I may possess into the service of the Conservative Party, the principles and policies of which I venture to consider as more vital at the present juncture to England's greatness and to the well-being of her people, than at almost any other time in her history."

Yet he hesitated. Throughout the year 1912 he was under severe pressure from several quarters. He had proved too valuable an asset as a reorganizer of railroads, America's foremost, in fact, now that Harriman was dead, for Kuhn, Loeb to let him go without a struggle. The Metropolitan Opera board was equally reluctant to lose their forceful and open-handed chairman. The amplitude of Kahn's adopted country, moreover, exerted a strong pull. At the same time Aitken was busily lining up Conservative support for Kahn's Parliamentary candidacy, insisting that the Gorton constituency would wait for him as long as a chance remained. The future looked promising. The chances were improving daily. Kahn must inform Aitken, before his arrival if possible, whether or not he planned to stand. If he did, his constituents should demonstrate on his arrival. Half the voters would know him by reputation, and he could count on an important position in Parliament.

At Kahn's request Aitken had tried to gain admission for Kahn's eight-year-old son Gilbert to Winchester, one of England's greatest public schools. Aitken found the task difficult. Priority, he explained, was assigned to the sons of old boys, and Winchester had become so popular that the sons of all its alumni enrolled there. Should conditions change, Gilbert might have no trouble getting in. Aitken promised to speak to the member for Winchester, Guy Baring, an old friend, and ask him to intercede with the headmaster. (After Kahn decided against playing a role in British politics, Gilbert attended not Winchester but Groton in Massachusetts.)

If he did run, Kahn reflected, would not his Jewishness militate against him? He sent Aitken a batch of anti-Semitic articles vilifying him. We do not know precisely what those articles said, but the following excerpts from diverse publications were typical:

The Silhouette, January 1906: "The violent and exclusive pursuit of gold had made of the Hebrew a human structure of one story and that floor a basement. . . . Behind his smiling mask of craft hides a grasping, avaricious hook for the main chance. He is the 32nd degree despoiler of trade and professional methods throughout the world."

Theodore Alfred Bingham, police commissioner of New York City, in *The North American Review*, September 1908: "They [Russian immigrant Jews] are burglars, firebugs, pickpockets and highway robbers—when they have the courage; but though all crime is their province, pocket-picking is the one to which they take most naturally. . . ."

George Kibbe Turner, in *McClure's Magazine*, June 1909: "[The Jewish pimp] vitiated more than any other single agency, the moral life of the great cities of America. . . ."

The March 1913 issue of *McClure's* contained a forty-page essay by Burton J. Hendricks entitled "The Jewish Invasion of America."

And at the Ivy League colleges the gentile students sang:

> Oh, Harvard's run by millionaires,
> And Yale is run by booze.
> Cornell is run by farmers' sons,
> Columbia's run by Jews.
>
> So give a cheer for Baxter Street
> Another one for Pell

And when the little sheenies die
Their souls will go to hell.

Anti-Semitism permeated Wall Street. Whenever the market averages slumped, rumor ascribed the blame to a Jewish conspiracy. "Shylocking" became a synonym for crooked securities dealings. Except for Kuhn, Loeb; Goldman Sachs; and Lehman Brothers, hardly any Wall Street firm would hire Jews. According to John Brooks in his *Once in Golconda,* "the Stock Exchange was widely known to have an informal quota system designed to prevent Jews from gaining a foothold in its power structure. And there were office buildings on and around Wall Street that consistently refused to rent to Jews."

Henry Ford carried his hatred of Jews to the verge of insanity. He published a weekly journal, the *Dearborn Independent,* chiefly as a weapon against the Jews and those serving them, "the greedy bankers of Wall Street."

Aitken hastened to reassure Kahn on February 12, 1912: "The newspaper articles you sent me are nothing at all compared with the attacks which are sometimes made on me. You can make up your mind for the future that you will have plenty of newspaper notices of this nature.

"On the other hand, you remember the night of my meeting in Ashton, and you remember the attention I got when I left the Town Hall after the meeting. That is your compensation.

"I do not think that attacks on Jews have the slightest weight in England, and I am quite sure that the Jewish members in the House of Commons will bear me out in this statement.

"The suggestion of German origin will not do any real harm. There are ten Members in the House of Commons born and educated in Germany. England is a tolerant country. Intolerance will only make you political friends."

Misgivings still troubled Kahn, so much so that on March 9, 1912, Aitken cabled: CHANGE YOUR PLANS WOULD CONSIDERABLY EMBARRASS ME AND OTHERS. . . .

Kahn replied by letter on March 11: ". . . I need not say that I shall, of course, observe whatever commitments I am under, unless and until I am released by those to whom I made them. On the other hand, the situation here, and with it my own views, have undergone a very material change since my return. I propose therefore that the whole matter stand over till I get back to England again. . . ."

By the fall of 1912, Kahn was so nearly sure of entering British politics that he began hunting for London real estate. The first property that seized his fancy was 2 Carlton House Terrace, a showplace of twenty-eight rooms with a price tag of $500,000. The owner, one of the world's wealthiest women, was formerly married to an American millionaire, Marshall Field, Jr., and also formerly to a Scottish multimillionaire, Maldwin Drummond. Kahn cabled Mrs. Drummond, expressing interest in the estate, then changed his mind. He preferred to take a year's lease for $20,000 (and later to buy for a million dollars) the Earl of Londesborough's Regency mansion, St. Dunstan's Lodge, standing amid twelve and a half acres at the center of Regent's Park, London's second largest private residence after Buckingham Palace. It was encrusted with legend. In the early nineteenth century it belonged to Francis Charles, third Marquess of Hertford, the prototype of both Lord Monmouth in Disraeli's novel *Coningsby* and the lecherous Lord Steyne in Thackeray's *Vanity Fair*. Near the entrance once loomed the clock that adorned the Church of St. Dunstan's before the Great Fire of 1666, on either side of which a gigantic figure holding a club struck the hours and quarter hours.

Mrs. Drummond, meanwhile, having mistaken Kahn's cable as a firm offer, accused him of bad faith. Incensed, he showed a copy of the cable to his attorneys, who assured him that it implied no such agreement. Thus armored in the conviction of rectitude, he made a typically Kahnian gesture. With St. Dunstan's already on his hands, he bought 2 Carlton House Terrace, never occupied it, and resold it at a loss. "I would much rather be burdened with a house I cannot use," he said, "than rest under the imputation of attempting to evade a moral commitment."

His mind made up at last, Kahn hurled himself into the political fray with a determination that deeply impressed his Gorton adherents. They liked his oratorical style. He resorted to none of the professional politician's theatrical flourishes. He won over the hardheaded Lancastrians with his subdued, genial approach to crucial issues, weighing them pro and con, handling them comprehensively. He showed himself to be as uncompromising a tariff reformer as Bonar Law, arguing that the sole means of raising British trade to a level equal to those of competitive nations was to develop a system of tariffs on merchandise manufactured abroad.

Gorton's representative during the preceding seven years had been John Hodges, a Scottish Socialist trade union leader, who spoke with a heavy burr. Like many another M.P., he visited his constituents only once or twice a year. To the thousands of Gortonites who first greeted Kahn in February 1913, he promised to be no stranger to them. He got a good press. A correspondent for *The New York Times*, cabling from Gorton, reported:

"Otto H. Kahn, it is confidently expected by his supporters here, will be returned to Parliament in the next general election. . . .

"Mr. Kahn's name is already on the list of every sporting club in the district, and he has contributed generously to charities and bazaars. He has given a massive silver cup as a challenge trophy for swimming teams of the district, swimming being one of the chief sports of the neighborhood. It is understood that both he and Sir Max have contributed heavily to party funds.

"A local Conservative leader says of Mr. Kahn:

"'He is one of the sincerest democrats I ever saw. Democratic Conservatism has never had a better champion. He seems to forget that he has a bank account except when a charity request comes along or a club secretary appeals for assistance. He is obsessed with a desire to end his life in the field of English politics, emancipating the workers, and this he believes with the rest of our party can only be obtained by a revision of the fiscal policy and practical legislation on lines of social reform.'"

In other speeches Kahn denounced the incumbent government leaders. Never, he declared, had he confronted a more disagreeable crew. They repeatedly violated their pledges to their constituents. They usurped autocratic power. The National Insurance Act, a form of unemployment insurance, was muddleheaded, the means of its passage corrupt, and he scoffed at its author, Lloyd George.

Kahn's political adventure lasted barely a year. Having transported quantities of art objects from New York to St. Dunstan's, having repaired and redecorated the famous old mansion, he announced in a letter to the chairman of the Conservative Association that he was withdrawing his candidacy. The cause he gave was greatly increased business problems at Kuhn, Loeb. "I discovered," he explained further many years after, "that my roots had gone too deeply into American soil ever to be transplanted. The microbe of America had entered my blood and could not be dislodged. I found I had been mistaken in thinking that I could forsake America for England. A little taste of leisure there convinced me that I wanted to and was bound to return to the strenuous life I lead here, to my work and associates, my duties, responsibilities, and aspirations, and do what little might be in

Otto Kahn, age eighteen, in the uniform of the Mainz Hussars. (Courtesy of Mrs. John Barry Ryan)

The three Eberstadt sisters with their husbands. The couple in the middle, Emma Stephanie Eberstadt and Bernhard Kahn, are the parents of Otto Kahn. (Courtesy of Mrs. John Barry Ryan)

Franziska Elisabeth ("Lili") Kahn, Otto's sister, as drawn by Edward Burne-Jones in 1889. (Courtesy of Mrs. Miriam Porter)

Abraham Kuhn. (Courtesy of Kuhn, Loeb & Co., copyright © 1955)

Solomon Loeb. (Courtesy of Kuhn, Loeb & Co., copyright © 1955)

Jacob Schiff. (Courtesy of Kuhn, Loeb & Co., copyright © 1955)

Abraham Wolff. (Courtesy of Mrs. John Barry Ryan)

At work. (Courtesy of Mrs. John Barry Ryan)

At sea. (Courtesy of Mrs. John Barry Ryan)

Addie Kahn. (Courtesy of Mrs. John Barry Ryan)

Addie Kahn with the four Kahn children (left to right): *Margaret, Roger, Maud, and Gilbert.* (Courtesy of Mrs. John Barry Ryan)

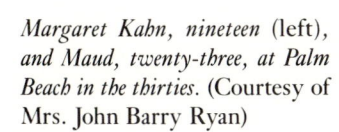

Margaret Kahn, nineteen (left), *and Maud, twenty-three, at Palm Beach in the thirties.* (Courtesy of Mrs. John Barry Ryan)

En route. (Courtesy of Mrs. John Barry Ryan)

my power to aid in constructive development, both in a financial and cultural way. Work is infinitely preferable to loafing."

But these explanations do not ring wholly true. Life as an M.P., if zealously pursued, would have allowed scant scope for artistic pursuits. The truth behind Kahn's sudden reversal remains a mystery. Two possibilities suggest themselves. He may have wearied of the frequent financial demands made upon him by the Conservative party. He may also have grown disgusted with the constant intraparty bickering. Whatever the reason, nothing the bitterly disappointed Aitken could say or do (though they remained close friends) nor any protests of Addie's budged him.

While Kahn never admitted it, his family came to believe that the real reason he withdrew was the likelihood of war with Germany and the embarrassment to which he would then be subjected as an M.P. of German birth.

12

War

World War I erupted on July 28, 1914. Kahn had sailed back to the States eighteen days earlier, restless as usual after his customary brief summer sojourn with his family abroad. Not long before, Joseph Duveen had sold him the famous portrait of Giuliano de Medici by Botticelli for $125,000.* Addie, cousin Ella Joshua, and the four children were still in Pont l'Evêque, near Deauville, planning to spend a few more weeks there, when, on August 5, England declared war on Germany. Through the ingenuity of an American Express agent, they managed not only to board a boat at Dieppe for Le Havre, thence another boat for England, but to take with them twelve servants and sixty-five trunks. They were obliged, however, to abandon two automobiles in France. Upon reaching London and St. Dunstan's that night, thirteen-year-old Nin wrote to "Dear Fathy": "My last letter I wrote from Pont l'Evêque and this one is written among the calm and trustworthy English. . . . You have never witnessed such excitement. Mother and Ella would sit in secret conference and if anybody went near them snapped. The ed† is stranded in Germany. . . . We had a beastly crossing. . . . We saw two English dreadnoughts, lots of torpidos [sic] and one adoreable [sic] submarine. . . ."

The same day Kahn, having learned by cablegram of his family's safe arrival, wrote to Nin:

---

* Now in the Crespi Collection, Milan.

† "Ed" for "The Educator," Fräulein Braun, who had taken her holiday in Germany and was forced to remain there for the duration. She later taught German elocution to voice students at the Juilliard School.

"I was very greatly worried about you til I heard from you at last this morning. I hope you were all calm and sensible about it and that you are now completely settled and well and cheerful. What a shame that you had to leave when you liked Deauville so much. The beach must have been lovely. I hope we shall repeat the visit next year, all of us together. Meanwhile, I do wish I was with you, but as this cannot be at present I trust you will be back here very soon. Much love."

The war divided the Kuhn, Loeb partners. On one side stood the Germanophile Jacob Schiff and the Warburg brothers, Paul and Felix; on the other, the anti-Prussian Otto Kahn, Schiff's son Mortimer, and Jerome Hanauer. With the firm's close ties to Europe's major banking houses, both sides feared a war that, the unimaginable slaughter apart, threatened to disrupt the whole international banking network. The third and eldest Warburg brother, Max, for example, headed the family firm, M. M. Warburg, in Hamburg, which maintained strong bonds with Kuhn, Loeb. Other European houses in the same orbit included Baring Brothers of London; the Rothschilds in England, France, and Germany; the Franco-Belgian Banque de Paris et des Pays Bas; and the Amsterdamsche Bank—to list only a few.

What Jacob Schiff prayed for was a negotiated Anglo-German peace, a compromise. Like many of America's German-Jewish elite, he bore the land of his birth, its music, its art, its literature, a profound affection. "My sympathies are naturally altogether with Germany," he wrote to a friend three months after the first shot was fired, "as I would think as little to side against my own country as I would against my own parents."

Schiff's Germanophilia was strengthened by his detestation of Russia's virulently anti-Semitic tsarist regime, an ally of England and France. For years he had refused to let Kuhn, Loeb lend the Russian government a cent. During the Russo-Japanese War of 1905 he not only participated in financing the Japanese, but absorbed the cost of disseminating antitsarist propaganda among Russian prisoners. Now, days after the Allies declared war against Germany, in a vain effort to dissuade Japan from joining them, he cabled his friend Baron Korekiyo Takahashi, the Japanese minister of finance and later premier, advising him that should his country oppose Germany, he might encounter obstacles in the path of financial support from American sources. According to *The Times* of London, Schiff had told its correspondent in 1914 that he was "willing to help the Kaiser rather than the Allies."

Though he did not soften his economic policy toward the Allies, the sinking of the *Lusitania* by a German U-boat on May 7, 1915, together with reports of German atrocities in Belgium, so profoundly shook him that he rushed over to J. P. Morgan's nearby office to apologize for the barbarism of his former countrymen. Morgan turned his back and refused to speak to him.

Wall Street remained predominantly pro-Ally. Morgan himself floated a half-billion-dollar Anglo-French loan. This exacerbated the conflict within Kuhn, Loeb. Schiff's thirty-five-year-old son, Morti, and Otto Kahn strove to mitigate the pro-German stigma attached to the firm, but Jacob Schiff stood fast. When Rufus Daniel Isaacs, Marquess of Reading, the Jewish Lord Chief Justice of England, arrived in New York at the head of the Anglo-French mission to arrange details of the loan, young Schiff and Kahn assured him that the money could readily be raised without security. Jacob Schiff weakened to the point of demanding, if Kuhn, Loeb participated, guarantees from both the British and French that no part of the loan would go to the aid of Russia. Lord Reading flatly rejected the terms, and a typical British headline proclaimed: KUHN, LOEB, GERMAN BANKERS, REFUSE TO AID ALLIES.

In *The New York Times*, on October 2, 1915, Schiff announced: ". . . with differing sympathies on the part of the individual members of our firm, we decided to refrain from financing public loans for any of the governments of the belligerent nations."

Nevertheless, as individuals, not as representatives of Kuhn, Loeb, lest they kindle the old gentleman's wrath, Morti Schiff and Otto Kahn each bought large amounts of the Anglo-French bonds—Kahn purchased $100,000 worth in the fall of 1915. Besides donating St. Dunstan's to the British government, Kahn gave tens of thousands of dollars to diverse Allied relief organizations; delivered pro-Ally, anti-German speeches; and wrote articles supporting the Allied cause.

In 1915, after Italy rejected the Triple Alliance, comprising Italy, Germany, and Austria, and entered the war on the Allied side, Kahn wrote rather naively to Toscanini, who was conducting concerts for Italian war relief:

"Italy by waiting and trading could probably have obtained from Austria most of what she wanted without firing a shot. But with Latin idealism she preferred to take the path of danger and sacrifice to achieve the attainment of her national aspirations and threw her sword onto the scale on the side of humanity and liberty in this fateful and awful fight which is to determine the spirit which will prevail in the world."

And to the French minister of fine arts: "I have always loved France (what man of culture does not?) and I cannot find words to express my admiration for the wonderful spirit and conduct of the French people, for their heroism in action as well—alas!—in suffering, for their superb dignity, calm and determination. It saddens me infinitely to think of all the noble French blood that is being spilled in this cruel war. It is the most precious blood in the world, for there is less of it than of other great races; and humanity needs more, I think, than that of any other race."

According to a myth advanced by Mary Jane Matz in her biography and perpetuated by Stephen Birmingham in *"Our Crowd,"* Kahn ordered Gatti-Casazza to remove German operas, especially Wagnerian operas, from the Met repertory. But Kahn had too much common sense to confuse music with the behavior of the country that nurtured it or of the composer who created it. As an Italian, Gatti-Casazza had greater cause to omit works by nationals of a country at war with his own, yet the idea never occurred to him. Between 1914 and 1917 the Met produced almost all of Wagner's operas and a good many operas by other Germans. Only after America entered the war did the Met exclude German operas.

On June 28, 1915, Kahn wrote a long letter to Felix Deutsch, the husband of his beautiful sister Lili, and then chairman of A.E.G. For many years of her married life Lili was the mistress of the company's brilliant, liberal president, Walter Rathenau—evidently the platonic mistress, according to the biographer David Felix: "Rathenau's sexual character was inevitably as ambiguous as the rest of him. . . . She [Lili] told his biographer [Count Harry Kessler] in 1927: 'To this day I have no idea *what* his love life was like.' Kessler noted: 'She spoke . . . very frankly about their relationship, which never got to the ultimate . . . although she was very sensual. . . .' Lili Deutsch concluded: 'He never had any real feelings. He just had a longing for feelings.' Actually, Rathenau responded somewhat more freely to men. An acquaintance of his told me that Rathenau took an active part in a milieu of homosexuals."

Kahn's letter to Deutsch, written in German, had a curious history. It was sent in response to a letter from Deutsch justifying Germany's position. Kahn wrote: ". . . the great majority of Americans are convinced that the ruling powers of Germany and Austria, though not perhaps the people themselves, are responsible for the outbreak of the war; that they have sinned against humanity and justice. . . .

"The conviction that everything, literally everything, which tends to ensure victory is permitted to her, and indeed called for, has now evidently assumed the power of a national obsession. Thus, the violation of innocent Belgium in defiance of solemn treaty; the unspeakable treatment inflicted on her people; the bombardment without warning of open places (which Germany was the first to practice); the destruction of great monuments of art which belonged to all humankind, as in Rheims, and Louvain; the *Lusitania* horror, the strewing of mines broadcast; the use of poisonous gases causing death by torture or incurable disease; the taking of hostages; the arbitrary imposition of monetary indemnities and penalties. . . .

"If, as you believe, England had been planning for years to attack Germany via Belgium, would she not then have had in readiness an invading force somewhere near adequate for such an undertaking? Instead she had the mere bagatelle of 75,000 or 100,000 men, which in the first months of the war actually constituted her whole available fighting force. . . .

"The theory of 'frightfulness' in the conduct of warfare which Germany now preaches and practices is no new discovery. On the contrary it is a very ancient one—so old, in fact, that long ago it had come to be discarded and superseded in European warfare and passed into the limbo of forgotten things. There, until resurrected by your countrymen, it lay for generations, along with much else which the human race had overcome and left behind in the progress of culture and humanity. . . .

"And what have you gained from your 'frightfulness'? . . . you have steeled your enemies to the utmost limit of sacrifice; you have embittered neutral opinion; you have disappointed and grieved your friends and 'sown dragon's teeth,' the offspring of which will arise against you many years even after the conclusion of peace. . . ."

Between New York and Berlin the letter was intercepted by a French military censor, how and precisely where we do not know. The censor copied it and sent the original on to Felix Deutsch, who replied with a brief note indicating that since his views differed so radically from Kahn's, further correspondence was futile. The censor delivered his copy to the French minister of information, who in turn relayed it to his opposite number in England. Here was stunning evidence that a German-American, a partner in one of the world's leading investment banks, was staunchly pro-Ally. Additional copies of the letter reached every Allied foreign office. On July 4, 1917, three months after the United States had declared war on Germany, *The New York Times* published passages of the letter, thereby conferring upon Kahn a fame that spread throughout Europe as well as America.

The letter was also reprinted in a book of Kahn essays entitled *Right Above Race*. They brought from Supreme Court Justice Louis D. Brandeis a letter dated May 18, 1918: "Possibly you may be interested in the enclosed address on 'Americanization,' in which I attempted to develop the thought of 'Right Above Race'—the thought which led me and I hope may some day lead you—to Zionism. . . ."

Kahn replied on August 12: ". . . I fear I must confess that I have not yet found the way to Zionism; perhaps, to be frank, because I have heretofore made no earnest effort to discover it. . . ."

Nor did he ever find the way.

The reelection in 1916 of President Woodrow Wilson, followed by his proposal of a League of Nations, filled Jacob Schiff with hopes for a negotiated peace. They were quickly dashed when Germany resumed her campaign of unrestricted submarine offensive. As America's entry into the war appeared inevitable, the Kuhn, Loeb partners buried their differences and reunited to aid the Allies.

One of history's bitterest ironies was the reaction of Jacob Schiff, capitalist of capitalists, to the Russian Revolution. He cheered. He cheered because it eradicated the stain of anti-Semitism from the Allies. "We should be somewhat careful not to appear overzealous," he wrote to Morti on March 22, 1917, "but you might cable Cassel, because of recent actions of Germany and developments in Russia we shall no longer abstain from Allied Governments financing when opportunity offers. . . ." To Boris Kamenka, president of the Banque de Commerce de l'Azoff-Don, he wrote on April 23, 1917: "May I say to you that nothing would give me greater satisfaction to be of advantage to the new Russia in all or any opportunities that may present themselves. . . ." On April 5, the eve of America's declaration of war, he wrote to the novelist Israel Zangwill: ". . . The Romanoff dynasty has ended, practically overnight, by a bloodless revolution which by a stroke of the pen has also brought forth the emancipation of Russian Jewry." In a letter to the great social worker Lillian Wald, he compared the revolution to the deliverance of Israel from its Egyptian bondage.

But when the Bolsheviks under Lenin routed the moderate Mensheviks and established their own Soviet government, his enthusiasm cooled.

The correspondence over the years between Otto and Paul Kahn reflected the ambivalence Otto felt toward his younger, chronically indigent brother, whom he partially supported. "Lili," Otto wrote from Cedar Court on August 8, 1911, "has told me that it would be a considerable contribution to your comfort and welfare if your annual income were increased by 5,000 marks and has suggested to me that *die Deutsche* ["the German woman," as he punningly referred to their sister Lili Deutsch] and I supply this sum jointly, to which proposition I naturally was happy to agree. The God of Israel . . . has been so kind to me that I can spare 2,000 marks per year without essentially limiting my own or my family's expenses, and I hope that you have just as few scruples about accepting this small service from me, as I would have accepting it from your brotherly hand if our roles were reversed. Even if, dear God, it has been 28 years since I left our Mannheim home, even if it would be dishonest to claim that time, distance, and the difference in my condition of life and interests have not estranged me, even if our—never very lively—correspondence died off quietly a few years ago with that last letter of yours that could hardly encourage me to respond (letter writing, except for definite purposes, is for the very busy person an invention of Satan, and becomes largely a matter of form, if the correspondents don't see each other from time to time, or have lively points of contact)—even so there remains, I'm glad to say, an instinctive, real, and easily revitalized feeling of fellowship and affection for you, you old 'pack rat' and 'miser.' —And so I lift my glass to you, wish the best for your wife and children and in the future. . . ."

The following year, 1912, a friend of Paul's showed him some El Greco paintings for sale. Paul pressed them upon Otto, expecting perhaps a commission from the owner. "What in the world?" replied Otto on March 22. "Absolutely not. Greco with his overly accentuated colors and his attenuated figures is little to my taste, and since I buy pictures not to flaunt them in a gallery but to enjoy them after a day's hard work, Greco may not enter my residence despite the respect I have for his work. So please politely decline on my behalf to your friend. And by the way, rumor has grossly exaggerated the extent and value of my collection, as it does about almost everything American, good and bad. With that I clasp you tearfully in my arms, give you a pinch in the rear, and hope that you, your wife, and children are well."

In 1914, when war came, Paul was forced as a German subject to return to Germany from Greece, and he joined the army. ". . . I am sorry to hear that these horrible times have struck you as well," Otto wrote on September 12, "and particularly that you have to leave your wife and children. . . . I have tried to cable you money from here, but that isn't possible at the moment. I will find a way to manage it in the next few days. The only thing I have been able to do up to now is give your wife 10,000 francs credit in Athens. . . . In case there is anything else in these times that it would be within my powers to do for you and her, let me know. . . . I will certainly do my best for the both of you.

"You are right to speak of the present tragedy of Europe as insanity. Criminal insanity! Woe to those who bear responsibility for it! . . . May you return to your family soon and in good health. You need not worry about their financial well-being. . . ."

Paul's military service did not last long. By January 1916, discharged, possibly because of poor health, he was back in Athens, jobless and penniless, turning again to Otto for succor. Greece was then torn by conflict between King Constantine, who favored the Germans, and the pro-Ally statesman Eleutherios Venizelos, between royalists and republicans. The brothers now communicated in English instead of German as they had before, a diplomatic precaution lest the Allies take over.

"This is the usual duplicate," Paul wrote on January 20. "I wrote you 2–3 weeks ago and asked you for £250 for my wife. Don't be angry. I cannot get money from anywhere else.

"I should be very glad if you could give me the money as a loan, to be repaid, with as much interest as you like, after the war. Of course this is only a very naive method, to save me from the horrible *disagio* [discomfort]; if it is *too* naive, then please don't give any attention to this."

The curt reply came not from Otto, who was beginning to weary of Paul's demands, but from a secretary, on January 31:

"In compliance with your request of the 3rd. inst., Mr. Otto H. Kahn has today remitted £250 to the National Bank of Greece, Athens, to the credit of Mrs. Euphrosyne Kahn."

April 1: "You would be very kind, to send another £250 to my wife Euphrosyne, or to let me know it by wire, if you will *not* send it. . . . When was the last money send [*sic*]?"

April 14: "This is only the usual duplicate of my last letter (of the 1st of April I believe), in which I troubled you again for another £250."

Otto's secretary responded again with a remittance.

September 5: "I am sorry that I shall have to trouble you again. But you may be sure, that I would not do it, if I could find out any other way. My demand is this:

"Could you send *to my wife* a declaration, valid in law and, if possible, certificated by the Greek consulate there, that you are ready to stand security for debts contracted by myself *or by my wife*, to the amount e.g. £1,000. You would greatly relieve our precarious situation. I thrust [sic] you don't expect further explanation, impossible to be given in a lettre [sic] just now. . . ."

Before filing the letter, Otto scribbled on it a note to his secretary: "Please have £250 transmitted as usual provided there has been an interval of three months since the last remittance."

Though Otto now bore his brother scant affection and did not care to carry on a protracted correspondence with him, though he regarded his remittances as no more than a family obligation, he could not, in his vanity, resist occasionally forwarding a copy of a speech he had delivered or an article he had written. Thus Paul, skilled in the arts of flattery and cajolery, wrote on June 28, 1916:

"Many thanks for your railway essay ["Strangling the Railroads," published in February of that year]. It is so clearly and almost excitingly written, that I could not help me [sic], with all my perfect innocence in this question, to take a great interest in it, especially in the fact that in the home-country of capitalism its influence on the legislation is much smaller than in most parts of Europe. . . .

"You would be very kind to send another £250 to my wife Euphrosyne. Our situation here is serious enough. Venizelos, no doubt, will be Prime-minister again within 2–3 months and very likely will drive us into war with Germany. So, as something may happen to me, I must beg you again, not to let my wife without money, if she should ask for it."

August 30: "Many thanks for your *High Finance* [an address before the American Newspaper Publishers' Association, New York, April 27, 1916]. I am very glad to learn something on America by a man who stands in the heart of its commercial life. And I am not less interested by some thoughts—or rather personal confessions—which throw a very curious light on the psychology of a millionaire, so difficult to understand by a poor dog like me. I hope your instinct of domination, who seems to drive you into politics, will not restrain you from giving us the results of your life and experiences in some great work, independent from political views.

"I trust you remitted to my wife the £250, for which I asked you some weeks before. If not, please do so. Things here are undecided still, but I fear the worst. So I beg you again, not to forsake my wife if something should happen to me."

On September 6, Venizelos having fled Athens to set up a pro-Ally provisional government in Salonika, Paul wrote: "What I feared has happened: I must leave Greece. Please, don't forget my wife."

He did not leave until the end of the month after cabling two last words to Otto: PLEASE MONEY.

Otto heard from him again in a letter dated October 24. He was living in Berlin with Felix and Lili Deutsch. "I do not know if my last lettre [sic] from Greece reached you. So, as the thing is of great importance to me, I wish to repeat I was forced to leave Greece (I am with Lili now) and that my family remains there still. I entreat you as intensely as I can with my bad English [why he still wrote in English defies explanation], not to forget my wife, especially to provide her with money. . . .

"I am sorry, that I have to trouble you again, but since the world is out of joint, I cannot help me."

"Prior to the war," Kahn told a courtroom full of newspapermen, "I had determined to become an American citizen. . . ." Actually, he had filed his intention of doing so as early as 1901, but took no further steps toward citizenship for fifteen years, probably because the thought lingered in his mind that he would sooner or later resettle in England for good, as Addie so dearly wished. The advent of war, however, prompted him to postpone still longer his renunciation of British nationality and his application for his final American papers, because to do so at that juncture would appear opportunistic, if not craven.

"In view of recent developments," he told the reporters, "I believe there is no longer room for such misunderstanding. Moreover, I feel that these developments have made it my duty now to assume formally the obligations and duties of citizenship in the country where I have worked and lived these many years and expect to live permanently, in which my children were born and expect to live and to which I have become deeply attached."

And so, on March 28, 1917, nine days before the United States declared war on Germany, having already severed diplomatic relations, Kahn passed his final naturalization examination before Judge Salmon of the Court of Common Pleas in Morristown.

"I must atone for my wealth."

In February 1915, Kahn performed an act of atonement, one of many that endeared him to the British and won him worldwide esteem. Five years earlier Sir Arthur Pearson, founder of the *Daily Express* as well as several popular periodicals, was forced to retire because of failing eyesight. He dedicated himself thereafter to the care of servicemen blinded in action. Kahn had kept St. Dunstan's, though he no longer used it as an occasional residence, and he turned over the entire estate to Pearson's Blinded Soldiers' and Sailors' Committee as a rehabilitation center. Workshops were added where volunteer instructors trained the sightless in dozens of occupations, among them typing, carpentry, weaving, and shoemaking. Braille was obligatory. To guide the trainees' steps, carpeted paths connected the buildings, uprights stood at the approach to forking walkways, handrails lined the gardens. On the vast acreage the blind learned to grow vegetables, raise poultry, farm for the marketplace, play sports and games. Most of the staff were as blind as Sir Arthur.

In New York, Kahn persuaded fellow philanthropists to help support the institution, and he periodically dug deep into his own pocket.*

The Kahn house at 8 East Sixty-eighth Street, spacious by normal standards, proved inadequate for the entire family, and so he bought the adjacent Number 10 for the children, their attendants, and teachers, linking the two structures with an underground passage. Having, with the loan of St. Dunstan's, demonstrated his affection for the English, he now showed how much he admired the French by converting Number 8 into the French Soldiers and Sailors Club. A housekeeper, chef, and waiters catered to the needs of any French personnel whose duties took them to New York. They paid nothing for meals. At their disposal, too, were English-language teachers,

---

* After the war, when the Blinded Soldiers' and Sailors' Committee moved its base, Kahn sold St. Dunstan's to the newspaper tycoon Harold Harmsworth, Viscount Rothermere. A fire destroyed the main building in 1936, and the rest of the property was auctioned off. Barbara Hutton bought it and built a Georgian-style three-story pink-brick villa of thirty-five rooms, which she named Winfield, after her grandfather Frank Winfield Woolworth. It is today the official residence of the American ambassador to the Court of St. James's.

rooms for dancing, shooting billiards, and playing cards, plus a library.

Yet false reports of pro-Germanism still plagued Kuhn, Loeb. They stemmed in part from an assurance Jacob Schiff had offered German colleagues that he would underwrite loans to German cities on condition that none of them be diverted to military supplies. When U-boats renewed their marauding, he immediately broke off negotiations.

The most savage denunciation of Kahn appeared in the letters column of the *Fort Worth Record* on May 14, 1914, under the signature of one W. J. Slade:

"To the Editor of The Record: Less than ten years ago Otto H. Kahn was a commissioned officer in the German army. The powers that be conceived the idea of overthrowing the United States government. They needed a military expert who could reach the high-ups. Kahn was selected and sent to England, where he learned the ropes first hand from the Rothschilds. He was then put in touch with E. H. Harriman in 1907. Harriman could not make a move. His holdings which were of the best railroad collateral were practically void until he associated himself with Otto H. Kahn. Then he could not name a sum of money Kahn could not produce. In that way Kahn gained the confidence of President Roosevelt. After acquiring such properties as the Rothschilds desired, Harriman conveniently died. It was then the military expert began his work. The first event was a convention of I.W.W.'s at Salt Lake City, Utah, who declared the bloodiest strike in the history of the United States. About the only casualty noted was when the strikebreaker guards at Houston killed several strikebreakers. At Jackson, Miss. one striker was killed, one locomotive was blown up. Kahn is still at work for his masters. We have no doubt but that he is behind the Carranza-Villa forces in Mexico. President Wilson can sit tight if he will, but action is what is needed, intelligent and unswerving, determined action, if President Wilson hopes to retain his authority."

Kahn appointed himself fund-raiser and propagandist for the Allies. In interviews, articles, and speeches that took him all over the country he assailed "the poison growth of Prussianism" that he had loathed ever since his youthful military training with the Mainz Hussars, and he called upon German-Americans "to rise, together with their fellow-citizens of all races, to free not only this country but the whole world from the oppression of the rulers of Germany. . . ."

In an address before the Merchants Association of New York at its

Liberty Loan meeting, June 1, 1917, two months after America finally joined the Allies, he said:

"It is the purpose of a common determination to fight and to bear and to dare everything and never to cease nor rest until the accursed thing which has brought upon the world the unutterable calamity, the devil's visitation of this appalling war, is destroyed beyond all possibility of resurrection.

"That accursed thing is not a nation, but an evil spirit which has made the government possessed by it and executing its abhorrent and bloody bidding an abomination in the sight of God and men. . . .

". . . Speaking as one born of German parents, I do not hesitate to state it as my deep conviction that the greatest service which men of German birth or antecedents can render to the country of their origin is this: to proclaim and to stand up for those great ideals and national qualities and traditions which they inherited from their ancestors, and to set their faces like flint against the monstrous doctrines and acts of a rulership that has robbed them of the Germany they loved and in which they took just pride, the Germany which had the good will, respect and admiration of the entire world. . . ."

The Chamber of Commerce, Harrisburg, Pa., September 26, 1917: "From each successive visit to Germany for twenty-five years I came away more appalled by the sinister transmutation Prussianism had wrought amongst the people and by the portentous menace I recognized in it for the entire world.

"It had given to Germany unparalleled prosperity, beneficent and advanced social legislation, and not a few other things of value, but it had taken in payment the soul of the race. It had made a 'devil's bargain.'

". . . we will say, with a clear conscience, in the noble words which more than five hundred years ago were uttered by the Parliament of Scotland:

"'It is not for glory, or for riches, or for honor that we fight, but for liberty alone which no good man loses but with his life.'"

Aside from the sincerity and effectiveness of his inexhaustible efforts to rally his fellow German-Americans around the Allied flags, Kahn prided himself on the scope of his erudition and the magnitude of his English vocabulary. The sound of his voice, the sight of his name in print delighted him. He held an opinion on practically every subject of importance—economics, politics, art, music, theater—and lectured or wrote incessantly about them. For advice on the tone and direction the thoughts he expressed should take, he retained Ivy Lee, the master publicist who helped to cleanse John D. Rockefeller's maculate image. For Kahn, Lee suggested appropriate topics to write or lecture about, assisted him in their preparation, and offered criticism of the manuscripts Kahn submitted to his shrewd eye.

Since 1910, Kahn had pasted newspaper stories about himself into huge leatherbound albums stamped O.H.K. Eventually they totaled eleven. During his mature years, *The New York Times* published 750 reports of his protean activities, while news stories appearing elsewhere on three continents ran into the thousands. He assembled fifty-eight of his articles and speeches into four books, none of which attracted a large paying readership (*Of Many Things*, published in 1926 by Boni & Liveright, yielded royalties for the first half of 1929 of $1.20), but brought him immense satisfaction. On February 5, 1924, for example, following a New York Drama League luncheon at the Hotel Astor, he delivered his speech on "Art and America." He then gave Ivy Lee a distribution list as follows:

Dramatic and Music Critics of First-Class Dailies	1,000 or more up to 1,500
Art and theatrical magazines	60
News reviews	60
Mr. Kahn's private mailing list	750
Selected list of prominent people	1,750
All libraries	2,050
Writers and men of letters	2,776
Officers of Women's clubs	2,500
Prominent patrons of art and music in America	
Prominent artists, musicians, theatrical people	3,000
Art clubs and Associations	
Members of (800) and supply for New York Drama League (200)—Communicate with Mr. Wilson or Mr. Dartt [secretaries] in Mr. Kahn's office about this distribution	1,000
Supply for Mr. Dartt (in Mr. Kahn's office)	100
Supply to keep on hand	600
Print a total of	15,750

Kahn's anti-Prussian blasts, such as his "Poison Growth of Prussianism" and "Prussianized Germany," had a different destination. In Switzerland a group of German expatriates had banded together as "The Friends of Democracy." Their business headquarters operated from New York, duplicating by the tens of thousands Kahn's articles, along with several by Jacob Schiff and others, and shipped bales of them to France's Service de la Propagande Aérienne. They were then scattered along the German front from planes and balloons. During the Germans' advance between the Aisne and the Marne they came upon several abandoned trucks loaded with the propaganda material and French orders directing its distribution.

The story circulated on both sides of the Atlantic that the Prussian high command ranked Kahn first among Germany's foes, and later, in 1918, when he set out dauntlessly to visit England, then France, which was under fire, every U-boat was ordered to watch for his liner and sink it. The Kaiser reportedly exclaimed that he would rather kill Kahn than either President Wilson or General Pershing. Improbably as the story sounds, Kahn never questioned it. "I wear the vilification of the Boche and pro-Boche as a badge of honor," he exulted. "My name has been on the blackest page of the Black Book of the German Government for four years."

The German press gave this claim some weight by quoting the Kaiser as calling Kahn, along with all anti-Prussian German-Americans, "filthy swine."

Kahn's energy was phenomenal. He did not confine his writings and speeches to anti-Prussian blasts; he also produced a wide-ranging quantity of both on topics of national significance, from "Art and the People," at the Shakespeare Tercentenary Dinner, New York, May 4, 1916, to "Government Ownership of Railroads," before the National Industrial Conference Board, New York, October 10, 1918. While he shared the conservative views of his fellow Republican capitalists on most financial issues, he shocked Wall Street from time to time with wholly unorthodox prescriptions. For example, he proposed at the annual dinner of the Association of Stock Exchange Brokers, New York, January 24, 1917: "Against unscrupulous promotion and financiering, a remedy might be found in a law which should forbid any public dealing in any industrial security . . . unless its introduction is accompanied by a prospectus to be signed by persons who are to be held responsible at law for any willful omission or misstatement therein. . . . The purchaser should not be permitted to be under the impression that he is buying a share in tangible assets when, as a matter of fact, he is buying expectations, earning capacity or good will. . . . The main evil of watered stock lies not in the presence of water, but in the concealment or coloring of that liquid. . . ."

He was sixteen years ahead of his time. Not until 1933 did Congress enact the Truth and Securities Law, which embodied Kahn's basic proposal.

In "High Finance," before the American Newspaper Publishers' Association, New York, April 27, 1916, he examined the reasons why the general public regarded the financial community with hostility. They were threefold. While exculpating the majority of his colleagues, he laid the blame at the door of a relatively few black sheep, what Matthew Josephson called the "Robber Barons." Second, he blamed the same rogues for their public-be-damned attitude, and finally he deplored the "cult of silence" that prevailed even among otherwise irreproachable financiers: ". . . some of its rites have been almost those of an occult science. To meet attacks with dignified silence, to maintain an austere demeanor, to cultivate an etiquette of reticence, had been one of its traditions. Nothing could have been more calculated to irritate democracy, which dislikes and suspects secrecy and resents aloofness. And the instinct of democracy is right."

"Art and the People," an idealistic outpouring that Kahn published in a brochure, exalted art as one of the most appropriate common meeting grounds available to all people, regardless of their incomes, occupations, or points of view. "For art is democracy in its very essence; not the counterfeit which, misunderstanding or misinterpreting the purpose and meaning of the democratic conception, seeks or tends to establish a common level of mediocrity and ultimately becomes the negation of liberty. . . .

"It is very far from being appreciated as yet by our wealthy men that art can be as educational as universities, that it is, or can be made, a strong element for civic betterment, that it has power of exhorting and stimulating and revealing and soothing and healing.

"European governments and municipalities have long since recognized this aspect of public usefulness and value inherent in art, and have given expression to this recognition by subsidising theatres and operas and other art institutions. Here, in accordance with the spirit and traditions of the country, this task to the largest extent is left to private initiative, to the generosity and public spirit, or, if you will, the enlightened selfishness of those who can afford to give. It is a duty and a privilege and ought to be a pleasure to fulfill it. . . .

"Maecenases are needed for the dramatic stage, the operatic stage, the concert stage; for conservatories and art academies; for the encouragement and support of American writers, painters, sculptors, decorators, etc. for all those things which in Europe have been done and are being done by princes, governments and communities. . . .

"Wealth is only in part a matter of dollars and cents. The visitor who pays twenty-five cents for a seat at a popular concert, if he brings with him love and enthusiasm for art, will be far richer that evening than the man or woman from Fifth Avenue if he or she sits yawning in a box at the Metropolitan Opera House. The poor man in a crowded tenement who feels moved and stirred in reading a fine book will be far richer than the man or woman sitting in dullness in a gorgeous library. If he goes to Central Park or Riverside Drive with his eyes and soul open to the beauties of nature, he will be far richer than the man or woman chasing through the glories of Italy or France in a luxurious automobile, the man thinking of the Stock Exchange and the woman of her new dress or next party. . . ."

A copy of the brochure reached Edith Wharton, who lived in Paris at 53 rue de Varenne. It prompted her to write to Kahn on March 23, 1917: ". . . What you have said needs to be said loudly and often, especially the point you bring out between the people who see and enjoy Central Park and those who tear through Italy thinking of bridge and the stock market. . . ."

In the same letter she appealed to Kahn for support in what she termed her "war-charities." ". . . When I started them I supposed they would not have to last more than a year . . . that I could keep them going without having to clamour for help. But the duration of the war, and the terrible misery among the French refugees and the tuberculous soldiers (the categories I work for) have compelled me (there is no other word, when one sees these things with one's own eyes!) to enlarge my task, and assume more and more responsibilities.

"If you have time, will you look over the summary of the work that I am enclosing [a description of the Franco-American hostels for Belgian and French refugees], and help me if you are not already pledged to too many other undertakings? . . ."

No doubt elated by the great novelist's complimentary words, Kahn sent her, on April 23, 1,500 francs and a letter couched in his most literary vein:

". . . Praise has value in exact proportion to the esteem which the praisee has for the person bestowing the praise, and by that formula I appreciate very highly what you are good enough to say regarding my speech.

"As to your war charities, I need not say how deeply I sympathize with your work. Your beneficent activities in France are amongst those things—all too few—to which, during the long two and one half years till America found herself and took her stand where she belonged, we were enabled to look with satisfaction and thankfulness as giving tangible expression to our *unneutral* feelings.

"Nor need I say how ardent is my affection, and how profound my reverence for France. There are some things for which only a great poet can find worthy and fitting expression. The emotions and sentiments which are evoked by France, glorious, heroic and alas! suffering, are amongst those things. . . .

"My daughter [Maud] is so sorry that, owing to some adverse circumstances, she missed the great pleasure of becoming acquainted with you during her stay in Paris. She has returned home filled with the inspiration of France and matured and deepened through her contact with the tragic realities of life and the sublime spirit of the French people. She is cajoling, manoeuvering and fighting to induce my wife and myself to let her go back to Paris, but for the present anyhow we do not feel that we should be justified in permitting her to take the risk of crossing the ocean. . . ."

13

European Mission

When, on May 9, 1917, the Anglo-French Mission, which included Marshal Joseph Jacques Césaire Joffre, the hero of the Marne, reached New York after military and economic conferences in Washington, Kahn was prominent among the bankers who greeted him. The Kahns' devotion to England and France was familial. The year before, Maud Kahn, who was then eighteen, had served as a Red Cross nurse in a London hospital.

On May 28, Kahn released a statement on war taxation hardly calculated to enchant his Wall Street brethren. He advocated a far higher tax on excess war profits than hitherto instead of a limited wartime income for everybody. "It is absolutely right that no man, as far as it is possible to prevent it, shall make money out of a war in which his country is engaged, but there is all the difference in the world between that doctrine and the unjust and immoral doctrine that no man shall be permitted to have more than an arbitrarily fixed income during a war. There ought to be an excess profit tax which might well be at a considerably higher rate than the present eight per cent, or even the proposed sixteen per cent, but it should only be applicable to the extent that business profits exceed the profits of, say, a certain average period before the war, and thus may justly be held to be attributable to war conditions. . . ."

He argued that an excess profit tax of perhaps 32 percent would yield a much greater return than the proposed 16 percent. In fact, figures he had analyzed indicated that a 40 percent tax on excess profits over and above the average earnings for the past three years would produce for the current year $800 million.

The Revenue Act of 1918 imposed, for that year only, a war profits tax scale ranging up to 80 percent.

In November 1917, President Wilson, himself a former professor of jurisprudence and political economy, summoned Kahn to the White House to explore with him the economic condition of the nation.

A week later, addressing a Liberty Loan rally in St. Paul, Minnesota, Kahn decried "the insinuation that big business had any share in influencing our government's decision to enter the war," and he added: "Perhaps you will be more inclined to believe in my disinterestedness when I say that I have made up my mind to keep no income for myself during the war, and whatever remains to me of income after paying my living expenses and taxes will be devoted to charity and war purposes as long as the war lasts."

He ran untrue to form again in an article on trade unionism. "I regard the labor union movement as an absolutely necessary element in the scheme of our economic life. . . . Trade unions have not only come to stay, but they are bound, I think, to become an increasingly potent factor in our industrial life. I believe that the most effective preventive against extreme State Socialism is frank, free and far-reaching cooperation between business and trade unions sobered and broadened increasingly by enhanced opportunities, rights and responsibilities."

Business must not begrudge labor its due, he argued, but recognize it as a partner. Every worker merits a decent living wage. Provision must be made for the unemployed, for those without means incapacitated by sickness, disability, or old age. The gulf between employer and employee, between businessman and farmer must be bridged. All must unite in an effort toward procuring for the masses greater ease and comfort, more of the rewards and joys of life. This was not simply a question of duty but of interest, because to preserve the present social system it must be made more satisfactory, more inviting. Kahn did not mean blue-collar workers only, but also white-collar workers —in short, workers in every field, from the unskilled to the professional.

"The building must be rendered more habitable and attractive to those whose claim for adequate houseroom cannot be left unheeded either justly or safely. Some changes, essential changes, must be made.

"I have no fear of the outcome and of the readjustment which must come. I have no fear of the forces of freedom unless they be ignored, repressed or falsely and selfishly led. . . ."

Within a year of America's entry into the war, Kahn, eager to observe developments at close range, sailed for Europe. Scared stiff, as he later confessed, lest a U-boat attack his ship, yet exhilarated, he landed first in England. Armed with letters from Theodore Roosevelt and Lord Reading, he spent much of May 1918 conferring with economic and military leaders, among them Prime Minister Lloyd George. He inspected St. Dunstan's, now the haven of hundreds of war-blinded veterans. He saw a good deal of Max Aitken, now Lord Beaverbrook.

On May 27 he crossed the Channel to France. Upon reaching Paris, which was under continual long-range bombardment, he donated 10,000 francs to the Société des Auteurs Dramatiques. An accompanying note read:

"I enclose a little essay I wrote that was published in America about eighteen months ago ["France," in *For France*, January 1917]. I have little to add, unless it is to tell you that it gives an inadequate idea of my love and my veneration for your glorious country. Only a great poet could find the words needed to express what I feel, as a man and an American, toward France, that nation so noble and proud, whose territory is the Holy Land of humanity."

He called on General Pershing and with his authority visited all the American bases and principal lines of communication. While the battle of the Chemin des Dames still raged seventy-five miles northeast of Paris, he moved near the front and dined in a castle that, an hour before, bombardments had partially demolished.

From France, on June 18, he proceeded to Madrid at the invitation of King Alfonso XIII, with whom he discussed plans under consideration for more active postwar economic interchanges between Spain and the United States.

The Legion of Honor is the only order France bestows. Its five classes range from Chevalier, or Knight, to Grand Cross. In 1918 Kahn was awarded the red ribbon and medallion of Chevalier, and three years later Premier Aristide Briand personally upgraded him to the second class, that of Commander. For Kahn's services before, during, and after the war King Victor Emmanuel appointed him Commander of the Order of the Crown of Italy, and Belgium's King

Albert awarded him the Cross of Commander of the Order of the Belgian Crown and made him Knight of the Order of Charles II.

When Kahn, having completed his tour abroad as a self-appointed ambassador at large, got back to America on July 25, he issued a statement summarizing his observations. Among those that struck him most forcefully was the British method of army salvage under Andrew Weir, director general of supplies. Through the salvage and recycling of materials that formerly ended on the scrap heap, Weir calculated, his system would realize within three years a saving of $500 million. Said Kahn: "If we find ways of applying after the war systematically in civil life the lessons now being learned as to the use and value of materials hitherto considered absolute waste, the possibility of wealth by that means in our country staggers the imagination."

Of France: "It was interesting and significant to notice how universally the French look to us for commercial cooperation after the war. Through our army's constructive activities they have seen at work on their own soil a race in which tradition, surroundings, and the principles and methods of personal initiative and individual enterprise have developed daring resourcefulness, self-reliance, adaptability and short-cut methods. They want us to join our qualities with their qualities and their opportunities. And, strange as it may seem in so old a country, France offers many and great commercial opportunities quite apart from the work of reconstruction. Moreover, their colonies are an empire of immense resources and vast potential wealth."

In Spain, Kahn reported, German intrigue and propaganda were rampant. Nevertheless, Spain was neutral and meant to remain so, "but I am convinced that her sympathies, on the whole, are more pro-Ally than otherwise and can be still more so . . . with understanding, tact, and sympathy toward Spain, coupled with a reasonably liberal policy in furnishing her the raw materials and other things she needs from us, we can obtain everything from her which we have a right to expect from a friendly disposed neutral."

The spruce banker disapproved of the doughboys' uniform, "the stiff color [*sic*; collar?] and general inappropriateness and discomfort . . . which, by the universal verdict of our own men, and those of other nations, is both the least well-appearing and the least practical of all uniforms."

Upon Kahn's return to America, President Wilson requested a detailed report of his trip. A long-standing admirer of the scholarly president, Kahn eagerly complied. Secretary of War Newton Baker appointed him chairman of the Military Entertainment Council Advisory Board to furnish diversion to the troops at home and abroad, a precursor of World War II's United Service Organizations. For the War Industries Board Council of Defense he produced analyses of foreign investments, conducted Liberty Loan campaigns, served as treasurer of the League for National Unity, an agency that opposed radicals and pacifists. To a Sunday evening gala in behalf of the United War Work Campaign, he contributed the use of the Metropolitan Opera House, its orchestra, and Caruso. Sunday evenings were among the Met's most profitable, and Kahn defrayed the loss out of his own pocket. He served on some two dozen relief and defense committees, among them the Hoover Commission for Belgian Relief, donating funds to them as well as to more than a hundred assorted war relief organizations. He never failed to answer the friendly letters he received from Allied soldiers and to help those of their families in need with a check. He set up a hospital near the front and sent large monthly sums to maintain it.

All of these activities failed to drain his energy. He continued to work as before at both Kuhn, Loeb and the Met. In fact, when Jacob Schiff died on September 25, 1920, it was Otto Kahn, not Mortimer Schiff, as Morti's father had dearly wished, who succeeded to the high command of the firm. As for the Met, through the collaborative efforts of Kahn and Gatti-Casazza, it enjoyed a 1917–18 season of high distinction, impaired only by the exclusion of German operas and German artists. (At London's Covent Garden, Sir Thomas Beecham, refusing to associate art with war, continued to conduct Mozart and Wagner, though as a concession to the general public he agreed to an English text, while the Carl Rosa Company toured Britain with Wagner.) The brilliant French conductor Pierre Monteux made his Met debut. John McCormack and Amelita Galli-Curci sang there for the first time, and Rimsky-Korsakov's *Le Coq d'Or* had its American premiere. As a token of appreciation for Gatti-Casazza's stewardship of the Met since 1908, Kahn, in the name of the board of directors, donated an ambulance bearing the general manager's name for use by the Italian army.

Though Kahn esteemed President Wilson, on one major issue he differed radically: the League of Nations, of which Wilson was the chief proponent. In a letter to Republican senator Miles Poindexter of Washington, dated November 29, 1919, Kahn set forth his opposition to the League of Nations Covenant, part of the Treaty of Versailles, as originally submitted to the Senate. While favoring any pact that promised to preserve peace, with America assuming her full share of its implementation, he rejected the entire concept upon which the Covenant rested.

"Nothing," he wrote, "that we fought for makes it incumbent upon us to entangle ourselves in the age-long racial squabbles and intrigues of Europe and Asia, or to become the guardians and guarantors of an arbitrarily and artificially remodeled world, put together in disregard, more or less, of the evolution of centuries and of the proven qualities and characteristics of races, according to the perceptions, predilections and compromises of a few men assembled in secret conclave, far removed from the informing and vitalizing currents of public opinion and not, perhaps, quite sufficiently removed always from considerations of domestic-political expediency.

"Nothing that we fought for makes it incumbent upon us to relinquish our fundamental national policies and traditions, and to transform the American eagle into an international nondescript. . . .

"America, the young giant of the free and unconventional west, cannot be put into a garment cut according to the manner and habits of old-time European diplomacy. She is not at her best when sitting around green tables in European chancelleries. . . .

"She will do far more and far better work for the world if she is left free to do it in her own way than if she is confronted and constrained by the rigid formulae and meticulous provisions of an instrument such as the one framed at Versailles. . . .

"I have been at pains to read through the Peace Treaty, including the Covenant, from beginning to end. I laid it away sore at heart and sickened. . . .

"I had hoped . . . that in place of creating a wholly novel and untried machinery of vast complexity, the United States, France and Italy would make a short, simple, solemn declaration to the world to the effect that the high and beneficent things we fought for, we mean to preserve and protect and that any one who assails them will find these great European powers and America again arrayed for the defense of liberty, peace and right. . . .

"Such a declaration, together with the utilization, strengthening and development of the existing machinery of The Hague Conferences and

Tribunal, would, I believe, accomplish it more effectively than an iron-clad document. . . ."

Kahn foresaw "the red flood of Bolshevism" threatening to engulf the nations, and believed that the Germans, still 60 million strong, could stem that tide if treated by its conquerors with mercy and humanity instead of destructive vengeance.

14

Oheka

The cold shoulder of the Morristown elite, the refusal of the Morristown Club to open its doors to him, may have been factors in Kahn's decision to seek a country seat elsewhere. The result was one of the most flamboyant displays of conspicuous consumption in American social annals.

He was drawn to Long Island where, in 1912, the year-old Piping Rock Club, which would rank among the most highly selective private clubs in the area, had admitted him. He doubtless owed his membership to the influence of the Kuhn, Loeb attorney Paul Cravath, a charter member. Mortimer Schiff, too, was a charter member. By nature a joiner, Kahn also belonged at one time or another to the Authors Guild, India House, the National Golf Links, the Pilgrims, the Essex Fox Hounds, and, among the clubs, in addition to the Piping Rock and the Morristown Golf, the City, the City Midday, the Lotos, the Army and Navy, the Baltusrol Golf (in Springfield, New Jersey), the Whippany River, the Southside, and the Princeton University Club (as the father of a Princetonian, Gilbert Kahn).

In 1914 Kahn acquired for a million dollars a 443-acre tract at Cold Spring Harbor near the North Shore, straddling the line between Suffolk and Nassau counties. The area was dotted with the pleasances of such potentates as J. P. Morgan, Clarence Mackay, and Harry Payne Whitney. Kahn intended to erect his demesne upon the island's highest rise of land, topping all these estates, but no such eminence being purchasable, he decided to build a mountain of his own. To move the vast tonnage of earth needed, he had a spur of track laid from the Long Island Railroad to his acreage. As architect he retained

William Adams Delano of the famed firm of Delano and Aldrich, and for the landscaping the Olmsted Brothers of Boston, whose founder, Frederick Law Olmsted, landscaped New York's Central Park and Washington's Capitol grounds. Deferring to his client's regal fantasies, Delano designed a castle incorporating aspects of the palace of Fontainebleau and the classic French castles of the Loire. The estimated cost was originally one million dollars; the actual cost, close to $9 million. He named the edifice Oheka, an acronym for Otto Hermann Kahn.

What Kahn envisaged, in his determination to stand topmost above the Long Island barons, was no mere turreted château but a mountain-top citadel. With America on the brink of war, work progressed slowly. Manpower was in short supply, imported materials of the sort Kahn wanted for the halls, courtyards, and patios no longer available. Moreover, such prodigality in wartime, and by a German Jew, threatened to inflame the kind of bigotry that had disenchanted the Kahns with Morristown. Sagely, they began retrenching a bit, and when America entered the war, construction stopped altogether. Addie Kahn, herself a gifted amateur landscape designer, informed the Olmsteds, on December 24, 1917, "all our . . . schemes have been temporarily abandoned."

The Olmsteds nevertheless replied: "We beg to ask what is your pleasure in regard to our continuing the development of plans for your place at this time. We believe that when the general situation clears and development work is resumed in this country we shall be overcrowded with commissions, and if such prove to be the case it would be distinctly to your advantage to have us develop some of your plans now so that they would be ready for you at a moment's notice."

On January 11, 1918, Addie reaffirmed her decision: "I discussed once, very fully, with my husband, the matter of further work. . . . I think, in fact, that even apart from war conditions, it will be far more satisfactory to me to plan the developments of the gardens when I am living at the place, and am familiar with every nook and corner of it." Rather than plant whole new stands of trees, she decided to transport those grown to maturity at Morristown, valued at $22,000, and had dummy trees made to mark the spots where she wanted to replant the real thing.

At length, two months after the Armistice, both building and landscaping were resumed. The year of total inaction, according to the architectural historian Robert King, had in part been meant to placate the community. "We have made up our minds," Addie told the

Olmsteds, "to continue the work very gradually and not in a pretentious way, owing to the enormous cost of labor and all materials now."

During the fall of 1919 the Kahns finally moved into their castellated aerie. America's second largest estate after George Washington Vanderbilt's Biltmore in Asheville, North Carolina, it presented a bird's-eye view so spectacular, with its French Renaissance tourelles, its Norman tower, its gables and roofs of varicolored slate, that Orson Welles included a stock shot of it, among other fantastic country seats, in *Citizen Kane* to suggest the grandeur of Kane's Xanadu. From the public road, past a stucco gateway, through wrought-iron gates, a driveway, lined with maple trees, led to a wide-walled turnaround and thence along an avenue flanked by tall cedars toward the main entrance to the château. The cedars were so positioned, according to Kahn's instructions, so as to spare Addie, whose bedroom overlooked the driveway, the sight of automobiles coming and going. Because she fancied eighteenth-century English conceits, a Greco-Roman ruin was constructed in the woods.

The château, which formed the letter *E*, comprised 127 rooms. To tend them, along with the ten-car garage, the stables, the tennis courts, the eighteen-hole golf course, the densely flowered grounds, required 126 servants, many of whom had worked in other Kahn residences. When old age or illness befell them, they were kept on without pay. As Addie Kahn once remarked: "Being a Kahn pensioner gives you everlasting life."

Of the household domestic staff few enjoyed greater prestige than the head butler. The city editor of the *New York Herald Tribune*, Dwight Perrin, on the track of a business story, telephoned the Cold Spring Harbor retreat to speak to Kahn. The footman who took the call explained that Kahn had retired for the night.

"Well, wake him up," cried Perrin. "It's an important message."

"Oh," said the footman, "only the butler is allowed to wake Mr. Kahn."

"Let me talk to the butler then."

"But he's asleep also."

"Wake him up. I've got to talk to Mr. Kahn."

"But I wouldn't dare do that, sir. Nobody is allowed to wake the butler."

The most arresting feature of the interior was the marble-paved entrance hall from which rose in great sweeping arcs a horseshoe staircase like the famous one at Fontainebleau. On the second floor, an immense reception hall and, adjoining it, a library at one end and a dining room at the other, each of them vast. The dining room could seat more than 200 people, though the Kahns preferred to limit their guests to fifty. At full-dress dinners a footman stood behind each guest's chair alert to his or her slightest wish. The food was brought up by dumbwaiters from basement kitchens to a huge pantry. What Kahn valued most in a guest was the capacity to amuse or enlighten, and should the general conversation turn dull, he was apt to slip quietly away.

The rest of the castle, three stories in all, contained sitting rooms, dens, studies, libraries, a Gentleman's Retreat (that is, smoking room), game rooms, master bedroom suites, three loggias, a sewing room, a schoolroom for the children and their tutors . . . There were two elevators and three other staircases. In that pre-air-conditioning era Kahn devised his own ventilation system. He installed conduits from the basement to grates on the hillsides, thereby creating passages for the flow of fresh air. They kept the rooms comfortable in even the steamiest summer weather.

Kahn was a restless man who, when not absorbed in work at Kuhn, Loeb or the Met, demanded constant diversion, and the appurtenances of his estate provided the means to pursue practically every hobby, game, and sport. What had initially been conceived as a greenhouse was converted into a swimming pool 70 feet long, bordered by marble tiles. Kahn commissioned an artist, Austin Purves, to decorate the walls of the stairwell with paintings on glass. Descending the steps was like descending to the bottom of the sea with multitudes of black, gold, silver, and blue fish swirling against a background of seaweed and coral. Aided by the eminent naturalist Charles Beebe and the live specimens in the New York Aquarium, Purves assigned each variety of fish to the level it would occupy in the ocean. Thus, conger eels appeared near the top, pompano below, and so on in gorgeous color alternations as one went deeper into the pool and different species succeeded each other.

Crisscrossing the acreage were several installations that accommodated Roger Wolfe Kahn's love of speed, which first manifested itself in his fourteenth year when he rode a motorcycle up the sides of bunkers on his father's private golf course in Morristown. At Cold Spring Harbor he tested cars on a speedway laid out for him. He owned a fleet of them, including a Lincoln, a Marmon, a Chrysler, a Duesenberg, a Ford, and a Bugatti fashioned to his specifications by Giuseppe Bugatti himself at a cost of $17,000. The Ford he dismantled and reassembled into a high-speed car with an underslung chassis. He used the speedway with its sharply banked turns for testing motorcycles as well.

Nearby were moored two or more of his father's boats. The largest was a yacht that Kahn also named *Oheka* (as he did other boats and several dwellings), a Maybach express cruiser 73 feet long with three twelve-cylinder gas engines, bought for $90,000. It carried a crew of six and could dine and bunk twelve guests. Its private burgee enclosed a yellow *K* against a blue background. The second craft was a fourteen-foot day cruiser costing $18,500. On one or the other of these craft Kahn would commute to New York City during the workweek. His chauffeur, John Punton, would drive him, usually in a maroon Rolls-Royce, from the castle to the beach club, then go on ahead to meet the boat at the Baltimore & Ohio dock, where Wall Street began, and drive him to the Kuhn, Loeb building. After work, the itinerary would be reversed.

Roger occasionally sailed with his father, but his ruling passion was aviation. While still in his teens, he was taught to fly by a bootlegger. Ultimately, his interest in jazz bands declined until, soon after his nightclub failed, he abandoned them altogether to devote himself to aviation. Kahn senior, while fearful for his son's safety, nevertheless built Roger a landing field on the estate and paid the salaries of airplane washers and assorted engineers. Roger piled up 2,700 miles of flight and after acquiring his pilot's license bought a series of planes, among them a Vought Corsair, a Bellanca Pacemaker, an Ireland Amphibian, a Fleet, and a hybrid Standard with a Sikorsky wing, which he kept in his own hangar named Roweka at Long Island's Roosevelt Field. He later joined the Grumman Engineering Corporation as a test pilot and flew such famed fighter planes as the Grumman Wildcat and the Grumman Hellcat.

In 1926 Kahn's cherished eighteen-hole golf course fell prey to a terrible threat, as did the lands of such affluent neighbors as the Phippses, the Whitneys, the Mackays, and the Vanderbilts, to name a few. Robert Moses, chairman of the New York State Council of Parks, a title that hardly suggests the tremendous political power he wielded, proposed to run the Northern State Parkway right through their properties, and in Kahn's case, through the middle of his golf course. Robert A. Caro tells the story in his magisterial *The Power Broker: Robert Moses and the Fall of New York*. Caro does not spare Kahn, according to whose often professed credo—"I must atone for my wealth"—all of the North Shore Midases had plenty to atone for.

"He [Moses]," Caro writes, "would not move the parkway route down out of the hills the barons held and onto the plains in the Island's center. This would mean that the parkway could never be truly beautiful. But, within the hills, there were many possible routes, and he was willing to compromise with the barons on which route would finally be chosen. He made deals: with at least a dozen barons he covenanted that he would move the parkway away from the homes to the edge of their property, out of sight of their castles, if they would in turn donate the right-of-way so that he would not need a legislative appropriation for it. . . .

"None found him more reasonable than financier Otto Kahn. Kahn . . . offered to secretly donate $10,000 to the Park Commission for surveys, if some of the surveys found a new route for the parkway in the Cold Spring Harbor area, a route which would not cross his estate at all. And Moses accepted the money."

In the end, the route of the Northern State Parkway was shifted to a comfortable distance from Kahn's golf course.

The Kahn estate was widely marveled at and admired, with a surprising exception: William Delano, the architect who designed the château. "I shudder to think of this folly," he said many years later. ". . . It grew and grew in size as his self-importance grew, and the gardens—which I must confess I delighted in designing—became more and more extensive. . . . When the place was finished and his chest fully inflated by the admiration of his friends, and while the last payment was still due on my fee, he called me one day on the telephone and asked me to lunch with him. I went—and his opening remark was that many of his partners had built houses and none of them had been charged more than six per cent by their architects, whereas I was charging ten. I explained that I had given most of my time for two years to the design and execution, often going to the site a couple of times a week with Mrs. Kahn (a widely traveled and very intelligent woman, and lover of beautiful things); in short, that I had always charged ten per cent for private houses and I thought his was one that had pleased him and his friends, and added, casually, that I had in my safe a longhand letter from him agreeing to my terms. 'In that case, I'll say no more about it,' and the lunch ended very agreeably."

The Cold Spring Harbor citadel was but one of numerous properties that Kahn acquired as either a dwelling or a real estate investment.

The first, in 1904, was a plot at the southeast corner of Fifth Avenue and Seventy-fifth Street, with a frontage of 57 feet on the avenue and 120 feet along the side street, for which he had paid half a million dollars. He planned to erect a town house that would eclipse in size and elegance that of its magnificent neighbors, such as the residence of Edward Harkness, financier and trustee of the Metropolitan Museum of Art. But Kahn changed his mind and sold the plot.

His next major real estate venture, five years later, was in Palm Beach, Florida, where he spent an average of two weeks every winter. He built a villa there, naming it Oheka, on Sunset Avenue fronting the ocean. It proved too small for his growing family, and he later built, for $250,000, a second Oheka, Italian Renaissance in style, at 691 North County Road.* The chief means of transport in Palm Beach was then a kind of wicker chair on wheels pedaled by a black attendant from the rear. It was called, with casual racism, an Afromobile, and every Palm Beacher of substance owned one. Kahn's pedaler, Miles, made an appreciative comment about the new Oheka that the family treasured ever after. When Kahn asked him what he thought of the villa, Miles replied: "It are equaled by few and surpassed by many."

In addition Kahn had purchased, for $75,000, a tract of land in Isleboro, Maine, on which to build a hot-weather retreat, and leased an Adirondacks camp from Mrs. Alfred Vanderbilt, Jr. He still owned the Sixty-eighth Street houses. Gilbert Kahn and his wife occupied Number 8 during the early years of their marriage. The only property Kahn bought abroad was St. Dunstan's. After disposing of it, he preferred to lease a grandee's estate like Cassiobury Park. In no place, owned or leased, did he linger long. After settling in Addie and the children, he would grow restive and bustle off to attend to the affairs of Kuhn, Loeb and the Met or to pursue his varied recreational pleasures.

In 1913 he had returned to his vision of a splendorous town house. The site he chose lay on the northeast corner of Fifth Avenue and Ninety-first Street, where he would erect a five-story mansion† facing Andrew Carnegie's four stories on the southeast corner.

It would cover an area of 100 feet on Fifth Avenue and 145 feet on Ninety-first Street. To design it, Kahn retained an English architect, J. Armstrong Stenhouse, and an American one, Charles P. H. Gilbert, whose notable works included the Felix M. Warburg house

---

*Now the Graham-Eckes School as well as a Historic Landmark.
†Now the Convent of the Sacred Heart, a Catholic girls' school.

(later the Jewish Museum), a block north of Kahn's purchase, and the Burden House on Eighty-fourth Street and Fifth Avenue (later the Marymount School). The Kahn structure, whose address would be 1100 Fifth Avenue, adopted the style of the Italian High Renaissance. Construction started in 1913 and encountered the same war-born obstacles as the Long Island house, not being completed until 1918, after World War I. A citation by the New York Chamber of Commerce following Kahn's death compared both structures to the Medici palaces.

The principal building material consisted of Caen stone, all of it imported from France. The two façades, the one on Fifth Avenue, the other on Ninety-first Street, rose from a high base of rusticated stone—that is, roughened masonry. Stenhouse introduced the continental contrivance of running a passage for vehicles behind the outside Ninety-first Street wall. Immense wood-paneled doors in arched entrances closed off this passage from the street. The main entrance to the house stood within the passage, and before it, night and day, a footman stood guard. When Addie's friends called he would escort them to an elevator that would waft them up to the fourth floor and Addie's Louis Quinze sitting room, the paneling, fixtures, and mirrors all imported from France. Nearby was a small room occupied entirely by Addie's hats on shelves at different levels. A bathtub of lapis lazuli adorned her bathroom. The elevator, too, had unusual aspects. Because Addie suffered from claustrophobia, the interior had been painted with motifs that gave a feeling of openness.

In her full matronly maturity Addie was a commanding figure despite her small size. She wore her hair in a high, upswept pompadour that increased her height but also exposed her large ears, making them seem larger. Her face and figure were lovely, her natural expression serene. Highly intelligent, she was well-informed in many areas.

According to the protocol established by Addie, dinner guests would ascend an Italian Renaissance Revival staircase under a richly painted quatrepartite vaulted ceiling and forgather in a walnut-paneled library among whose handsomest furnishings were two matched writing desks, facing each other, covered in red leather, with gold-tooled drawers, one desk for Kahn, the other for Addie. Thence the assemblage moved into the Gothic, or Italian, Room for reception amenities. Furniture was sparse here lest it detract from the cream of the Kahn art collection adorning the walls. Before proceeding to the dining room the guests were expected to pause and admire the paintings. Along with the putti cavorting on the ceiling was a little pictorial jest conceived by Kahn—a group of classically nude sportsmen playing pool, baseball, tennis, and golf. A small window in Kahn's study on the floor above afforded a full view of the Gothic Room, and he would peer through it from time to time, delaying his entrance until all the most important guests were present.

Life at 1100 Fifth Avenue was highly formal. With or without guests, the family dressed for dinner. Though each of the girls had her own maid, their appearance seldom entirely satisfied their mother. To Addie they often looked disheveled, improperly turned out. She regulated the activities of the youngest children, Gilly and Pips, with the rigorousness of a drill sergeant—so many hours for lessons, so many hours for games, so many for repose.

15

St. Peter's, St. Bartholomew's, St. John's

By the end of 1919 the Kahns had abandoned Cedar Court and were dividing their time between the New York mansion and the Cold Spring Harbor château, each a frame for some of the most effulgent social events of the period.

On February 16, 1920, Walter Hewlett, the treasurer of Cold Spring Harbor's St. John's Episcopal Church, wrote to Kahn thanking him for a donation of $580 and welcoming "you and your family as members of St. John's Parish." Hewlett meant parish only in the secular sense. The Kahns had also rented a pew in St. John's for their four Episcopalian children and bought burial plots for themselves in its nondenominational cemetery, but neither ever became communicants in any church, though the fiction persists that they worshiped, successively, at St. Peter's in Morristown, St. Bartholomew's in New York, and St. John's in Cold Spring Harbor.

From these falsities arose a body of misconceptions about the elder Kahns' religion. According to one of the most widespread myths, Kahn was walking along New York's Park Avenue, accompanied by Marshall Wilder, a dwarfish hunchback who had become a national vaudeville star because of the witty monologue he delivered about his own deformities. As they passed St. Bartholomew's Church on Fiftieth Street, Kahn exclaimed: "Marshall, isn't it beautiful? It always gives me a thrill when I look at my church. You know, I used to be a Jew."

"Indeed," Wilder supposedly replied. "You know, I used to be a hunchback."

Addie Kahn remained indifferent to all places of worship. What church benefactions she and her husband bestowed were intended to embellish the social status and widen the future opportunities of their children. Though Addie bought for them, in 1918, pew number 21 at St. Bartholomew's for $3,850, she never sat there with them; until they were old enough to attend church by themselves, one of the governesses accompanied them.

Kahn, however, was increasingly fascinated by the external elements of both Episcopalianism and Catholicism, by their elaborate architecture, music, and art, unlike the comparative esthetic simplicity of Judaism. Of his sense of spirituality, of the depth of Christianity's attraction for him, he left scant indications in his voluminous writings and speeches.

Kahn numbered several close friends among the Catholic clergy and donated funds to their charities. Perhaps the closest was Father Francis Patrick Duffy, the "Fighting Chaplain" of New York's 69th Regiment during the war, whose statue dominates Duffy Square at Broadway and Forty-seventh Street, a few blocks from his postwar pastorate, Holy Cross Church. Another clerical intimate was Father John Kelly, the tuberculous, epileptic chaplain of the Catholic Writers Guild. A year after the Versailles Treaty, many of whose terms Kahn had deplored, especially those imposing harsh German reparations, he traveled in Europe with a group of like-minded Americans, participating in conferences of economists, bankers, and statesmen on the general spread of discord and dissension. Father Kelly, who was present at one conference, recalled later that when a member of the gathering ventured disparaging observations about Pope Benedict XV and the Vatican, Kahn rose in wrath and declared: "Gentlemen, all my life my greatest joys have been in the music and arts which have been saved for us since the early centuries through this church. If another such remark is made here, my colleagues and I shall withdraw."

Father Kelly remembered, too, a curious dialogue between Kahn and himself regarding the great exemplars in the history of man. There were three whom Kahn considered the greatest of all. He expatiated on St. Paul and St. Francis, then fell silent.

"And the third?" Father Kelly prodded him.

"I do not feel worthy to mention his name."

"You mean Jesus?"

"Yes."

"But if you revere him so, why did you never follow in his footsteps?"

"Because for that one has to have a special call, and I do not feel that I have had one."

During the postwar decade Kahn contributed funds to a variety of Catholic churches and organizations. To list a few: St. Catherine's Welfare Society; St. Hugh's Church in Huntington, Long Island, along with funds for the construction there of a parochial school; the Society of St. Vincent de Paul; the Catholic Diocesan Choristers; the Catholic Big Brothers League; and St. Christopher's Inn, a Franciscan hospice at Garrison, New York, that sheltered and fed the destitute and homeless irrespective of race or creed.

Father Anselm di Pasco, the chaplain and later spiritual director of St. Christopher's Inn, wrote to Kahn on March 13, 1929: "When I received your very generous donation [actually, it was only $25], I did not know what to admire more, your faith, your generosity or your broadmindedness, hence to show my sincere and profound appreciation for your sympathy in my discouraging work, I am sending you under separate cover a blessed medal of St. Christopher as a token of gratitude.

"Attach the medal to your car, Col. Lindburgh [sic] has one on his plain [sic] and may St. Christopher, the Patron of Autoists, guide and protect you on all your journeys. . . ."

Upon Kahn's return from a trip abroad, Father di Pasco wrote on October 31, 1930: "I am wondering whether you stopped at Assisi the cradle of Franciscanism and the birthplace of the 'Poverello'? The next time you go abroad you should not miss the treat. Mr. Charles P. Howland of the Council of Foreign Relations told me that he enjoyed the stay at the Convento very very much. . . ."

Kahn replied five days later: "I did not have the occasion, unfortunately, . . . to visit Assisi, which I know well and love. I envy Mr. Charles P. Howland his stay at the Convento in the midst of the loveliness of its surroundings, the beauty of its art and the vivid spiritual presence of the 'Poverello,' whom I revere as one of the very few greatest and noblest of men, perhaps the most appealing and loveable of all figures in history. . . ."

Kahn often considered conversion, but always drew back, restrained perhaps by a sense of loyalty to his forebears. Or was it a fear of appearing opportunistic? On November 27, 1927, he wrote to the *Jewish Chronicle* correcting an editorial that claimed that he had joined the Episcopal Church. "Permit me to say that you are mistaken. I have not joined the Episcopal or any other church.

"A year ago I made the following statement for publication: 'Religious observance is instilled in one's youth. My parents were not practising Jews and did not bring me up to be a practising Jew. But I never left Judaism and I have no idea of doing so.'

"That statement continues to hold good."

When a semiliterate namesake, Sidney Kahn, wrote to him on December 5, 1928: "Will you please stop changing your religion. You have to go to church if you change. Pope of Rome goes here too. Henry Ford said over and over again the best Hebrew wasn't born," Kahn's secretary, James Dartt, hastened to reply: ". . . I beg to inform you that Mr. Otto H. Kahn is a Jew, and has no intention of affiliating himself with any other religion. . . ."

The first of Kahn's children to marry was Maud. In her early twenties she had fallen in love with an officer of the Scots Guard attached to the British embassy in Washington, Captain and Brevet Major John Charles Oakes Marriott. In accordance with her father's instructions, Sir George Lewis notified Kahn on June 1, 1920:

"I send you enclosed the marriage articles which I have prepared and in which I have followed the lines in the recent marriage of the Duke of Devonshire's daughter. I think it is drawn in such a way that no difficulty can arise in the terms in which the settlement will be finally drawn up.

"You understand, I think, that if the settlement is to be an ante-nuptial marriage settlement it must be signed by yourself, your daughter and her intended husband before the marriage. . . ."

Under the terms of the final agreement Kahn would transmit to a trustee £100,000 for investment in government securities of England, America, India, or any English colony, of which Maud would enjoy the income for life. Should Marriott survive her, he would receive half of the income for life. The rest of the agreement dealt mainly with the division of capital, after both husband and wife died, among any children born to them.

The marriage took place in St. John's Church on June 15, 1920, with Maud's sister, Margaret, serving as maid of honor, and as best man Major General Hugh Bethell, military attaché to the British embassy. Hundreds of guests attended the reception afterward at the Kahn castle, having journeyed from Boston, New York, and Washington. They included former ambassador to Germany James W. Gerard; the British and French consuls general; Mrs. Bainbridge Colby, wife of the secretary of state; the American-born author Princess Julia Cantacuzene; Mrs. William Vanderbilt, Jr.; the conductor Artur Bodanzky and his wife; the August Belmonts; the Bernard Baruchs; the Hamilton Fish Armstrongs; the Mortimer Schiffs; the Paul Cravaths; the Felix Warburgs . . .

The New York Times devoted more than a column to the event. Moved to lyrical heights, its society correspondent reported: "There were several marked innovations at the church ceremony in the way of quaint English customs. Standing at the entrance to the church was a Scots Guard in his flaming red coat and busby.

"The path of the bride as she left the church was also strewn with white sweet peas, so thickly that her path became a veritable carpet of flowers.

"The church was one mass of bloom. The pews of the center aisle were festooned with huge clusters of white roses, and the great masses of white peonies and smilax half concealed the chandeliers. . . . During the ceremony the song of birds could be heard outside. Preceding the ceremony a quartette [sic] consisting of harp, violin, cello and organ played some of the favorite selections of the bride.

"The bride walked to the chancel with her father. She wore a gown of soft ivory satin with a very long train of satin depending from the shoulders with a wide flare at the end. The train was edged with orange blossoms and was trimmed with old rose point lace studded with seed pearls. There were also motifs of the lace, which was worn by the bride's mother at her wedding, on the gown, which had short wide flowing sleeves of cascaded satin. The veil of tulle was fitted over the dark coiffure, with a circlet of orange blossoms, and fell almost to the end of the train. Her only ornament was a string of pearls, the gift of her parents. She carried a bouquet of white orchids. . . ."

From the managing director of two movie theaters, the Rialto and the Rivoli, Kahn received a letter a week after the ceremony: "We are showing on the screen at the Rialto Theatre this week, pictures of your daughter's wedding. The pictures were exceptionally well taken and give a splendid view of the affair.

"If you would care to see it, I would be pleased to arrange a special private showing in our projection room. I could also let you have a copy of this film which would be a souvenir of this momentous occasion."

The theater corporations, as it happened, had borrowed from Kahn since January 1920 a total, including interest, of $48,593.68, and would borrow by the fall $32,285 more. It is not known whether Kahn viewed the newsreel or accepted a copy of it.

Next of the Kahn children to marry was Gilbert, a twenty-one-year-old Princeton University dropout. On September 24, 1924, before he began his senior year, his father informed Princeton's president John Grier Hibben "of the to me regrettable and disappointing fact that he will not return to the University.

"The fact is that, for more than one year, it has been a question whether Minerva or Venus would determine his immediate course of action, and finally the latter has won. More soberly expressed, Gilbert became engaged a year ago to a charming and in every way eligible young lady, Miss Anna Whelan [Anne was the correct name; she was the daughter of Charles Whelan, who headed the United Cigar stores]. My wife and I have been trying to convince the two young people of the wisdom of postponing their marriage until after Gilbert's graduation, but for a variety of reasons we have had to yield at last, and the wedding is to take place within two or three months. Neither Gilbert nor the future Mrs. Gilbert can reconcile themselves to the idea of his continuing a student as a married man, and so my wife and I have reluctantly consented to his leaving college and entering business.

"I trust that his younger brother [Roger], who aspires to enter Princeton next fall, will prove a more faithful son to his Alma Mater. . . ."

Father Kelly married the couple. Gilbert then went to work for the Equitable Trust Company and later Kuhn, Loeb. He wanted to buy the partnership offered to him by the zesty "21" Club, but his father would not hear of it.

The marriage lasted until January 1933. A month later Gilbert married Sara Jane Heliker, a beauty-contest winner and acrobatic dancer. In November the first Mrs. Gilbert committed suicide by jumping out of the window of her New York apartment. The second marriage, too, ended in divorce, and in 1938 Gilbert married Polly Ann Stover, a perfume company executive.

In its Sunday feature section of June 26, 1910, *The New York Times* carried an article wherein the great monopolist Thomas Fortune Ryan named the seven young men whom he viewed as "America's future kings of finance." Among them was Otto Kahn, "not only a highly successful Wall Street man, but his very catholic tastes and varied interests have long served to bring him before the public." It must have gratified the old buccaneer when, seventeen years later, his grandson, John Barry Ryan, a reporter for *The Newark Ledger*, became engaged to Margaret Kahn. Margaret being Episcopalian and John Catholic, the marriage could not be celebrated in a church. The neutral ground chosen was the Kahns' New York residence, and on February 9, 1928, Father Duffy performed the rites.

The bride had always held a special place in Kahn's heart. "It is my deliberate conviction that you are the nicest girl in this here republic," he wrote, typically, a year after her marriage, when she and her husband were vacationing in Oheka Cottage in Palm Beach and Kahn was preparing to embark for Europe. "I should love to be with you in the pink palazzo by the southern sea but there is really no sense your being in this relentless city because during the day the evil spell of the office claims me and in the evenings and on Sundays I have several thousand accumulated things to do."

Roger Kahn never matriculated at Princeton. Jazz and aviation absorbed his energy. On February 8, 1931, at Oheka in Cold Spring Harbor, a justice of the peace married the youngest Kahn offspring, then in his twenty-third year, and a twenty-year-old musical comedy singer, Hannah Williams, a performer in a Billy Rose revue, *Sweet and Low*, who had achieved a measure of celebrity singing its most popular number, "Cheerful Little Earful" (music by Harry Warren, lyrics by Ira Gershwin and Billy Rose). An earlier marriage, when she was sixteen, had ended in an annulment. Only members of the family attended Roger's wedding, for his father, who wanted Hannah to quit *Sweet and Low*, hoped to keep it secret. But rumors of the union reached Broadway, and at length Billy Rose announced the termination of Hannah's contract. This was followed by a reluctant public disclosure from her father-in-law: "Miss Williams has retired from the stage and the young couple have left for an extended wedding trip." A divorce ensued within two years. Hannah then married the former heavyweight boxing champion Jack Dempsey. Roger married Edith May Nelson, a chorus girl from Augusta, Maine. At the Grumman Corporation he rose to the executive level and remained there until his death in 1954.

16

Adventures in Theater

"Reinhardt's greatest spectacle . . . The sensation of London . . . a marvelous living tableau . . . we are struck by Prof. Reinhardt's mastery of stage crowds, his skill in grouping colors and costumes harmoniously, his knowledge of what can be done with stage-lighting, and his instinct for effects that are grandiose and dramatic, as well as his feeling for beauty. . . ."

Thus the critics acclaimed *The Miracle*, a combination of mime, dance, and music, without spoken text, that opened at London's vast Olympia Exhibition Hall on December 23, 1911, before an enthralled audience of some 30,000. The German playwright Karl Vollmoeller contrived the scenario, Engelbert Humperdinck, the composer of *Hänsel und Gretel*, wrote the music, and the Austrian theatrical prodigy Max Reinhardt staged and directed it.

Based upon an ancient legend, *The Miracle* is the story of a young nun who, succumbing to the lures of the temporal world, forsakes her vows and flees the cathedral where she has been praying daily before a statue of the Madonna. She carries off with her the figure of the Christ Child in the Madonna's arms. The Madonna, in her compassion and understanding, descends from her niche and takes over the nun's duties during the years of her absence. When the nun returns, her spirit broken, penitent, the baby she has borne dead beside her, the Madonna resumes her place in the niche. The dead baby is transformed into the image of the Christ Child. The nun falls at the feet of the statue, as angels sing in the air above her, a sign that her sins are forgiven.

Reinhardt constructed the nave of a Gothic cathedral in Olympia Hall, which normally accommodated automobile shows and sporting events. His cast and extras numbered 2,000, and he made his immense audience part of the play. All the action took place at the center of the cathedral. There was no curtain. Instead, arrangements of lighting successively brought to view the eight different scenes.

In mid-January of 1912, Otto Kahn, having returned to London on business, attended *The Miracle*. He hurried backstage afterward, introduced himself to Reinhardt, and exclaimed: "Max Reinhardt, come over to us! I'm inviting you. Everything you need will be at your disposal. You've given Europe enough and Europe has nothing more to give you."

Incredulous, Reinhardt declined the offer. Already crowned with laurels, he saw no reason to leave Europe. The London run of *The Miracle* would earn close to $2 million, and the spectacle would captivate audiences all over the continent. He grew to regret his refusal, however, and eventually entered into negotiations with Kahn for a 1914–15 New York season. Kahn formed the American Miracle Company, in which he hoped to enlist the support of other rich men. He proposed to rent Madison Square Garden for *The Miracle*, but it was too late—war ended the project.

Kahn believed with missionary faith, and somewhat naive optimism, that the American people needed and wanted greater exposure to the arts, and that they were capable of valuing them. He had reached that conclusion while journeying back and forth across the country by railroad, sometimes for the sheer pleasure of it, sometimes, like his mentor Harriman, to inspect a network of lines to be reorganized. He found, to his dismay, an enormous cultural vacuum. "The people of all sections are keenly eager for nourishment of mind and soul," he wrote in October 1913. "But the opportunities offered to them to meet these spiritual desires are as yet far from adequate. This being the case, *faute de mieux*, they take what they can find, and not all of it is worthy. Some of the substitutes, indeed, are distinctly deleterious. . . .

"Our people have frequently demonstrated the faculty and willingness to recognize, whenever it exists, genuine merit in the artistic offerings placed before them. They are open-minded, always on the alert for improvement and possess the great advantage of having no ingrained artistic prejudices or superannuated traditions to overcome. . . .

"Unfortunately, among the people who could help most materially in the direction I have indicated [that is, the millionaires] there are still relatively few who look upon art as the strong, educational, social and moral factor which it is, who take it as seriously as it deserves to be taken as a potent agent in forming and guiding the thoughts and sentiments and conduct of the people, and a great boon to vast numbers in making their lives fuller, happier and more beautiful. . . .

"In this huge country of ours, we need not one, but a dozen theatres of the type of the Comédie Française, a dozen opera houses, permanent orchestras, etc., that shall know no consideration except to serve and steadfastly to adhere to the highest standard of artistic endeavor. We need institutions to train and guide aright the amazing quantity of all kinds of artistic talent which is latent among the people of our country, and so much of which, alas! goes to waste for lack of opportunity, inspiration and guidance."

Kahn's first venture into nonoperatic theater had occurred in 1910 when, a year after seeing Anna Pavlova and her partner Mikhail Mordkine dance at the Châtelet in Paris, he engaged them for the series of performances at the Met, then backed them in their country-wide tour. Ballet still struck most Americans as bizarre, especially in the hinterlands. Pavlova herself enjoyed enormous personal popularity, but the ballets as a whole eluded the public, and the financial returns were slender. Kahn partly subsidized both the Met appearances and the tour at a loss of many thousands of dollars.

He turned to the legitimate theater. He was indifferent to profit or loss. As an investor, he consciously avoided what promised to be Broadway hits (George Gershwin's *Lady, Be Good!* was an exception). They simply failed to interest him. What drew his support was the challenging, the innovative, the experimental. On February 19, 1915, a new theatrical group inaugurated its first season at the Bandbox Theatre, 205 East Fifty-seventh Street, with the following announcement:

"The Washington Square Players have founded an organization for those who cannot find response to their demands for quality of play and production in the usual New York playhouse. . . . There will be no restrictions to the type of play produced except that the writing must be sincere, truthful and effective. American plays will be encouraged in order that a stimulus may be given to dramatic interpretation of life about us, but no play will be accepted simply because it is American. . . .

". . . performances will be given every Friday and Saturday evening—one new production to be made each month for five months.

"The price of each ticket is fifty cents.

"The price of a subscription of ten tickets (two for each performance) is five dollars."

The Players evolved from informal discussions among young artists, playwrights, and stagecraft novices who gathered at the Washington Square Bookshop in Greenwich Village and at a nearby restaurant. Sharing a disgust with the meretriciousness of the commercial theater, they planned to specialize in one-act plays by foreign as well as native authors. Their first program included *Interiors* by the Belgian symbolist Maurice Maeterlinck. The Bandbox Theatre, with only 299 seats, proved too small for the audiences they attracted, and the following season the company moved to the larger Comedy Theatre close to Broadway. Until the war forced them to disband, they produced sixty-one one-acters and seven full-length plays. The former included Oscar Wilde's *Salome*, Chekhov's *The Bear*, and Eugene O'Neill's *In the Zone;* the latter included Chekhov's *The Seagull*, Molière's *Sganarelle*, Ibsen's *Ghosts*, and Shaw's *Mrs. Warren's Profession*. Among the performers who went on to stardom were Katharine Cornell, Walter Hampden, and Roland Young.

Kahn helped the Players from the start. During their first four seasons he gave them, outright, $12,500 in addition to a series of loans totaling several thousands more. When, after the war, they reemerged as the Theatre Guild, he proved still more generous. The Guild had set out with the ludicrously inadequate capital of $2,160. Every member of the company received the same salary—$25 a week. In desperation, the co-founder, Lawrence Langner, and the actor Rollo Peters called on Kahn at Kuhn, Loeb. He had, they knew, rented the Garrick Theatre to the prodigious French director Jacques Copeau and his Théâtre du Vieux Colombier. Now that Copeau had returned to France, would Kahn rent it to the Guild? How much could they pay, he wanted to know. "As little as possible," the two men replied in unison. "Very well," said Kahn, "when you make the rent, you will pay the rent. When you do not make it, you need not pay it!"

Kahn both backed the Guild and served as its financial adviser. When, on December 2, 1924, the cornerstone of a new Guild office building at Fifty-second Street and Broadway was laid, Kahn, relishing the publicity and the opportunity to orate, delivered the principal address:

"When I first met them [the founders], they held in their arms a frail infant. They had barely enough means to give it the most frugal sustenance for a few weeks or months. They asked for some kind of garment, however rude, to cover its nakedness and it will always be a particular satisfaction to me that I was able to meet their modest request."

The reason earlier efforts to establish such a theater had failed, he insisted, was that though financially and socially powerful, they were spiritually feeble.

The most hapless outcome of Kahn's theatrical philanthropies befell Jacques Copeau, who, under Kahn's patronage, staged at the Garrick Theatre, during the 1917–18 season, twenty-one plays from the repertory of the renowned Vieux Colombier. When the two men first met in Paris in 1913, the financier was so entranced by Copeau's brilliance and the originality of his ideas that he decided then and there that New York should have a permanent French theater. Kahn was already involved in a dozen Franco-American organizations to which he donated substantial sums. But in his Francophilia he neglected to take into account the paucity of French-speaking audiences in New York. At the January 23, 1918, matinee of Copeau's version of *Les Frères Karamazov* the box office grossed $225.50. A week later a double bill of Jules Renard's *Poil de Carotte* and Auguste Villeroy's *La Traverse* sold $223.75 worth of tickets.

Undaunted, Kahn proceeded to underwrite a second season in the conviction that it would benefit the general public. Between the two seasons he lodged the entire troupe at Cedar Court. There they pursued Copeau's rigid routine of eurhythmics, gymnasium exercises, mime, dance, improvisation, rehearsals, diction, and discussions of the week's plays.

Gaston Gallimard, the brilliant young business manager of the important *Nouvelle Revue Française* as well as director of its burgeoning book publishing arm, had accompanied the Copeau company to New York and was also a guest at Cedar Court. Amid those bucolic surroundings, Gallimard meditated on the sloth of his earlier years and, very likely under the influence of Kahn, the businessman and intellectual, realized that his firm must expand its publication of books, which thus far had remained the tail wagging the *NRF* dog, and establish itself on a sounder commercial basis. He became France's greatest publisher, whose authors included Proust, Cocteau, Camus, and Sartre.

The second Copeau season failed as dismally as the first, and Kahn abandoned the prospect of French repertory for New York.

The Washington Square Players had earlier split into two factions. George Cram ("Jig") Cook, a Greenwich Villager and one of the most vociferous Players, felt that the company concentrated too heavily on foreign dramatists. With his wife, the playwright Susan Glaspell, he broke away to seek American talent. In the summer of 1915, in the living room of a cottage at Provincetown, Massachusetts, they produced four one-act plays: *Change Your Style* by Jig Cook himself, *Suppressed* by Cook and Glaspell, *Contemporaries* by Wilbur Daniel Steele, and *Constancy* by Neith Boyce.

The Provincetowners then took over the Wharf Theatre, which remained their summer base for years to come, and during the winters they established themselves first at 139 MacDougal Street in the Village, then at 133, calling the theater the Provincetown Playhouse. By the 1916–17 season they had expanded their repertory to twelve plays, four of them by a haunted reformed drunkard named Eugene O'Neill. They were *Bound East for Cardiff*, *Before Breakfast*, *Fog*, and *The Sniper*, and the author acted in the first two. O'Neill became the most prolific of the Provincetown playwrights, turning out for them nineteen plays, including *All God's Chillun Got Wings*, *The Emperor Jones*, and *Desire under the Elms*.

Kahn was now contributing to both factions, the Washington Square Players and the Provincetown Players. His largesse to the latter began with money to open a restaurant for the company in the same building as the theater. The monthly rent was $45, which he regularly paid. Kahn's subsidies over a period of ten years totaled $63,000. Offered a directorship, he refused on the grounds that if he were to accept responsibility for the artistic direction, he would inevitably prove a disturbing element. "I have extended financial support," he wrote, "but I am taking no part in determining the management or influencing the artistic production." Indeed, he disliked *Fiesta* by Michael Gold, the Communist editor of the *New Masses* (though he liked Gold personally and was untroubled by his politics), yet he handed the Provincetowners $15,000 toward its production. It foundered amid critical scorn and public hoots. Kahn himself merely smiled and observed that he would have enjoyed writing a scathing review.

The Provincetown thrived, thanks largely to Kahn's bounty, a good many of its actors, playwrights, and directors rising to world prominence. The financier happily watched it grow into one of the most courageous, innovative, and influential companies in the annals of the American theater. "God shows what he thinks of wealth by the people on whom he bestows it," said the financier, attributing the epigram to Oscar Wilde.* Perhaps I can give the Divine Powers a slightly better opinion."

In 1920, at fifty-three, with his soldierly bearing and confident stride, his full head of silky gray hair and pointed mustachios all meticulously barbered, Kahn looked the image of glowing health, but the appearance was deceptive. As early as 1913, at a Chicago banquet, he had collapsed, presumably with a slight stroke. He suffered from high blood pressure and occasional chest pains. Seven years after the first collapse he was felled by a serious stroke. He himself ascribed it to overactivity. In a single week, as chief partner of Kuhn, Loeb, he would oversee the complex operations of that firm, while he himself specialized in the reorganization of railroads and the purchase and sale of railroad securities, guide the fortunes of the Metropolitan Opera, participate in half a dozen little-theater endeavors, help support innumerable institutions as well as talented individuals, and vigorously pursue the pleasures of first nights, golf, tennis, sailing, horseback riding, and hunting. Upon recovering from his stroke, and, heeding his doctors' advice to prolong his customary summer European jaunt, he slowed down somewhat. For example, in Scotland the gentry were appalled to see him shooting birds, not standing on his two feet like the sportsman and gentleman he was purported to be, but seated, shotgun at the ready, in the rear seat of his Rolls-Royce.

Unlike the Copeau misadventure, language proved no barrier to the success of Kahn's next dramatic importation, which he sponsored together with the brilliant, flamboyant producer Morris Gest and Gest's partner, F. Ray Comstock. The Moscow Art Theatre, founded

---

* Probably a misattribution. Leslie Frewin, the British biographer of Dorothy Parker, ascribes a similar epigram to the early-nineteenth-century cleric Sydney Smith: "If you would learn what God thinks about money, you have only to look at those to whom he has given it." Richard Steele wrote in *The Tatler*, No. 203: "It was very prettily said that we may learn the little value of fortune by the persons on whom Heaven is pleased to bestow it." And Jonathan Swift, in a letter to Miss Vanhomrigh, August 12, 1720, wrote: "If Heaven had looked upon riches to be a valuable thing, it would not have given them to such a scoundrel."

in 1897 by Constantin Stanislavsky and Vladimir Nemirovich-Danchenko, transcended language by the power of the actors' portrayals and the directors' new concepts of dramatic interpretation in Russian as well as foreign plays, in classic as well as modern. "The Moscow Players need no language," said Gest; "their silences are louder than other people's words." Wherever the company performed, it exerted an artistic influence that profoundly affected, and in some aspects altered, traditional theatrical methods and philosophies. America was no exception.

During the 1922–23 season, beginning in New York, then playing Chicago, Boston, and Philadelphia, the Moscow artists presented Tolstoy's *Tsar Fyodor*, Gorky's *The Lower Depths*, Chekhov's *The Cherry Orchard* and *The Three Sisters*. They fared so well that for the first time in his experience as a theatrical investor Kahn not only recovered his original stake, but actually realized a profit, which totaled $24,515. The Russians returned the following season with a repertory of twelve plays and bookings in eight cities, but this time they lost money—$47,772 of it Kahn's.

Part of this second-season debacle may have resulted from the campaign of vilification launched by a small organization of mindless superpatriots styling themselves the American Defense Society. They had tried to bar the Russians' entry by charging them with espionage for the Soviet government. Failing that, they continued to spread malicious rumors about the visitors, accusing them of undercover machinations. Kahn, one of many objectors, speaking as honorary chairman of the Committee of Patrons for the American Season of the Moscow Art Theatre, proclaimed:

". . . Americanism is not so frail a growth that it needs to be protected from contact with the Moscow Art Theatre.

"The visit of that organization can not, by any remote stretch of the imagination, be connected with Soviet propaganda. It is an event of distinct significance, but that significance is solely and wholly of an artistic character.

"By common consent, the Moscow Art Theatre stands supreme among organizations devoted to dramatic art. It is looked upon with something resembling reverence by leaders of the dramatic profession in all countries.

"The Moscow Art Theatre has just completed a two weeks' season in Paris. Among all the world's Governments, none has been more determined in discountenancing the Soviet Government than that of France. No people has been, and is, more opposed to Bolshevism than the French people. No authorities are more strict in controlling the admission of Russians than those in charge of the issuance of passports to France.

"Yet, the French Government not only permitted the visit of the Moscow Art Theatre to Paris, but the artists composing that troupe were treated with distinguished consideration in official quarters. The people and the press of Paris were unanimous in the manifestation of their enthusiasm anent the performances of these artists.

"Our own Government, which has permitted the visaing of the passports of the Moscow Art Theatre to this country, would certainly have refused to do so if its own investigation had not fully convinced it that there is no relationship whatsoever, open or hidden, direct or indirect, between the aims and activities of these visitors and the aims and activities of Bolshevik propaganda. . . ."

The troupe from Moscow spoke of Kahn as "the faithful Maecenas of Russian art."

In a gross misunderstanding of the capitalist Kahn's political orientation, Moissaye J. Olgin, director of *Izvestia*'s Editorial Bureau for the American Continent, wrote to him on October 16, 1924:

"The seventh anniversary of the October (Soviet) revolution is at hand. For seven years a new order has prevailed in Russia. New human relationships, new social activities, new ideas and aspirations have marked this momentous era in the history of the Russian people.

"Whatever one's attitude may be towards the best methods of solving social problems, one cannot escape the conviction that the change in Russia has exercised a deep and lasting influence over the minds of a vast number of thinking people the world over.

"At this solemn hour of the approaching seventh anniversary, public opinion in Soviet Russia is enormously eager to know the attitude of the world towards the Revolution, particularly as regards its cultural aspect. This paper is, therefore, conducting an inquiry among the creative minds of every country as to *what, in their opinion, has been the influence of the Revolution and the Soviet System on the general culture of the world.*

"We should be very grateful to you for an expression of your opinion on the above subject. The results of the inquiry will be published in a special Anniversary Literary Supplement to this paper. The most significant opinions will be cabled to Moscow immediately. . . .

"P.S. Your photograph will be appreciated. . . ."

Kahn forwent the pleasure of replying.

17

Paul Robeson

"Mr. Otto H. Kahn—[March 13, 1923]
"I am Paul L. Robeson, Rutgers 1919, Columbia Law School 1922, Negro, Phi Beta Kappa, and Walter Camp's All-American End 1918.

"I am very anxious to get before any theatrical managers and playwrights, especially those who may possibly have Negro roles: (Eugene O'Neill). Last year I played the title role in Mary Hoyt Wiborg's 'Taboo' [an unsuccessful play about voodoo practices] in New York opposite Margaret Wycherly, and in England opposite Mrs. Patrick Campbell. Both the New York and English critics were very kind in their comments on my work. Augustin Duncan, who directed the play here, Miss Wycherly and Mrs. Campbell were all enthusiastic about my acting ability and my voice.

"I know that you are a power both in theatrical and musical circles and I am hoping that you will be kind enough to use your influence in getting me a hearing. It may be that you might find an opportunity for me to sing on some of the programs of your free concerts.

"I am enclosing two clippings concerning my work since I left college. If at some time you could give me a short interview, I could perhaps explain to you better just what I hope to do. However if you wish to get some definite idea about what I can do, Augustin Duncan, Miss Margaret Wycherly, or Miss Wiborg would be glad to tell you.

"I am approaching you because I know that you are a trustee of Rutgers, and might be interested in me as a Rutgers graduate.
Gratefully yours,
Paul L. Robeson."*

* The letter was actually written in his wife, Eslanda's, hand.

Kahn's immediate response to this letter was not only to draw the gigantic young black man to the attention of the Provincetown Playhouse, but to enlist the interest of such consequential figures as Alexander Woollcott, Carl Van Vechten, Heywood Broun, and W. E. B. Du Bois. It chanced that the Provincetown had scheduled a revival of O'Neill's *The Emperor Jones*. A quarrel broke out between the author and Charles Gilpin, the black actor who had created the title role of Brutus Jones, when the latter, resenting the frequent repetition of the epithet "nigger," substituted innocuous words. O'Neill, who had seen Robeson perform at the Harlem YMCA, found him an ideal replacement for Gilpin. As the bull-roaring fugitive convict who stows away to a Caribbean island and there terrorizes the natives into acknowledging him as their emperor, Robeson electrified audiences and critics.

The opening night was May 5, 1924, and three weeks later, he starred in another of the prolific author's plays, *All God's Chillun Got Wings*. The theme was miscegenation. Jim Harris, a young black law student, marries a white girl, Ella Downey. A prey to her own mistrust and bigotry, fearful lest Jim pass his exams and thus establish his mental superiority, she goes insane. Jim, unable to concentrate on his studies, flunks. Ella, triumphant in the face of her husband's defeat and his promise to care for her, bends over his hand to kiss it.

O'Neill was inundated by letters and telegrams threatening to kill him, his wife, and his children. The district attorney of Manhattan, a Deep Southerner named Joab H. Banton, swore to destroy the playwright. The Ku Klux Klan wrote, promising hideous reprisals if the play went on. O'Neill returned the letter, scrawling across the envelope "Go Fuck Yourself." The president of the Society for the Prevention of Crime denounced *All God's Chillun* as "a damnable thing to put on the stage." William Randolph Hearst's *New York American* led the racist press. It predicted riots and reported, among other falsehoods, that two Provincetown champions, Mrs. Willard Straight, widow of the distinguished diplomat, and Otto Kahn, had withdrawn their subsidies. In reality both had increased theirs.

It was at Kahn's urging that the Provincetown introduced Robeson as a singer. His first concert, on April 19, 1925, consisting chiefly of spirituals, with his close friend, a pianist named Lawrence Brown, as an accompanist who also often sang a tenor part, roused the audience to lusty bravos. The James Pond Bureau contracted Robeson and Brown for an extensive tour. The terms included 55 percent of the box office and the freedom to accept theatrical offers for part of each season. Robeson's wife, Eslanda, who served as tour manager, wrote frequently to Kahn, sometimes to seek financial aid, sometimes to keep him abreast of the tour's progress.

"My husband, Paul Robeson," she informed him on June 21, 1925, "is at the brink of what we hope will prove to be a very remarkable career. If you could see your way clear to act as his patron and back him for two years, we would surely try to make you never regret it in any way—in fact we would earnestly try to make you feel very proud to have helped him. . . .

"What we would ask of a patron would be a straight loan of $5000 for a period of two years. The only security we can offer at present for such a loan is Mr. Robeson's future, which has crystallized to the following extent. . . ."

And she listed a contract to appear in *The Emperor Jones* in London, the Pond Bureau tour, six recordings for the Victor Talking Machine Co., and a one-third interest in a full-length statue of Robeson by Antonio Salemme.

"We want to accomplish the following things with the money—

"1. We want to send Paul Robeson's partner, Lawrence Brown, south for the time we are in London, so he can collect new songs, compose new songs and study Negro music, so we will have our material all ready when we begin our concert tour. Mr. Brown also wants to publish and copyright all the songs he has already composed and arranged. That will take about $1500.

"2. We want to clear up our own debts, so that we will be free to leave for London and fill our contract there. These debts total . . . about $1500.

". . . Paul Robeson wants to be able to study voice all he can. This will take about $500. . . .

"I am sure if you could hear Paul Robeson sing *with Lawrence Brown*, you would realize what enormous possibilities there are in their work, which will be exclusively Negro Music, and further, if you could talk with both of these boys about their plans and their hopes, I am sure you would feel convinced that they are fine honest earnest ambitious young artists, fully deserving of any help you might give them.

"This could be arranged for you (hearing them sing and talking with them) any time that would be convenient to you, at the home of our mutual friend Carl Van Vechten, or at any place you might designate. . . ."

Four days later Kahn dispatched through Van Vechten one of his typical invitations: "Just a line to confirm that my boat, the 'Oheka,' will be waiting for you at the foot of East 23rd Street at two o'clock on Sunday next to take you and your guest and Mr. and Mrs. Paul Robeson . . . to our place at Cold Spring Harbor. . . ."

Evidently Kahn admired Robeson the man as highly as he did Robeson the singer and actor, for on June 29 he loaned him $2,500 without interest (though he accepted Robeson's $5,000 life insurance policy and his Pond contract as security), and agreed to advance another $2,500, if needed.

"It all happened so quickly," Eslanda wrote to him on July 1, "that we are all stunned by our good fortune. . . .

"Paul and I appreciated very much the opportunity of meeting you and Mrs. Kahn at your home, and we are very glad to know that Paul's singing gave you so much pleasure.

"Paul wants me to say that he will be glad to sing for you or for Mrs. Kahn at any time you wish him to do so—without charge. We feel that this would be an opportunity to express in some small way our gratitude for your interest and generosity."

On July 28, in a letter requesting the promised additional $2,500, she wrote: ". . . Paul and I have been very happy these last few weeks, secure in the knowledge that we are at last on a firm financial footing—thanks to your kindness and generosity. . . .

"Paul and I fully appreciate how kind you have been, and hope from time to time beginning in the very near future we will be able to send you very satisfactory artistic and financial reports. . . ."

August 19, aboard the R.M.S. *Berengeria*, bound for England: "This is our second day out, the sea is calm, and Paul and I feel splendidly. We are in our chairs on deck. Paul is deep in his script of 'Emperor Jones' . . . ."

September 17, London: "I have just mailed you a set of clippings from the London newspapers describing the opening of the 'Emperor Jones.' Paul gave the finest performance I have ever seen him give at the premiere and at the final curtain was forced to take 12 bows and finally make a speech. The audience stood up and cheered and shouted. You can imagine how happy we were. The house was packed with a paid audience. I mean people who bought seats—with the exception of critics. . . ."

November 17, on vacation at the Welcome Hotel in Villefranche-sur-Mer: ". . . We spent an afternoon at the home of Matisse, the great painter, and his daughter was in tears over Paul's singing, tho she scarcely knows a word of English. We had tea with Mary Garden yesterday, and she too adored his voice. . . ."

18

The Miracle

In the early twenties Kahn reanimated a cherished prewar hope: he would at last bring *The Miracle* to America. Max Reinhardt, with whom he resumed negotiations in the former's Salzburg castle, came to New York in 1922, as eager as Kahn to revive the colossus. They chose the Century Theatre as the only house big enough to accommodate the spectacle. They turned to Morris Gest to produce it and to the scenic designer Norman Bel Geddes to create the interior of a Gothic cathedral.

Gest was a master publicist, and he fed the press a dazzling plethora of facts and figures about the magnitude of the cast, the Niagaras of paint and forests of materials consumed for the scenery, the fortune spent on costumes, the research into Catholic religion and Gothic architecture. The leading ladies, however, scarcely required hyperbole so far as their persons were concerned. Lady Diana Duff Cooper, daughter of the Duke of Rutland and adoring wife of the Conservative Parliamentarian Alfred Duff Cooper, was among the most ravishing women in England. She was also witty, warmhearted, and endearingly eccentric. Though no professional actress, barring appearances in two obscure movies, she struck Reinhardt, with her looks and youth, as the perfect Madonna. The original Madonna was Maria Carmi, the exquisite wife of *The Miracle*'s author, Karl Vollmoeller. Divorced, then married to Prince Matchiabelli, she had contracted to resume the role. A compromise was reached. The two beauties would alternate as the Madonna and the Nun. But the princess shortly withdrew, and for the Nun, Reinhardt chose a teenage American girl he happened to notice on an ocean liner. Rosamund Pinchot, the niece of Pennsylvania's governor Amos Pinchot, had no theatrical experience whatever, but Reinhardt exclaimed: "There's my nun!"

One imagines the pleasure that Kahn, a connoisseur of female pulchritude, took in the proximity of such goddesses. He grew especially fond of Lady Diana, though her devotion to her husband precluded romance with Kahn or any other man. They became fast friends, however. He acted as her financial adviser, and when she had $5,000 to invest, advised her to buy Florida real estate. Within a few weeks he had increased the capital fivefold. He proposed to back any production she might care to appear in on the London stage. He notified his secretary, James Dartt, that he wished to protect Lady Diana Cooper if any of the investments he made for her failed to pay interest or passed dividends, and Diana, in her autobiography, recalled: "Clever and godfatherly [for he was the godfather of her firstborn] Otto Kahn was coping with my savings to some jingling tune. 'The boss made you a thousand dollars, seemed to be often told me—an unwearying repetition." He became "a man I was attached to and trusted completely."

Another member of *The Miracle* company became one of Kahn's few intimate male friends. This was Reinhardt's chief deputy, Rudolf Kommer, whom Lady Diana described as "the funniest, the most fantastical, spherical figure in Lederhosen and sky-blue, silver-buttoned jacket, shirt open on a fat child's neck, round nose, round dark velvet eyes, thick semi-circular eyebrows and ruthlessly shaved round head." To Reinhardt's son Gottfried, Kommer was a "Bukovinian world citizen [having originated in Czernowitz, the chief city of the Romanian region of Bukovina] . . .ex-littérateur, suspected spy, half man, half coffeehouse, serving the restless, bored and lonely of high and cafe society."

Kahn first met Kommer when Reinhardt sent the Bukovinian ahead to New York to prepare the ground for *The Miracle*, and he took him virtually on sight. Kahn detested bores and fools, and at the approach of either was known to shed his normally gentle manner and cry out: "Don't talk to me!" Kommer he found supremely entertaining. He became Kahn's bridge partner and backgammon opponent, called him "dear boss," introduced him to delectable ladies . . .

The Miracle opened amid tumultuous excitement on January 16, 1924. At every performance thereafter it filled the Century Theatre. Kahn recovered his $300,000 within the first three months, then began to realize substantial profits, a novel and exhilarating experience for him. Will A. Page, in his memoirs of a career as press representative to

Broadway's leading producers of big musical revues, hailed *The Miracle* (which he never represented) as "the most gorgeous, imposing and stupendous offering ever shown on the American stage, or any other stage in the world."

On December 1 the company embarked on a tour that lasted five years. From Cincinnati Lady Diana wrote to Kahn the following October:

"A 1000 thanks for your delightful letter of last week. I apologise for answering so late but life in Tchintchinati [sic] is not the calm & dignified routing it is in New York— No, its [sic] a wild rush from Barbecues to Cafeterias, from the 'Club of the Stage and Screen Scribes' . . . to the Soda Fountain—from 'Residential Mansions' on the heights, to the nether regions of Music Hall. And I hardly know how to thank you for your overwhelming kindness. I once asked Kätchen Kommer* to tell me what I had accomplished to deserve so much attention—& he sang 'There came 3 kings from the East. King Otto, King Max and King Morris'—I do not recognise the kingliness of the last two, (much as I admire them) because to Max Reinhardt I was an instrument of his art, & to Morris Gest just an object of his salesmanship. But to you I am nothing—from an utilitarian point of view; your kindness towards me is l'art pour l'art—It is kindness for the sake of kindness. It is kingly. Hail King Otto! The inhabitants of this 'gate to the south' seem to be most enthusiastic about The Miracle—(which they also owe to you) & yet, somehow I shall be most happy to see New York again, my friends, & you. . . ."

The Madonna and the Maecenas corresponded through the years. On November 5, 1929, three weeks after giving birth to a son, John Julius Cooper (later Viscount Norwich), she wrote in a letter she headed with the famous old jingle about the Gunpowder Plot to blow up the English Parliament in 1605:

> Please to remember
> The 5th of November
> Gunpowder, treason and plot . . .

"Dearest Boss. It was wonderful of you to agree to become my baby's godfather [upon learning of her pregnancy, Kahn had told Kommer he intended to be the godfather]—especially as it is against your principals [sic] to exercise so middle aged a function, also because

---

*A nickname Diana, who loved the odd little man, bestowed on him, having derived it from a Viennese cafe owner who constantly told his cat: "Ah, Kätchen, Kätchen, it is useless for you to park und crowl."

you could hardly tell at the time what my poor brat would look like. It might for all you know have resembled a monkey—But thank God this baby's beauty is as exceptional as your consent. (Let me beware of boring you with the age-old extasies [sic] of new—not young—mothers.) Yet with the fine intention to be judicial, to avoid with iron determination what my darling germans call 'affenmutterism' [doting motherism], I feel it would be equally silly to blink at *facts*, ignore the virtues of your godchild-paragon. With a heart brimming full of charity and desire I now study his contemporaries—with what result! 'Lousy!'—behavior, looks. 'Lousy!' *'Moderate'* I have said to myself a 1000 times but before the shaddowy [sic] smile of yr godchild my resolutions melt as snow in spring, my heart beats in tempo delirico—if there is such a term. For familly [sic] & illiteration [sic] reasons (Cesarian also) he is to be called John Julius—His points are 1 Remarkable strength—2 self possession 3 wide apart thoughtful blue eyes, 4 fair hair 5 9 lbs of weight, 6 a desire to please 7 pancake ears—His fault—only human—is insatiable appetite—and unfair critisism [sic] since I alone suffer from this intemperance. Standing between you two—an interpreter, as it were,—I extend to you his first greeting, & also a message about all he expects from you. 'Vater werden ist nicht schwer—Vater sein dagegen sehr' [To become a father is not hard—To be a father, on the other hand, is very hard]. He doesn't know the author but he feels it applies to godfathers—If John Julius is at present proud of having O.H.K. as a godfather, we are trusting the day will come when O.H.K. will be proud having J.J. as a godson. To bring this desireable [sic] reversal of attitudes about it is essential to plan earnestly the life-scheme of this darling 'citoyen du monde' and that is where you come in. Whilst my poor baby was making, his father lost his seat, & joined the long queue of unemployed statesmen. Of course then John Julius' eyes are prejudiced against politics. In days to come he will meet, or rather Lady Colebox [i.e., Coalbox, Diana's nickname for the London hostess Sibyl, Lady Colefax] will bring to his nursery, poets, painters, musicians, actors, doctors, lawyers. He will tolerate them, for his heart is kind—but as I read him he will not aspire to become one of them. If there is anything in pre-natal influence or in up-bringing, if there is any harmony between his hopes & my wishes, if your godfathership is the good omen I take it to be—then J.J. will strive to become a man in the city, a man in Wall St. John Julius Cooper—financeer [sic]!

"This tedious scrawl is therefore written to inform you that my Hope is to be christened on *Nov. 23rd* in the chapel of Belvoir, in water from Jacob's Well poured from a Benvenuto Cellini ewer & that Diana & J.J.C. are expecting you to have a job ready for the latter with the good old firm of Kuhn Loeb & Co. & that he will report at 52 William St. on his 18th birthday (15th Sept. 1947).

"Whatever you may think of your profession or of my son's aptitude for it, I as the prophetess mother, see him as a partner in Kuhn Loeb & Co. May God will that this comes to pass, that he may protect you both.

"All loving gratitude & a welcoming, if still slightly timid grin from your (most) junior partner.

Yrs as ever
affectionately,
Diana."

Kahn replied on the twenty-third: "My most dear Diana, don't tell Kommer of that appellation, because if you did he would probably fly into a paroxysm of jealous rage. Still the 'most dear' is strictly in accordance with the facts, even though I have never before been vocal about them, in contrast to the blatant exhibitionism of Kommer, but have wrapped myself into the mantle of Ritter Toggeburg (see your anthology of German poetry). In the spirit of said Ritter I hereby declare you a paragon and masterwork of creation. If there is any flaw in you, diligent search over many years has failed to disclose it. And those assertions I stand ready to maintain and defend in mortal combat against anyone daring to question them.

"This outbreak and disclosure on the part of one who has kept silence all these years, is the reaction to your delightful letter of November 5th. When Kommer mentioned to me last summer that you meant me to be godfather to your first-born who had not then emerged from the mysterious recesses of the infinite, I confess that I did not take his announcement quite seriously, because I was not conscious of any action on my part which warranted my being singled out for that conspicuous mark of friendship and confidence. Now that, in your letter, I have proof that you meant it and mean it let me say how genuinely I appreciate your thought of me and how proudly and gladly I accepted the charge of being godfather to your son.

"May he grow up to be a joy and a blessing to you and your husband always. If there is anything in eugenics, he ought to set every female heart aflutter, as he grows to young man's estate, and he ought to aid K.L. & Co. to heights undreamed of hitherto.

"Will you please transmit to John Julius the enclosed check, which I have made out to your order (inasmuch as I do not feel sure that, notwithstanding his brilliancy, he has mastered as yet the art of writing), and explain to him that, if he will invest it at 5% and will give instructions that the coupons, as they come due, are likewise to be invested at 5%, he will have, when he reaches 21 years, a nest egg of £2821. at his disposal (provided he does not have to pay any income tax in the meantime). If he should prefer to have me attend to the investing, I am, of course, at his disposal, in which case I leave it to him to return the check.

"In this connection, you may be interested to learn that neither you nor I have been busted by the recent debacle in the New York Stock Market. Your funds, having been invested in non-speculative securities, did not participate in the dizzy rise of the defunct boom, but neither did they come down to earth with a sickening thud. I did take a very modest flyer or two on your behalf, when the picking seemed good during the recent wreckage. The total result is that your account is today worth slightly more than it was at the end of last year.

"With all my love to you and John Julius, and my kindest remembrances to his father, who, I feel sure, will very soon rejoin the conservative phalanx at Westminster and resume his course towards the heights of political leadership. . . ."

19

Of Parties, Premieres, and Grand Tours

He was everywhere, a small, soft-spoken, compact figure, tirelessly on the move by Rolls-Royce, private railroad car, yacht, or ocean liner. The humorist Franklin P. Adams, a charter member of the fabled Algonquin Hotel Round Table of wags and wits, to which Kahn was occasionally invited, penned this couplet in his *New York Herald Tribune* column:

> The sun it never shone upon
> A busier man than Otto Kahn.

He nevertheless found time to read whatever he felt was worth reading, but so as not to offend people who sent him tedious books they had written, he devised a soothing little deception. In his letter of acknowledgment, he would quote a line or two from the last chapter, thus deluding the proud author into believing that Kahn had read the entire book.

At his Kuhn, Loeb command desk, beneath the portrait of Edward Harriman, he played the big game of railroad reorganization or, as eyebrows rose among his partners, strove to placate some irate prima donna.

Kuhn, Loeb and the presidency of the Metropolitan Opera together absorbed only part of Kahn's intellectual life. Another sizable part was devoted to speechmaking before official groups in the United States and Europe. The scope of his topics varied extensively: art, music, economics, banking, foreign affairs, to designate a few. In his lightly

Germanic accent, lecturing on "The Value of Art to the People," he quoted Walter Pater, one of his guiding spirits: "We have an interval and then our place knows us no more. . . . Our one chance lies in getting as many pulsations as possible." Fascinated by the relatively new art of the cinema, having financed and reorganized several film companies, including Paramount, of which he was a member of the board of directors, he told another gathering, sincerely, if naively: "Mix a degree of idealism, even of romanticism, with your practical considerations. . . . Don't underestimate your public. . . . Don't get into a rut. Vary your formula. Strike out along new paths. . . . Wastefulness is a mortal economic sin and moreover, a standing invitation to competitive attack. . . ." In Paris, at the American Club, he vigorously opposed the United States joining the League of Nations.

During the twenties he served as spokesman or officeholder in about 170 different projects, dealing with federal legislation, agriculture, railroads, industry, labor, capital, taxes (with no war to be fought, he recommended reducing them). His appointments, often a score or more a day, sometimes kept him at work (or play) long after the last curtain had fallen on Broadway. One wonders whether his hyperactivity may not have contributed to his bouts of illness. Max Schuster, a journalist before he founded a publishing firm with Richard Simon, wrote: "When an honorary committee is about to be launched, the members do two things. First they make Otto Kahn chairman. Then they decide what they are organizing for." In 1921 Kahn became a director and the vice president of the Philharmonic-Symphony Society (now the New York Philharmonic), devoting himself to its affairs, artistic as well as financial.

A self-appointed envoy, he journeyed abroad continually, combining economic missions with recreational pleasures, and was feted by leading statesmen of the countries he visited. He played a crucial role in arranging American loans for the reconstruction of war-torn countries. In Italy, during a press conference, he warned that the prevailing measures against inflation were inadequate. In France he propounded a plan to fund her $4.2 billion debt to the United States.

Toward the end of 1922 the octogenarian former premier of France Georges Clemenceau, who had undertaken a goodwill tour of the United States in hopes of revivifying her fading interest in European affairs, lunched with the Kahns at Cold Spring Harbor. As he boarded the S.S. *Paris* for the voyage home, he received a telegram from his host:

PEACE HATH VICTORIES NO LESS RENOWNED THAN WAR. IN MAKING THE SPLENDID EFFORT AND UNDERGOING THE FATIGUES AND RISKS OF YOUR JOURNEY TO AND THROUGH AMERICA YOU HAVE CONDUCTED A BRILLIANT CAMPAIGN WHICH WILL NOT FAIL TO BEAR FRUIT AND HAVE ONCE MORE DEMONSTRATED THOSE GREAT QUALITIES AND THAT STOUT HEART AND THAT ARDENT PATRIOTISM WHICH DID SO MUCH TO ACHIEVE VICTORY IN THE fiELD MAY YOU HAVE A SAFE JOURNEY AND A PLEASANT HOMECOMING AND MAY THE KIND FATE WHICH HAS KEPT YOU YOUNG AT EIGHTY [actually, eighty-one] CONTINUE FOR MANY YEARS TO PRESERVE YOUR HEALTH YOUTH AND VIGOR PLEASE ACCEPT THE EXPRESSION OF MY PROFOUND AND ADMIRING SYMPATHY AND OF MY MOST CORDIAL AND SINCERE GOOD WISHES.

Clemenceau replied the following day at sea: I CAN BUT THANK YOU AND EXPRESS ALL MY GRATITUDE FOR ALL YOU HAVE DONE TOWARD THE GREAT WORK OF INTERNATIONAL PEACE AS IS THE EVERLASTING WISH OF FRANCE AS WELL AS OF AMERICA I KNEW YOU HAD DONE YOUR BEST FOR THE CAUSE ALLOW ME TO CONGRATULATE YOU IN ADVANCE FOR ALL THAT YOU WILL CONTINUE TO DO.

Kahn's favorite diversions were elaborate, costly, and far-ranging, and were usually linked to some international banking enterprise. In early March 1925, for example, he organized a tour of Morocco, the object of which, along with the fun, was to discover such concessions in the French colony as would be acceptable to American investors. To accompany him as guests he invited Georges Bénard, head of Paris's Banque Bénard, who had already entered into negotiations for a loan to be floated by Kuhn, Loeb; Percy Peixotto, president of the American Club in Paris, who agreed to act as courier; Comte Marc de Beaumont, president of the Cercle Inter-Allié; and Jo Davidson, the black-bearded American sculptor who the year before had modeled a bust of Kahn.* Following Kahn's instructions, they gathered in Marseille and sailed thence to Casablanca. The great Maréchal Louis Hubert Gonsalve Lyautey, the Lawrence of Morocco, received Kahn and Davidson at his residence in Rabat, where Davidson persuaded Lyautey to sit for a bust. From Rabat, Kahn led his companions to Fez, then to Marrakech, all the while gathering data about the colony's railroads, its shipping, its industries.

---

* Now in the National Portrait Gallery, Washington, D.C., a gift from Kahn's daughter Margaret.

In the rough. (Courtesy of Mrs. John Barry Ryan)

🙵 Homes Sweet Homes 🙵

Cedar Court in Morristown, New Jersey. (Courtesy of Robert King)

Oheka in Cold Spring Harbor, Long Island. (Castle Ventures Limited)

1100 Fifth Avenue, New York City. (Convent of the Sacred Heart)

Oheka II in Palm Beach, Florida. (Courtesy of Robert King)

"Il Ottokan" and his favorite singer, Caruso. (Courtesy of Mrs. John Barry Ryan)

Paul Robeson as Othello. (Courtesy of Paul Robeson, Jr.)

Lady Diana Cooper in The Miracle. (Cecil Beaton photograph, courtesy of Sotheby's, London)

Jo Davidson sculpts Kahn in Paris, 1924, while Rudolf Kommer looks on. (Courtesy of Mrs. John Barry Ryan)

*Otto Kahn's great and good friends:
Maria Jeritza as Tosca . . .*

. . . and Grace Moore as Manon.
(Metropolitan Opera Archives)

NOTED FINANCIER BECOMES EXCITED AS YANK DOUGHBOYS WALLOP GERMANS AT ST. MIHIEL; GRABS MARY ASTOR'S HAND

WEDNESDAY, OCTOBER 20, 1926.

"Are movie battles exciting? They must be, for at the height of the St. Mihiel engagement, fought Tuesday at Camp Stanley for the picture 'Wings,' the photographer found Otto H. Kahn, noted financier and art patron, holding the hand of Mary Astor, screen star, as they watched the action. Miss Astor played a part in 'The Rough Riders,' and is now on her way back to Hollywood. Kahn is touring the Southwest with a party of financiers and writers." (San Antonio Express-News)

Kahn on Fifth Avenue with Fritz, a gift from Maria Jeritza. (Courtesy of Mrs. John Barry Ryan)

Otto Kahn as caricatured for Vanity Fair *in October 1933 by Covarrubias.* (Courtesy of Vanity Fair, copyright 1933; copyright © renewed 1961 by Condé Nast Publications, Inc.)

The Kahns at home at 1100 Fifth Avenue in 1932. Addie stands beneath Rembrandt's Portrait of a Young Student; *Joos van Cleve's* St. John on Patmos *is on display in the corner of the room.* (Erich Salomon, Bildarchiv Preussischer Kulturbesitz)

"My memory of our stay in Morocco is like the echo of an Arabian Nights entertainment," Davidson wrote in his autobiography. "We were invited to a banquet at Marrakech by [El Hadj Thami] El Glaoui [the feudal pasha of Marrakech and Caid of the Berber tribes known as the Glaoua]."

They passed through wrought-iron gates into a flower garden of arresting beauty. The remote sounds of music and the voices of unseen women charmed their ears. El Glaoui, a commanding figure in his snow-white djellaba, welcomed them at the portals of a vast reception hall and escorted them into a dining hall richly carpeted and lined with deep cushions on which the guests reclined. "Our host did not join us in the feast," Davidson recalled, "but moved among us, urging us to partake. We watched our Arab friends removing dainty morsels with their fingers. . . . The feast was endless, and dish followed dish. . . . I have never attended such a sumptuous meal anywhere in the world!"

Kahn wanted to prolong the expedition with a train trip through Spain, but Davidson preferred to return to his wife, Yvonne, in Paris. His host, however, irresistibly insisted he stay with the group, especially as the Comte de Beaumont had left it and Davidson was needed to make a fourth at bridge. Kahn, though no crack player himself, undertook to coach the sculptor. He must not forget, he warned, to lead "from strength into weakness." The first session proceeded smoothly enough until Davidson, who could not take the game seriously, committed a grievous blunder. Kahn angrily flung down his cards. "Hold it, boss," said Davidson. "I'm afraid I will have to do your bust all over again." Why? Kahn demanded to know. Because, Davidson explained, "here is an expression I have not seen before, and I must put it in."

Shortly after Kahn got back to Paris, on May 8, the French colonial minister, André Hesse, presided at a dinner given in his honor at which those interested might hear his views on Morocco. Among his listeners were several cabinet members and many senators, deputies, and bankers.

Kahn's next hegira began on September 1, 1926, at New York's Grand Central Station. Ten guests, three valets, two black chefs, and a courier from the Raymond & Whitcomb travel agency filled three railroad cars, the "Yosemite Park" and the "Washington" along with a third car for the domestic staff and the baggage, coupled to a

Toronto-bound Canadian Railway train, the first leg of a transcontinental jaunt that would last two months and cover 11,708 miles. The serious part of Kahn's purpose was to deliver as a lecture his essay "Art and America" in various cities along the way. The guests included the magazine publisher Condé Nast and his *Vanity Fair* editor Frank Crowninshield; Rear Admiral Ernest August Taylor, retired, who had commanded the cruiser *Renown* when it carried the Prince of Wales on his round-the-world "friendship tour" in 1920; Arthur Loasby, president of the Equitable Trust Company; David Gray, a playwright (and later U.S. ambassador to Ireland); Leonard Cushing, a scion of New York millionaires; Lieutenant Colonel Norman Thwaites, a much-decorated British veteran; and Kahn's secretary, James Dartt, and Dartt's wife of two months, Helen, to whom Kahn had assigned a compartment for their honeymoon.

On the first night Kahn, gorgeously attired in monogrammed silk lounging pajamas, of which his English valet, Cooper, had packed several colorful variants, knocked at the Dartts' door. Did Helen require a sleeping pill? At the age of twenty-two, having led a sheltered girlhood on an Ohio farm, she had never imagined the need for a sedative, and she shyly declined. A perceptive woman, however, she realized that what Kahn really wanted was her admiration for his elegant apparel. Kahn loved clothes. Every morning Cooper would lay out half a dozen ensembles for him to choose from.

In Toronto, on September 2, the directors of the annual Canadian National Exhibition applauded the art lecture. Next day, switching to another line, the voyagers went on to Detroit, then to Chicago. Altogether, they rode thirteen different lines through fifteen states. When not due to sleep in their compartments, they were booked by the Raymond & Whitcomb man into the city's finest hotel. One quality they shared, the Dartts excepted, was skill at contract bridge, which they played continually at five cents a point.

Glacier National Park, Montana, September 12: A band of Indians bestowed on Kahn the name Chief of Many Horses (probably signifying wealth) and staged a ceremonial circle dance, arms linked, which courtesy obliged Kahn to join.

Los Angeles, the Beverly Hills Hotel, September 30: Kahn was entertaining a starlet in his suite when he inadvertently spilled a cocktail over her gown. Panicky lest somebody intrude while the starlet withdrew to the bathroom, slipped out of her gown, and tried to wash out the stain, he summoned Dartt to act as both lookout and chaperone.

San Marino, California, October 6: The railroad magnate Henry Edwards Huntington personally conducted the sightseers through his fabulous collection of rare books, paintings, and sculpture, which, after his death the following year, would be opened to the public as the Henry E. Huntington Library and Art Gallery. The English members of the party felt that Gainsborough's far-famed *Blue Boy* had been overcleaned.

San Antonio, Texas, October 19: Paramount's William Wellman was shooting a reenactment of the battle of St. Mihiel for the film *Wings* (which, in 1927, would be the first film to win an Academy Award for Best Picture). "Yosemite Park" and "Washington" carried their passengers into the desert to Camp Stanley to watch the action. Kahn found himself in a director's chair beside Mary Astor, who, having finished *The Rough Riders*, was en route back to Hollywood. Kahn happily held her hand.

Fort Worth, Texas, October 24: In that eighth year of prohibition, Amon G. Carter, the exuberant publisher of the *Fort Worth Star-Telegram*, had a mammoth tent pitched on his estate for a party in honor of the travelers. The bootleg beverages of choice were called "Kuhn, Loeb cocktails," and the tent shook with shouts of "Amen, Amon." Each reveler received a five-gallon hat and a hollow cane to secrete the forbidden liquid.

The junket ended in New York on October 29.

"Mr. Kahn was a strange and essentially pathetic mixture of arrogance, pseudo-sophistication and insecurity, childishly anxious to make a good impression," so Helen Dartt recalled. "The whole expedition, the special train, his speech, his distinguished guests, as well as his pajamas, were all a reassurance for his ego, still seeking admiration and acceptance, unsatisfied by financial success."

Of all Kahn's pleasure-cum-business peregrinations, the most extensive occurred in the spring of 1927. He chartered for one month the Duke of Westminster's yacht, the *Flying Cloud*, at a cost of £1,000, then equivalent to about $19,400. A four-masted twin-screw auxiliary schooner, 177 feet long and 38 feet 4 inches wide, with luxuriously appointed staterooms, a dining salon, and two card rooms, she was a floating palace.

The guests were to rendezvous in the Sicilian coastal city of Siracusa. Their qualifications, as always for a Kahn tour, included the capacity to entertain and, ideally, to play decent bridge. They numbered six: David Gray and Frank Crowninshield again; Rudolf

Kommer (with Kahn, this ensured at least one bridge table); Paul Dougherty, painter and brother of Walter Hampden (Dougherty); Jo Davidson, reputed to be, despite Kahn's lessons, the world's worst bridge player; and the novelist Arnold Bennett, who played no bridge at all. The absence of women aboard was customary. Helen Dartt had been a rare exception. Not even Addie Kahn went along; her tastes and temperament were, in the main, too dissimilar from her husband's. Kahn told Bennett, "When women are about, men are always stupid," as Bennett reported in a letter to his friend, the pianist Harriet Cohen.

Bennett described the excursion in his journal, in letters, and in a little book, *Mediterranean Scenes: Rome-Greece-Constantinople.** His estimation of Kahn was considerably less harsh than Mrs. Dartt's. In an affectionately tongue-in-cheek vein, he wrote: "Otto, the host, comparatively a pauper, but the most thoughtfully dressed young man on two continents. . . . Cooper had to organize two thousand pairs of Otto's trousers, a hundred and fifty pairs of boots and shoes, forty dressing gowns, six thousand shirts, and neckties countless as the stars or as the moods of Rudolf and Paul. . . ."

Bennett was bemused by Kahn's passion for bridge, which Kahn sometimes played all day and far into the night before adjourning to the dining salon for a champagne supper. One night, as the *Flying Cloud* sailed along the coast of Ithaca, the beauty of the moonlit seascape moved Bennett. He burst into the card room, exclaiming: "We're passing Ithaca! Ithaca! The island of Ulysses!"

Nobody looked up. The only words Bennett heard were "Three spades . . ."

But what impressed him most about Kahn was his energy and punctuality. He had told his guests he would meet them in Siracusa at 6:30 P.M. He appeared on the dot of 6:30 P.M. Before boarding the yacht, "we swept through many thoroughfares into the Greek theatre and enjoyed exactly one hundred minutes of Aristophanes. Thence swiftly to the quarry called 'Paradise.' Thence swiftly to the other neighbouring sites. Thence to the Duomo-Temple-Mosque. Thence swiftly to shops. Thence swiftly to the hotel, where we swiftly ate. (How Otto, grandmaster of the Metropolitan opera [*sic*], had contrived in the intervals between these activities to interview *prime donne*, I

---

* A bibliographic curiosity. The edition consisted of one thousand numbered copies handsomely illustrated with engravings. Only the first twenty-five, however, had a preface that recounted the voyage. The author sent the first copy to Kahn as a kind of bread-and-butter token.

cannot say; but he had.) Thence swiftly to the Siracuse [sic] Opera, for a performance of *La Tosca*. At something like midnight we all left Otto still indefatigably savouring Puccini and the voices of the American stars. . . . I fell dead into bed. . . .

"The brief but pregnant jottings in my Journal comprise many such entries as: 'Bridge at 10 p.m. Otto proceeded with his mail'; 'Nobody went ashore except Otto'; 'Went to bed exhausted; Otto was still working.'"

Kahn once told Bennett, with some exaggeration, considering his occasional illnesses: "I have never in all my life felt the sensation of being tired."

In a letter from Constantinople to his nephew Richard Bennett, written on May 5, the novelist noted: "The governments of all the countries we visit apparently have hopes of a big American loan from Kahn. He does nothing to kill this illusion, so we are vastly well treated."

Kahn's appearance in Constantinople created a riot among the tourist guides, who fought for the prestige and profit of serving him. Rumors of his approach to any city tended to set the financial sector aflame. The mighty American banker was about to bring off another coup!

Kahn's involvement with theatrical, literary, and artistic enterprises brought him a kind of satisfaction he had experienced in no other milieu. His association with his Kuhn, Loeb partners was largely confined to the office. He shared neither their religious upbringing nor their social status, and indeed, fell under the suspicion of being an anti-Semitic Jew. Unfairly. He did not scorn Judaism, he simply did not subscribe to it. Catholicism captivated him, and he was several times on the verge of conversion. Though the Social Register listed the Kahns, and he belonged to the exclusive Piping Rock Club, the summit of New York society—where the Astors, the Vanderbilts, and the Morgans reigned—was not accessible to him. But among theater people, among writers and artists, he found a comfortable position where questions of social levels or ethnic origins did not weigh. Here he encountered gratitude for his selfless philanthropies and investments from which he seldom expected and hardly ever received any returns, respect for his intellect, and genuine fondness.

His ubiquity, together with his love of publicity, made him a national character, his public utterances and journeyings newsworthy, his personality and appearance the subject of caricaturists, comedians, and jokesmiths. During the single year of 1926, *The New York Times* carried forty-six stories about him.

In her first talkie, United Artists' *Be Yourself!* (1930), Fanny Brice warbled a ditty, lyrics by Billy Rose and Ballard Macdonald, entitled "Is Something the Matter with Otto Kahn or Is Something the Matter with Me?" wherein she portrayed a would-be prima donna rejected by the master of the Met.*

A story that Wall Streeters gleefully circulated concerned a tailor who hung a sign in his window: MAX KAHN, COUSIN OF OTTO KAHN. Incensed when he passed the shop in his Rolls, Kahn commanded his chauffeur to halt the car, burst into the shop, and forbade his nonkinsman ever again to take the name of Otto Kahn in vain. Meekly the tailor removed the offending sign. The next time the financier passed the shop he beheld a new sign: MAX KAHN, FORMERLY A COUSIN OF OTTO KAHN.

The caricaturist Ralph Barton drew for *Vanity Fair* (April 1922) "a typical first-night audience in New York." He placed Kahn in the third row between the dancer Irene Castle and the playwright Zoë Akins. For the same periodical's "Private Lives of the Great" series (October 1933 issue), another caricaturist, Miguel Covarrubias, showed Kahn in his bathtub singing "You're an Old Smoothie" as he scrubbed his back and a tiny mermaid, perched on his knee, strummed a banjo. The November 2, 1925, issue of *Time* magazine pictured him on its cover. *The New Yorker* for February 20, 1926, carried a "Profile" of Kahn by Waldo Frank under the nom de plume of "Search-Light," a sensitive, perceptive eulogy that reflected the affection in which the knights and ladies of the Algonquin Round Table held the subject:

"The key to the man is a virtuosic grace," Frank wrote. "Grace of harmony and of *at-homeness*. Through the Wall Street canyon, Kahn blows like a zephyr. Under the looming granite walls, he walks with round cheeks. Our world is a delirium of electric blares: Kahn's eyes twinkle. Our world is a holocaust of dying civilizations, dead millions. Kahn knows not of death, he is a happy lover, lyrical and unattached. . . .

"Most men who achieve power do so by laborious study of the world they aim to conquer, and by ruthless excision of those traits in themselves which do not chime with their world. Not Kahn. He had at the outset qualities, the vices to make him what he is. That is why his face reveals no struggle. That is why he can say sincerely: 'I feel as

---

* Movie audiences never heard the parody for it wound up on the cutting-room floor.

young as when I was twenty-five: I hope I am not much wiser.' He is not much wiser. He ignores the wisdom which he does not need. That is why he is seldom nervous, usually happy. He is at no odds with himself. He is this dapper, personable gentleman—so full of individual judgments and tastes and traits; and ways of talking and ways of enjoying life. And yet, deeply, he is no individual at all: he is a swift and lyric symbol of the world he thinks he has conquered. He is an element of modern life. He is fate for once smiling and having a whale of a time. . . .

"A subtle, dynamic nostalgia moves Kahn into those realms from which his technical mind would seem to bar him. It is not true that Kahn can give mere cash to artists. He has a restless conscience. He is pitifully moved by spiritual effort in these realms beyond him. He gives to artists, both good and bad, because he gives to the impulse of the artist."

Kahn's wardrobe was the source of never-ending wonder. The nine-act pseudo-Freudian Eugene O'Neill drama *Strange Interlude*, which premiered at the John Golden Theatre on January 30, 1928, began at 5:15 P.M., broke at 7:15 for dinner, resumed at 8:30, and ended shortly after 11:00. Accompanied by the actress Elsie Ferguson, Kahn arrived for the first part wearing dark striped trousers, a dark-gray tailcoat, and a gray cravat. He returned for the second stretch, this time with Max Reinhardt as his companion, wearing white tie and tails. Presumably he sacrificed dinner, for he had only an hour and a quarter to ride all the way uptown to Ninety-first Street and Fifth Avenue, change, and ride back to the theater. At his reappearance Alexander Woollcott, then theater critic for the *New York World*, whispered to his neighbor, Mrs. Herbert Bayard Swope: "Kahn must have inadvertently hung Elsie Ferguson in his clothes closet."

After the first performance, at Carnegie Hall, of George Gershwin's symphonic poem *An American in Paris*, Jules Glaenzer, head of Cartier and an inveterate first-nighter, gave a party in honor of the composer, at which he received a silver humidor inscribed with his name, the title of the piece, and the date of the premiere—December 13, 1928. The occasion roused Kahn to one of his loftiest flights of oratory. "George Gershwin," said he, "is a leader of young America in music, in the same sense in which Lindbergh is the leader of young America in aviation. And in more than one respect, he has qualities similar to those of the gallant and attractive Colonel, qualities which we like to consider characteristic of the best type of young America. He has the same unspoilableness—if I may coin the word—the same engaging and unassuming ways, the same simple dignity and dislike of show, the same absence of affectation, the same direct, uncomplicated, naive, 'Parsifalesque' outlook upon life and upon his task. . . ."

He went on to recite with the aplomb of a professional actor the first stanza of Thomas Hardy's poem "On an Invitation to the United States":

> I shrink to see a modern coast
> Whose riper times have yet to be
> Where the new regions claim them free
> From that long drip of human tears
> Which peoples old in tragedy
> Have left upon the centuried years

"The 'long drip of human tears,' my dear George! They have great and strange and beautiful power, those human tears. They fertilize the deepest roots of art, and from them flowers spring of a loveliness and perfume that no other moisture can produce. . . .

"And just because of that I could wish for you an experience—not too prolonged—of that driving storm and stress of the emotions, of that solitary wrestling with your own soul, of that aloofness, for a while from the actions and distractions of the everyday world, which are the most effective ingredients for the deepening and mellowing and the complete development, energizing and revealment, of an artist's inner being."

A marked contrast to his informal conversation which could be both laconic and dryly witty, as when a client inquired about another client: "Is he absolutely honest?" and Kahn replied: "Honest, yes. Absolutely honest, no."

Kahn occasionally extended his weekend hospitality to a motley array of fun-lovers, such as Robert Benchley, the Marx Brothers, Franklin P. Adams, who had nothing in common with the *hautes mondes* of Fifth Avenue, Mayfair, and the Sixteenth Arrondissement. The *Oheka* once conveyed to the Brobdingnagian retreat the three rowdy clowns the Ritz Brothers, the youngest of whom, Harry, at first glimpse of the lush interior, exclaimed: "Let's louse the place up!" Roger Kahn brought the jazz pianist Zez Confrey, who inquired at the massive dinner table, as he eyed the platoon of servitors: "Tell me, Mr. Otto, what do you do when you want a single boiled egg?" Franklin Adams wanted to know: "Can I order from the menu, or do I have to take the blue-plate special?"

Addie did not participate in these highly informal gatherings.

Kahn was a subject particularly appealing to the writers of *The New Yorker*'s "Talk of the Town" pages, who, during the magazine's early years in the twenties, continually inserted bits about him, so much so that editor Harold Ross posted an enjoinder on the office bulletin board: "Otto Kahn has been mentioned six times in Talk recently. There will be no more mention of him for six months."

An occasional luncheon guest at the Algonquin Round Table, he became the butt of gentle joshing by such normally acidic jesters as Dorothy Parker, George S. Kaufman, and Alexander Woollcott. As guests at Kahn's Fifth Avenue residence, Charles MacArthur and Ben Hecht were perusing their host's volumes of classic authors when it occurred to them to embellish the flyleaves with such inscriptions as "To dear Otto, without whose help this could never have been written, Plato," or "To Otto, in memory of our wild and wonderful weekend at Cape Cod, Shelley." Love to Otto was also inscribed from Cicero, Shakespeare, and Oscar Wilde.

For practically anybody bright and intelligent enough to stir his imagination, no lengthy acquaintance was essential to win the coveted invitation to Cold Spring Harbor, such as the one he issued to the ballerina Tamara Geva in June 1928: "My boat, the Oheka, will await you at eleven o'clock on Sunday morning at the New York Yacht Club, foot of 26th St., to take you to my place on Long Island. . . ."

Kahn instituted an annual social event when, in the fall of 1924, he appointed Alexander Woollcott a substitute host at Oheka, with the privilege of organizing a weekend party, the guests to be of Woollcott's choosing. The first group of these yacht-borne merrymakers consisted of Jack Baragwanath, mining engineer, playboy, and Algonquin Round Table regular, and his wife, the fetching illustrator Neysa McMein; the Ziegfeld Follies beauty Justine Johnstone, who married the Hollywood producer Walter Wanger; Dorothy Parker; and Charles MacArthur. "Are any of them married to, or divorced from, one another?" Kahn, in an unwonted burst of levity, wrote to Woollcott beforehand. "One can never know nowadays."

Prior to the next get-together commanded by Woollcott, Kahn, ever the celebrity hunter, wrote: "If it be not gluttonous when such tasty and satisfying fare is provided, to suggest an additional course, I wonder whether the chef would feel disposed to endeavor adding Miss Katherine [sic] Cornell and her husband [the director Guthrie McClintic] to the menu. Of course, this is merely an humble suggestion. The chef is absolute boss, and, being responsible as he is for the repast, all the ingredients must be of his untrammeled selection."

The largest number of ingredients, fourteen in all, composed the 1928 menu and included—with the accommodations assigned by Kahn:

Beatrice Lillie	Grey room
The Baragwanaths	Mrs. John Marriott's suite
Helen Hayes	Green room
Cole Porter	Uncle Felix's room
Charles MacArthur	Mauve room
Alexander Woollcott	Gilbert Kahn's room
Mrs. George Kaufman	Flower room

Kahn had known the young British writer Beverly Nichols barely a few minutes at a New York party before he bade him join another private railroad journey, this one to Palm Beach, then to New Orleans, across Texas and New Mexico, to Hollywood, and back to New York.

"You play bridge, of course?" Kahn confidently asked when he issued the invitation.

Nichols scarcely knew the difference between a renege and a little slam. So he took a crash course from a professional player during the time remaining before the departure on February 22, 1928.

"Otto Kahn was my ideal American millionaire," Nichols recalled in his memoirs. "He used his millions with taste, kindliness and understanding. . . . There was a cosy feeling when traveling with him, that one could request the engine driver to stop so that one could admire the view. (Once we actually did this, to the fury of earnest business men, who, for reasons best known to themselves, were desirous of arriving punctually in—of all places—Philadelphia.)

"But apart from these obvious appurtenances of wealth, he was a patron of the arts in a sense that has been little understood since the days of the Renaissance. He was one of the few supporters of the Metropolitan who was more interested in music than in tiaras; he had a poetic vision about Hollywood which he pathetically persisted in treating as though it were worthy of his intelligence; and in England he will always be remembered by the men of St. Dunstan's home for blinded soldiers, which he gave to the British nation at the end of the First World War.

"He was, in short, a very considerable dear."

"I talk about art to businessmen," Kahn told Nichols, "and about business to artists. That is why I still have a certain reputation for wisdom in both camps."

In Hollywood, Cecil B. De Mille gave Kahn and his entourage a private screening of his 1923 supercolossal biblical extravaganza *The Ten Commandments*. Following one of the most spectacular sequences, the dance of the golden calf, De Mille asked how many extras he thought were used. Kahn had no idea. "Two thousand five hundred," said the director, full of pride. "What do you think of that?"

"Economic waste" was what Kahn thought. "Artistic ill-judgment! . . . Have you ever seen Velasquez' picture of 'The Surrender of Breda'? If you look at that picture, you will have an impression, in the background, of a veritable forest of spears and lances. If you count those lances you will find that there are, if my memory serves me right, precisely eighteen. [There are actually twenty-eight.] Velasquez was an artist!"

In the early Paramount Famous Lasky film *Glorifying the American Girl* (1929), a combination of musical revue and drama about the Ziegfeld Follies, Kahn made a brief appearance as himself along with scads of other incurable first-nighters, among them Ring Lardner, Florenz Ziegfeld, Mayor Jimmy Walker, and Texas Guinan.

20

Patronage

On December 3, 1925, Hart Crane, the homosexual, alcoholic poet whose sparse body of works rank among the finest in twentieth-century American literature, wrote to his father:

". . . For the last six weeks I've been tramping streets and being questioned, smelled and refused in various offices. Most places didn't have any work to offer. . . . My shoes are leaky, and my pockets are empty; I have helped to empty several other pockets, also. In fact I am a little discouraged. This afternoon I am stooping to something that I know plenty of others have done. . . . I am writing a certain internationally known banker who recently gave a friend of mine five thousand dollars to study painting in Paris, and I'm asking him to lend me enough money to spend the winter in the country where it is cheap to live and where I can produce some creative work. . . ."

The internationally known banker was Otto Kahn, and the same day Crane wrote to him. ". . . My first collected poems [*White Buildings*] are about to be published (probably next spring) with a Foreword by Eugene O'Neill. . . . I am not yet well enough known to reap any substantial benefit from what I have written. I am twenty-six years of age, and for the last seven years I have been entirely dependent on my efforts as an advertising copywriter for my living. . . .

"Besides the poems collected into my forthcoming volume I have partially written a long poem, the conception of which has been in my mind for some years. I have had to work at it very intermittently, between night and morning, and while shorter efforts can be more successfully completed under such crippling circumstances, a larger conception such as this poem, *The Bridge*, aiming as it does to enumerate a new cultural synthesis of values in terms of our America, requires a more steady application and less interruption than my circumstances have yet granted me to give it. . . .

"If the suggestion seems worthy and feasible to you I should like to borrow the sum of a thousand dollars, at any rate of interest within six per cent. . . ."

He appended a list of writers who valued his poetry. They included Waldo Frank, Allen Tate, Marianne Moore, and Eugene O'Neill.

What Kahn read of Crane's poetry he must have found hard to understand, for it was extremely complex, full of connotative allusions, mystical and visionary. Impressed, however, by the commendatory comments of O'Neill and Frank, whose critical reaction he sought, he asked the poet to call at 1100 Fifth Avenue on December 6, only three days after Crane's appeal. They talked for three hours before Crane, ecstatic, left the richer by a thousand dollars and the promise of another thousand when needed. This was supposedly a loan, but Kahn did not seriously expect repayment. For the next five years Crane struggled to finish his masterpiece, *The Bridge*, meanwhile hastening his self-destruction through drink and orgies with waterfront sailors. Kahn, ignoring the poet's sordid private life, continued to advance money, usually a few hundred dollars at a time. Dartt reminded him in a memo dated December 11, 1926: "Re Hart Crane . . . note for $1000. The above note is due today with interest. What action do you want me to take?" Kahn scribbled across the memo: "Do nothing." Altogether he wrote off $2,392.42.

Crane kept his benefactor apprised of his progress. He prepared for him an elaborate schema of the long, difficult poem and later sent him completed parts as he forged ahead. He wrote to his father, Clarence Arthur Crane, on October 11, 1927: "I have just had an interview with Otto Kahn, following his reading of the manuscript of 'The Bridge' [that is, the final section]. Kahn is very enthusiastic about what I have accomplished and is most anxious that I keep on with the composition until it is finished. I told him about your willingness to extend me the assistance of the monthly allowance of $50, and he has come forward with an additional $300. . . ."

Crane wrote the last lines on December 26, 1929. The following year, in Paris, Caresse Crosby's Black Sun Press published *The Bridge* while Horace Liveright brought out the American edition. Crane dedicated a special deluxe edition to Otto Kahn. The reviews were, for the most part, laudatory. In *The Nation*, Granville Hicks pronounced it "as important a poem as has been written in our time." But praise did not alleviate the author's inner anguish, nor did the meager royalties relieve his poverty. On April 27, 1932, sailing back to the United States from Veracruz, Mexico, Crane, at the age of thirty-three, threw himself overboard. His body was never recovered.

On May 22, the poet's mother, Grace Hart Crane, wrote to Kahn: ". . . I wish to take this occasion to express my sincere gratitude for the great assistance you rendered him at a time when he was desperately in need of an opportunity to be free to write. If it had not been for your understanding and generosity, 'The Bridge' might never have been written. . . .

"No words can adequately convey the agony of mind and heart I have endured since the shocking news of Hart's tragic death. He was my only child—my chief interest in life, and I feel there can be no compensation for such a loss. . . ."

Neither the painter Alexander King nor the playwright Paul Green, when both were young and needy, solicited help from Kahn. He offered it unasked. Horace Liveright introduced King, who had been doing book illustrations, to the banker. Not long after, in December 1926, they met again in the publisher's office. For half an hour beforehand Kahn had been studying a few of King's paintings that hung there. "You ought to go abroad for a while," he advised. "You should see what is happening in the art world of Paris and Italy." But King had a wife and two children, and much as the prospect of such a trip excited him, he could not bring himself to leave them behind. Kahn suggested he call on him at Kuhn, Loeb, where they could explore the situation further.

When King showed up the next day, the meeting lasted barely half a minute. Kahn began without preamble: "I have decided to take care of you for a year, in France. Later on we will see."

The money he gave without strings of any kind sufficed for the entire family, and a week later they sailed for France aboard the liner *Rochambeau*.

"That was Otto Kahn," King wrote in his memoirs. "May the earth rest lightly on his generous heart. You will search in vain for his like today. He saw my work and approved it. We met face to face. He sized me up. He made up his mind. And that was the end of it."

Paul Green was teaching philosophy at the University of North Carolina and writing his early plays (*In Abraham's Bosom* would win the

1927 Pulitzer Prize) when he received a letter from Kahn, whom he had never met, enclosing a check for $1,500. "Green, I have been following your work," the letter read, "and I would like to just send you a little something. Use it any way you please." A bit later he wrote: "When you are in New York, come and have dinner with me down on Wall Street. . . ." They ate in the Kuhn, Loeb private dining room, attended by liveried footmen. Afterward Kahn took his guest for a walk on Wall Street and through the Stock Exchange. "Mad," Kahn remarked. "We're mad in America and some day we are going to pay for it."

One month after Marc Connelly's Pulitzer Prize–winning *Green Pastures* opened at the Mansfield Theatre in 1930, the author sent Kahn a check for $450 representing the repayment of a loan plus 6 percent interest. Kahn acknowledged it the next day:

"It is indeed a source of most genuine satisfaction to me to be able to feel that I have had some little part, however indirect, in enabling the creation of 'The Green Pastures,' the greatest and most moving play, in my opinion, since 'Cyrano de Bergerac'; and my head is slightly swelled through the consciousness of the fact that, when I read the script last year, I realized immediately the beauty and uniqueness of the play, as well as its compelling popular appeal, while, from what I understand, several 'eminent' managers did not see what seemed to me so patent.

"And what now? You are young; you have genius; the world is at your feet; the American stage, beset and menaced, needs you; and so forth. What are you planning?"

He enclosed a check of his own and a postscript: "I find that your check errs by undue generosity to me. Your note (enclosed) ran at the rate of 5%, not 6%. The exact interest to date amounts to $335.55. Consequently, there is due you a refund of $114.45, for which I enclose my check herewith."

During the two years, 1930–32, that Sergei Eisenstein, the prodigious Soviet film director, spent in the United States and Mexico, he was a prime target of right-wingers. Though when he arrived in New York, on May 12, 1930, under contract to Paramount, he was greeted by effusions of studio publicity, though honored at major universities where he lectured, he was also subjected to a campaign of vilification by reactionary cabals. In Hollywood one Major Frank Pease, an anti-Semitic anti-Communist, agitated for his deportation. Paramount terminated his contract. Disheartened, Eisenstein was about to return to Russia when he decided to make a film about Mexico. He found a sponsor in the leftist novelist Upton Sinclair, who proceeded to seek investors. Sinclair's wealthy wife, Mary, provided the initial source of funds. Eisenstein then began filming *Que Viva Mexico!*, which, as he originally conceived it, was to depict poetically the history and culture of the country. The project proved disastrous from the start. The director and two members of his company were arrested on arrival in Mexico for no understandable cause. Innumerable complications, political, financial, technical, impeded progress. As Eisenstein's obsession with the Mexican mystique deepened, the shooting continued for almost a year. Sinclair, meanwhile, sought additional investors. Otto Kahn, conservative, Republican, anti-Communist (with whom Eisenstein had dined at 1100 Fifth Avenue the year before) put up $10,000.

Amid the turmoil, conflict, and chaos the money ran out, and the director and sponsor ended their relationship in acrimony. On February 17, 1932, the Eisenstein unit left Mexico for Russia via the United States. At first they were denied admission to the United States, then given a transit visa good for one month. The negative of *Que Viva Mexico!* remained with Sinclair, who had promised to forward it to Eisenstein in Moscow for editing. Instead he had it edited into a feature film, *Thunder Over Mexico*, and two shorts, *Death Day* and *Eisenstein in Mexico*, which brutally distorted Eisenstein's original concept. Ironically, Kahn, who had invested $10,000 because he admired Eisenstein's artistry, but without hope of seeing a penny of it again, recovered $5,000 from the bloody remnants.

The religious institutions and causes in which Otto and Addie Kahn participated financially or personally were predominantly Christian. During the decade 1920–30, for example, Addie contributed a thousand dollars to St. Bartholomew's offertory, and Kahn donated modest sums to various Catholic and Episcopalian churches and charities. He subscribed a thousand dollars toward paying off the mortgage on St. Bartholomew's land and building and $5,000 toward a boarding school for actors' children to be established by the Episcopal Actors' Guild.

During the same period one of his few investments in or donations to Jewish organizations was the purchase of five shares for $250 of the *Jewish Daily Bulletin* plus $500 toward a sustaining fund. Yet when the Yiddish Art Theatre requested an interview, he replied, on October 26, 1931: ". . . if the purpose of your proposed interview is to enlist my financial cooperation, I am bound to tell you in advance that the simply overwhelming demands and commitments under which I am in these trying times make such cooperation quite impossible for the time being. . . ."

Kahn's widespread reputation for openhandedness emboldened a number of peculiar petitioners to seek his support. Some of the more preposterous letters from Europe he preserved, perhaps as orthographic curiosities, after dictating a reply to his secretary. Consider the case of a Romanian who wrote from his home in the town of Medias on April 30, 1928:

"My request is the following: Lend me please One hundred and fifty dollars. This money is in need for several experiments. It is a matter of experiments for the more cheap production of chocolate and pastry for Diabetes. I must buy a great variety of things. (Spezial flour imported of England), chemical preparations, anise, etz. . . .—My salary is previous very little, in this manner, that I make barely a living. But I will and I must advance. Ideas and energy are at my disposal. I am besides well acquainted with the nature of articles for Diabetes and I feel thoroughly convinced, that I shall gain my end.—I beg you therefore once more very hard to help me the only time. You are wealth and I am poor. You would make with that amount a man so happy and you will perhaps lay the fondation stone for a errection of a new life. You would it never repent. I shall repay the money very exact.—I am sorry to say you, that I have not any safeguarding, than my word of honour, to act honestly. In case, that my experiments will turn well, I shall find in Austria men, who will be partner in my business. It would be me possible to pay back you money in 4–6 months. If all turn ill, I shall work and work and you will receive this amount perhaps in several years—but it is sure, that I retourne it you. . . . At all events I would be happy, if you will me answer. It is better to have not a hope, than to hope without any prospects. . . .

"P.S. Exuse, Sir, my bad English. I have learned that language alone and I can not well it. . . ."

Dartt replied: "On behalf of Mr. Otto H. Kahn, I acknowledge receipt of your letter . . . and regret to say that Mr. Kahn cannot comply with your request."

21

Women

On November 24, 1923, the stunning blond Viennese wife of Baron Leopold Popper de Podhurgen, better known to opera buffs throughout Europe as Maria Jeritza, touched off a cannonade of *bravas!* with her acrobatic performance at the Met as Tosca. To soften the heart of the lustful Roman chief of police Baron Scarpia, who has offered to spare her lover's life in return for her favors, she flung herself prostrate before him and in that position, sang the demanding aria "Vissi d'arte," a feat never attempted by any other soprano.

Jeritza became Kahn's mistress, a relationship that both Addie Kahn and Baron Popper accepted with outward composure, in the style of European aristocracy, thereby avoiding a major public scandal. Kahn liked to take a constitutional on Fifth Avenue of a Sunday morning with a dachshund named Sieglinde. Jeritza later gave him a companion for Sieglinde, another dachshund, Fritz by name.

Though the affair was an open secret, few periodicals mentioned it. An exception was the weekly *Amerikai Magyar Nepszava* (The American Hungarian People's Voice). The following paragraph appeared in April 1924, of which a translation into English as awkward as it was false somehow found its way into the Kahn archives:

"The first news of international interest: Marie [sic] Jeritza, at present starring in New York, is obtaining a divorce from her husband, Baron Popper [they remained married until 1935] and will be married to Otto H. Kahn, New York millionaire [who was never divorced]. With this Kahn-combination [play of words, literally not translatable, notes the anonymous translator] she will conclusively terminate her singing; henceforth, she will live for the happiness of her home. Jeritza, the Hungarian [she was born in Austria] will henceforth the more forcefully support the English-Hungarian friendship, and will smoothen [sic] out any complications arising in those quarters."

Fifty-five years later the Kahn legend prompted *The New York Times* to perpetuate an equally baseless rumor. It involved Rose Cumming, an interior decorator with exotic looks as arresting as the decor she contrived for the homes of the rich. Her famous shop stood at 515 Madison Avenue. A Pekinese named Cantor lived in the window. In an article about the women leaders of the profession, the *Times* reported on May 31, 1979: ". . . And finally, there was the beautiful Rose Cumming. Reputedly the mistress of Otto Kahn, the financier, and given to wearing chiffon over her nakedness. . . ."

The decorator's younger sister Eileen protested in a letter to the *Times*:

"Rose Cumming never even met Mr. Kahn, but she was fortunate in having Mrs. Kahn as a client; nothing prodigious but helping to refurnish her very beautiful New York house.

"Mrs. Kahn liked and admired Miss Cumming's work and enjoyed coming to the shop to discuss the work in progress. She nearly always came bearing gifts of rare flowers or fruit from her greenhouses. . . . In answer to the many queries as to where she found such perfection out of season she would say proudly, 'They came from the Kahn greenhouses.' Enter here the beginnings of the canard.

"The second remark is also most unfortunate, 'chiffon over her nakedness'—it was, of course, not true but it gives a picture of a very different person from one who wore her décolletage with a bit of daring and of beauty!"

At a New York dinner party given in the spring of 1924 by Sir William Wiseman, a British associate and later partner of Kuhn, Loeb, a picture-pretty musical comedy star found herself seated beside Otto Kahn. She was Grace Moore from Slabtown, Tennessee, who the year before, in the *Music Box Revue*, had jollified audiences with her rendition of "Yes, We Have No Bananas." Kahn struck her, she recalled in her memoirs, as "a rather pompous, dignified man, interested in too many things to get a great sensation out of any of them." She nevertheless determined to charm him. Had he, she coyly asked, ever fallen in love with the Met's prima donnas? He professed total indifference to all of them except as singers. "The Opera itself is too alluring," said he, according to Moore.

So alluring was the spell she cast over him that before the party broke up he promised to introduce her to both Gatti-Casazza and the Met's assistant manager, Edward Ziegler. At 4:30 P.M. on April 10, the time fixed for an audition, Kahn escorted her to the rehearsal room, where Gatti, Ziegler, the conductors Artur Bodanzky and Wilfred Pelletier, and the composer Italo Montemezzi awaited her. Pelletier sat at the piano, prepared to serve as Moore's accompanist. Montemezzi had already offered to coach and tactfully chose for the occasion an aria from his first opera, *Giovanni Gallurese*. Polite applause followed. Gatti allowed that she had a good voice, but needed another year of training.

She spent the year in Europe, studying with Mary Garden. Her opinion of Kahn changed after she met him in Venice and he acted as her artistic tour guide. For nearly fifteen minutes, she recalled years later, they stood silently in the Palazzo Dorigo Giovanelli before Giorgione's painting *The Tempest*. "You know," said Kahn, "this is one of the few things in my life that I have been unable to buy. Everything has its price but this."

Kahn's age—he was then fifty-eight—saddened him, Grace believed, for he loved life and saw age as the beginning of its end. In a transient mood of depression, he told Moore: "I feel the romance of Venice. I only regret I'm not fifteen years younger and you ten years older."

In the spring of 1925, Moore telephoned Kahn in Palm Beach to ask, now that she had trained hard, if he would arrange a second audition for her. The request was granted, but the outcome was dismal. After Gatti dismissed her with a curt "thank you," she sat weeping on a bench outside the opera house. Ziegler was the first to find her there, but he had no consolation to offer. "Your voice," he said, "has lost color, resonance and pitch . . . it isn't as good today as it was a year ago."

Bodanzky appeared next. Grace, he predicted, would probably never learn to sing on key. Tears dried, resolute, she thereupon called Kahn and wagered $100 that she would sing at the Met within two years.

Late next winter she telephoned him collect at the Ritz Hotel in Paris. As a result, he agreed to meet her on the Riviera in the home of a mutual friend. She sang for him four arias from *Manon*, *La Bohème*, *Louise*, and *Roméo et Juliette*. "There has been a remarkable improvement," Kahn conceded. "I see also you are more serious than ever and more unwavering in your ambitions for opera. I am sure Mr. Gatti will want a third audition, and I shall keep my fingers crossed that this third time will work the charm."

Her singing did more than charm Kahn. It ravished his heart as well as his ears. JUST HEARD GRACE MOORE, he cabled Gatti from Paris on March 15, 1927. SHE HAS MADE REMARKABLE PROGRESS RATHER CONTRARY TO MY EXPECTATION AND DESERVES IN MY OPINION SERIOUS CONSIDERATION ESPECIALLY FOR FRENCH PARTS EVEN LOUISE.

Gatti replied two days later: WILL KEEP GRACE MOORE IN MIND HOPING TO HAVE OPPORTUNITY OF HEARING HER SOON STOP AM HAPPY TO TELL YOU OUR SEASON CONTINUES MAGNIFICENTLY EVEN REVIVAL OF MIGNON THE RESULT OF WHICH I EXPECTED MODERATE WAS INSTEAD A GREAT ARTISTIC AND FINANCIAL SUCCESS.

June 3, a letter from Kahn to Gatti in Milan: "I am writing these few lines to let you know about several artists whom I heard in Paris.

"First: Grace Moore. I believe she is the most promising young American artist now in the field, and worthy of your serious attention. She is scheduled to sing Louise at the Opéra Comique next autumn. Before that she will sing either at Aix-les-Bains or at Vichy, probably in August or September. Her voice has developed greatly, and she is getting to be a lyric-*dramatic* soprano. I hope very much you will surely hear her when you visit Paris, or, if you prefer, she will go and sing for you anywhere you like. She can always be reached at her permanent address: 53 rue Pergolèse, Paris."

". . . She sang for me a good audition," was Gatti's verdict, on July 27, after an audition in Milan. ". . . She sang well, with art and expression and with a sympathetic voice in pitch and sure. I do not believe that we can count on her for dramatic roles, but only lyric ones. Considering the ensemble of her qualities and the impression she made on you as well as upon myself and the Maestri, I gave her a contract for the coming season at terms very advantageous for us and for a period of about two and a half months, with our right to prolong the contract and renew it for the following years. . . ."

She collected her hundred-dollar bet, having, on February 7, 1928, made her Met debut as Mimi in *La Bohème*. Kahn, carried away, stood up in his director's box and cheered. He later maintained it was the most important debut since Rosa Ponselle's Leonora in *La Forza del Destino* ten years earlier.

To a friend who once asked Grace Moore what interested her most next to singing, she replied, "Love."

In her memoirs she testified: ". . . the unvarnished truth about my love life is that it has always been perfectly normal, happy, and enormously successful. . . .

"Unlike a great many women, I really like men. I don't think they're 'heels,' and I don't think, as the female Jeremiahs say, that a woman is a fool to trust them. But then men have been good to me, good friends. Perhaps it is because I have been fortunate enough to have known only the most attractive men. . . . I cherish people who are important, well-informed, literate. I reach out towards the experience of others and find them much more fascinating than any I may have had myself. As I listen I become impressed; as I become impressed I feel emotional sympathy: soon, because I am an incorrigible romanticist, I am in love. . . .

"My greatest good fortune has always been that the men I have loved have been so full of vigor, wit and experience that sitting back quietly has been the better part of fun."

Her affair with Kahn was brief compared to his years with Jeritza, but Kahn had the gift of retaining the friendship of the women he had loved. His fondness for Grace Moore lasted through her marriage in 1931 to Valentin Perera, a Spanish actor, and until his own death.

Like a number of women who attracted him, Moore benefited from his financial acumen. A wretched speller, she wrote to him from Hollywood, where she had starred in two MGM films, on February 3, 1934: "Dear Boss, I am sending this little note to you hoping you can give me a little advise—I have a small french account of 300,000 fcs. [francs] which I wish to pay as soon as possible but to change my dollars into fcs. at this time almost requiring doubling the original amount, so I am hoping that the French will soon leave the gold standard the franc will be reevaluated and I can buy my 300,000 worth & not at the sacrifice of so many more dollars than originally invested at 25 fcs. to the dollar. So I come to you my only financial adviser with the hopes that you can help a *struggling movie star* so far from her real home. If you think advisable I can arrange with the bank or any place you advise me to buy francs at the opportune moment & I can send a check for the dollars. This amount covers a morgage on my Cannes property & I do want to settle as soon as possible as it is my one and only debt.

"We had a divine winter here, giving concerts getting thinner & preparing for my musical film [her third, *One Night of Love*]—The story is charming & we have secured the rights to 'Butterfly' Score, So I hope and pray this time I can do something worth while—We made many charming friends here & feel that even in Hollywood one can find delightful & intelligent people which of course is contrary to all reports—I do hope my darling that you are feeling very well—I miss my dear old Metropolitan & do hope to be back there Again soon & to look up & find you either applauding or scolding from your perch on high. My greetings to Willie Wiseman & to you always much affection Grace Moore Perera."

For once Kahn was stuck. He replied somewhat sheepishly on February 24: "My dear Grace: Alas, I do not know the solution of the riddle concerning which you do me the honor of consulting me. In the case of any nation other than the French, I might venture a fairly definite guess, but one of their picturesque and attractive qualities is to be incalculable, in spite of, or perhaps because of, their proverbial logic. Such being the case, and several other elements peculiar to the French situation and French mentality entering into the problem, I find myself unable, in the present aspect of affairs, to express an opinion as to your problem. I feel somewhat mortified to thus disappoint your flattering faith in my financial wisdom, but it is better to be humble than wrong, especially when the affairs of friends are concerned.

"I am delighted to learn that you are happy in Hollywood and that you are pleased with the story of your forthcoming film. I am greatly looking forward to seeing and hearing you in it. Namely, I expect to invade Hollywood next June or July and am praying that you may still be there at that time. R.S.V.P. . . .

"Incidentally, I hear from impartial witnesses that you look more lovely than ever and that your voice is in admirable shape, as it was indeed when I heard you sing at the Metropolitan about a year ago. . . ."

France did not go off the gold standard until 1936. On January 26, 1947, after considerable success as both film and opera star, Grace Moore died in a plane crash near Copenhagen.

Like many rich, influential men with ready access to the leaders of the performing arts, Kahn was a prime target for overambitious women. During the mid-twenties his conflict with two of them began. An obscure coloratura named Rosalinda Morini sued Kahn for impairing her professional reputation when he publicly retracted the high marks he was purported to have accorded her. A darkly pretty twenty-six-year-old medical student at the University of Pennsylvania, Morini had decided to switch to a musical career. She managed to persuade

Kahn to attend a concert she gave at Carnegie Hall on August 1, 1927. She subsequently placed an ad in *The Musical Courier* quoting Kahn's lavish praise: "One of the most beautiful voices I have ever heard." Kahn promptly reproved the periodical: "To the best of my recollection I made no comment on Miss Morini's vocal qualifications on the one and only occasion I ever heard her sing." The coloratura took this as libel and sued Kahn for $250,000. She ultimately accepted a settlement of "considerably less than $10,000" and a second letter from Kahn for publication in *The Musical Courier:*

"I . . . made favorable comment upon your singing. The difficulty was, as we both recognized, that a misunderstanding arose as to what were the exact words used by me, and as to your advertising matter, resulting in my letter to *The Musical Courier*.

"I had no purpose to reflect unfavorably upon your integrity or your ability.

"It is my policy never to permit the use of my name in connection with advertising, to which policy I shall strictly adhere."

The most Byzantine artifice to extract both professional and financial benefits from Kahn was conducted by Lydia Lindgren, a soprano *manquée* who styled herself "the second Swedish Nightingale." Tall and blond, a Valkyrie, she came to New York from her native Stockholm in 1912. Her early weeks in New York were marked by passion and melodrama. Rudolf Sulzberger, a Dresden merchant in town on business, became her steady escort until he confessed that a wife and four children awaited him at home. Lydia ended the relationship, whereupon Rudolf tried to kill himself by inhaling the gas from the gas jets in his hotel room.

According to what Lindgren told newspapermen, she had obtained an audition at the Met in 1914. (No record of the effort survives, if, indeed, there ever was one.) Kahn heard her and asked to be introduced. "Madame Lindgren," her lawyer, Irving Mariash, interposed, "is willing to tell about her relations with Mr. Kahn from that time on." But for the moment she ventured no further.

She sang briefly with the Chicago Opera Company and gave a concert or two, but never performed an operatic role of any importance. In 1926 she married a short, pudgy Brazilian tenor, Raoul Querze. The following year she, too, attempted, or pretended to attempt, suicide. While staying at the Copley Plaza Hotel in Boston, she swallowed a few drops of iodine. After calling a cab that sped her to a hospital, she quickly recovered. The hospital attendants found clutched in her right hand a letter addressed to Kahn, beseeching his aid in the advancement of her newly acquired mate's career. "It was my own trouble," she explained to the press. "Always when I am unhappy I go to Boston. I have friends there connected with Harvard. They console me. . . . Once I thought I could sing."

Five years later Lindgren embarked on a new course. This time she involved a third "Swedish Nightingale," Julia Claussen, a mezzo-soprano of distinction. According to Lindgren's 1931 court testimony, scandalous gossip had reached her ears concerning Kahn and herself. The stories spread through America and Europe, the Number 2 nightingale charged, and it was Madame Claussen who had circulated them. They so affected Lydia that she developed an inferiority complex and could no longer practice her vocal technique. She filed a slander suit against the mezzo-soprano for $250,000.

Kahn entreated her to drop the suit for the good of the Met, and she consented. She felt entitled, however, to some sort of compensation. On February 11, 1931, Kahn, his mink-clad ex-inamorata, and their lawyers—he retained four of them—convened to discuss the terms of a possible settlement. When Mariash, then twenty-seven, a minnow among whales, approached lawyer Sol Stroock, hand outstretched in amicable greeting, Stroock pulled back, saying: "I don't shake hands with people like you." His meaning was clear: Mariash represented a blackmailer. Kahn's innate gentlemanliness moved him to apologize to the adversary lawyer for Stroock's behavior. Later he fired Stroock.

During the ensuing arguments, Kahn and Lydia glanced at each other, then disappeared into an anteroom. They emerged smiling. They had reached an agreement. "The matter is settled and I choose not to discuss it," announced the beautiful Swede, and Kahn nodded happily. She refused to tell even Mariash, her own lawyer, how much Kahn had promised to pay. Whatever the sum, she later complained, Kahn paid only a small portion, and on September 30 she sued him in Queens Supreme Court (Queens because she and Raoul Querze were residents of that borough), Justice Charles J. Druhan presiding.

"At the request of Mr. Kahn," Mariash set forth, "Madame Lindgren withdrew the slander suit against Madame Claussen. Mr. Kahn promised to pay her $160,000 in cash and also to obtain a competent manager for her and her husband and launch them on a career. He paid $13,000 in accordance with the terms of his verbal agreement [referring to their behind-closed-doors parley] and then stopped. She has not seen him since he persuaded her to withdraw the slander suit.

"This suit is to recover the $160,000 which Mr. Kahn promised to pay and for damages sustained by Madame Lindgren by reason of his failure to do so."

This time Kahn added to his team of counsel the formidable Max Steuer, one of the most astute trial lawyers in American legal annals. The interchanges between Steuer and Mariash grew so vicious that Judge Druhan halted the proceedings and summoned the attorneys to his chambers along with their clients. "I don't want this kind of thing in my courtroom," he said. "Why not get rid of the case?" In short, pay the woman. Kahn pledged $160,000 with the understanding that no publicity ensue.

Returning to the bench, Judge Druhan delivered an extraordinary ruling. Though he knew that a settlement had been agreed upon, though he undoubtedly understood the nature of the farce confronting him, he granted a motion to dismiss Lydia's complaint. "I shall hold as a matter of law," he said, "that the plaintiff has failed to prove that on the day in question the alleged agreement was entered into between the plaintiff and the defendant. I shall hold, moreover, that the so-called slander action was based upon a fraudulent claim. If my conclusion in this respect be correct, it follows that the discontinuance of the slander action was not a valid consideration for the promise which the plaintiff now claims was made in the anteroom of the defendant's attorneys. . . ."

Nevertheless, Lydia pocketed $160,000.

22

Mussolini, Harding, and Hoover

Kahn held strong opinions about virtually every major issue of the day, and he expressed them in a steady flow of interviews, lectures, pamphlets, articles, and books. While he remained a staunch Republican, he frequently took a position that flouted the Establishment. His views on employer-employee relations, for example, struck some of his peers as downright socialism, though many of his proposals would one day be adopted.

"The worker is neither a machine nor a commodity," he wrote. "He is a collaborator with capital. He must be given an elective voice in determining jointly with the employer the conditions under which he works, and whenever practicable, and desired by employes, to have representation on the board of directors. The employer should avoid patronizing treatment of employes. The employers should infuse interest in tasks to be performed and maintain the closest possible contact with employes.

"A worker's living conditions must be attractive to himself and family. If the employer has not the necessary means to provide this, then it becomes the duty of the State to do so.

"The worker must be relieved of the dread of sickness, unemployment and old age. The community must find ways and means by public works or otherwise, for any man fit and honestly desirous to do an honest day's work to have an opportunity to earn a living. The only ones to whom a civilized community has a right to turn its back are those unwilling to work.

"The worker must receive a wage which not only permits him to keep body and soul together, but large enough to enable him to lay aside a portion to take care of his wife and children, to share the comforts and recreations of life, and to be encouraged to obtain the rewards of thrift."

Association with Communists did not repel Kahn, providing the meeting ground advanced the cause of art. He remained the friend and patron of the card-carrying Michael Gold, and it was with Kahn's backing that Gold and others of his Marxist persuasion formed, in 1926, the Workers' Lab Theatre, the first dramatic organization consecrated to the creeds of the extreme left. During the two years of its existence, 1927–29, it produced twelve Marxist-oriented plays, all of them box-office and critical catastrophes. Kahn, who had poured more than $50,000 into the enterprise, remained smilingly unruffled. After attending a play that excoriated capitalists and glorified the workers, predicting the latter's ultimate triumph, he observed: "I give my money gladly to artistic enterprises. I am willing to take a chance on thereby upsetting the social order."

Despite the political chasm that lay between them, Kahn and Gold remained genuinely fond of each other, respected each other. They took pleasure in the irony of their situation, and amiably joked about it. Once, as they left Kahn's New York mansion to amble down Fifth Avenue, Gold fell back some twenty paces. He could not, he explained, walk side by side with a capitalist.

Kahn subscribed to Gold's *New Masses*, a mouthpiece of the far left. Gold hoped, he wrote in a bantering note of appreciation, that "the butler was able to withstand the monthly shock of delivering our 'scandalous sheet' to your hands." In his correspondence with Kahn, Gold addressed him as "Emperor" and signed himself "your class enemy."

Speaking to a group of Gold's fellow radicals, Kahn, in a more serious mood, said: "You are Socialists and Communists, but I don't mind as long as you are faithful to art." Gold pronounced him "the only millionaire with a soul."

"The greatest statesman in Europe is Benito Mussolini."

So Kahn proclaimed on May 30, 1925, in a Paris press interview after concluding a politico-economic tour of thirty-one European cities. It was a conviction he shared with many financiers. "Contrary to all that has been written against him, Mussolini is not the enemy of liberty. He is, however, a man that realizes that liberty can, like every good thing, be abused and that likewise it must fit itself into the structure and welfare of the nation. The Roman premier is one of the very few statesmen who has had the courage not to bend the knee before the eighteenth century conceptions of government, conceptions which were resolutely rejected by the wise men who framed the American Constitution. . . . I congratulate the Italian people upon their splendid and fearless leader, who, supported by the masses, has restored order and tranquility, has strengthened the national spirit, has brought efficiency, reform and progress into the administration of government."

Order . . . tranquility . . . reform . . . progress. These were the supposed achievements that blinded big business, bankers, and many fundamentally decent lesser mortals to the terrorism that Il Duce and his Fascist bullies sowed throughout Italy. Few of his admirers were more thoroughly deluded than Kahn, who declared that the Italians "should be grateful to him for the incalculable services which he has restored to Italy."

The House of Morgan floated an Italian loan of $100 million and extended credits of $50 million for stabilization.

On March 25, 1925, Kahn had copies of a laudatory speech he had delivered on Italy and fascism translated into Italian and distributed to Metropolitan Opera singers and conductors of Italian extraction.

In an address before the Foreign Policy Association, on January 23, 1926, Kahn insisted: "[Mussolini] is no dictator in the generally understood sense of the word. . . . The Fascista movement was in the nature of a patriotic revolution—be it remembered—singularly little marred by bloodshed. . . ."

When in Rome, Kahn seldom failed to pay his respects to Mussolini at his headquarters, first situated in the Palazzo Chigi, then in the Palazzo Venezia, where they would exchange ideas on world problems. During his Roman sojourn of April 1927, he was received by the minister of finance, Count Giuseppe Volpi; little King Victor Emmanuel III; and Mussolini, who tendered their gratitude for his services to their country. Mussolini made him an honorary member of the Fascisti, and Kahn wore the party emblem as a boutonniere. He continued to speak and write in praise of Mussolini, and nothing indicates that he ever suffered any disillusionment, that, along with many others, he ever perceived the extent of the dictator's megalomania.

On the question of taxation Kahn again championed measures atypical of investment magnates, who before 1913 had paid no income tax at all. "I have received several letters," he said during the war, "stating that, owing to the excessively high cost of living and for other reasons, men of small means could not afford and should not be asked to bear additional taxation in any appreciable extent and that therefore the proposed vast increase in the income tax is a necessity. Economics are stubborn things and cannot be successfully dealt with emotionally. I quite agree that the financial burden of the war should be made to weigh as little as possible upon the shoulders of the poor and those of small means." Many of Kahn's recommendations, strengthened by a number of economists who shared his views, were adopted.

Soon after the Armistice, Kahn began crusading against the nonproductive millionaires who sheltered their fortunes in tax-exempt securities. "To those who take the view that criticism of our existing surtax schedule is necessarily the squeal of the rich man or affected by the bias of greed, I would point out that the rich man has little to squeal about on the score of taxes provided he will join the ranks of the idle rich. All he has to do, if his conscience and disposition permit it, is to turn his back on work, risk and constructive effort and place as much of his capital as is or can be liquid into tax exempt securities and to the extent that he does so all direct taxation ceases to trouble."

From 1914 to 1921 the loans extended to the Allies by the United States totaled $20,780,732,000. Kahn, whose pronouncements were referred to by *The New York Times* as "state papers," along with J. P. Morgan and other far-seeing financiers, called for the cancellation of the entire debt. On February 9, 1922, at a meeting of the National Institute of Social Sciences held in his New York home, Kahn announced: "I am in favor of doing everything in our power to help Europe straighten itself out. . . .

"Now as to our debts. I believe they are just debts. We did not come into the war from the same motives as other people. We did not enter because menaced or because as Colonel Harvey [George Brinton McClellan Harvey, journalist and diplomat] so ingloriously said, we were afraid not to. I wish we had gone in sooner, but when we did we went in to be on the side of right and humanity.

"But I am entirely clear in my mind that from a moral point of view and from a business point of view we ought to cancel those debts. . . . It would be the best investment this nation ever made, and it would yield to us fabulous sums of money, aside from what it would yield in recognition of our generosity and fair-mindedness."

He added four provisos: the debtor nations must balance their budget; militarism must be abolished and heavy armament eliminated; useless barriers to trade removed; currency stabilized. "We would insist on these preliminaries to giving up our debts."

The United States at first insisted upon the repayment of all Allied debts. A schedule for repayments, aggregating $22,220,188,000, was fixed, but of that barely 12 percent had been met by 1932, when all payments ceased.

The Treaty of Versailles had obligated Germany to pay reparations to the Allies. The liability fixed upon was 132 billion gold marks payable in annual installments of 2 billion plus a sum equal to 26 percent of Germany's yearly exports. Kahn was dismayed. He figured prominently among a group of bankers, economists, and financiers who foresaw that such harsh penalties would reduce Germany to utter chaos and open the door to Soviet aggression. The prediction proved well-founded. When Germany defaulted in 1923, French and Belgian troops occupied the Ruhr. With the deprivation of this rich mining area, the Germans were even less able to produce funds to pay reparations. Whenever they tried to convert marks into foreign currency, the value of the mark diminished, leading to a cataclysmic inflation. Kahn propounded several solutions, including a moratorium. But the world depression of the thirties destroyed Germany's ability to pay any reparations at all, and with the rise of Hitler, virtually every condition imposed at Versailles was disowned.

From Berry Brothers & Co., wine merchants by Appointment to H.M. the King and Queen Alexandra, established in the XVII Century at 3 St. James's Street, S.W., to Otto H. Kahn Esq. on July 22, 1914:

"We have the pleasure to enclose our account for the wine consumed in London this season.

"The unused quantity has been removed from St. Dunstan's and your account credited accordingly.

"With regard to 1900 Vintage Champagne, we fear that next year when you come to London it may be very difficult or probably impossible to procure for you the finest Champagne of the Vintage.

Among the wine which we collected from St. Dunstan's were 17 bottles 1900 Pommery and 44 bottles 1900 Louis Roederer. We venture to suggest that if you would care to take these small quantities of this fine Champagne we would be happy to sell it to you now, and store it for you until next season free of charge, delivering it then when instructed.

"With regard to our 1830 Grande Fine Champagne Brandy which, as we think you will agree, is the finest to be found in the present day, we would say that we are now selling our last puncheon of this, and it is more than likely that by this time next year it will all be gone. We therefore propose putting a further dozen of this on one side for you for delivery when convenient to you. . . ."

And on August 24:

"We have to acknowledge with thanks receipt from our esteemed favour of the 11th inst., with cheque for £37.16 in payment for 12 bottles of 1830 Grande Fine Champagne Brandy, which Brandy we will keep here for delivery as required."

Though Kahn regaled his guests with the finest wines money could buy, he himself drank sparingly and seldom touched hard liquor. In 1926 he offered his friend and fellow Long Islander, the Hearst columnist Arthur Brisbane, $28 a bottle for the tens of thousands of bottles filling the latter's cellar at Hempstead. Brisbane declined.

Such was the quality of his ardent spirits that the popular British writer of thrillers E. Phillips Oppenheim, whom he had met on the Riviera, wrote to him on August 18, 1928, months before embarking for New York: "I am taking you at your word and sending you my address, which . . . is . . . in New York, the Biltmore Hotel, where I expect to arrive on November 9th. . . .

"If you should happen to think of it, and would let your secretary send me just a line there of introduction to the bootlegger of whom we were speaking, I should be exceedingly obliged. I know there are plenty to be found in New York by casual enquiries, but I was at the Ritz Carlton Hotel in New York when those two motor men died there, and I have had a horror of getting hold of the wrong stuff ever since. . . ."

Kahn, who was also vacationing on the Riviera, promised to furnish the bootlegger's address.

Kahn deplored the Eighteenth Amendment, ratified on January 16, 1919, prohibiting "the manufacture, sale or transportation of intoxicating liquors within, the importation thereof into, or the exportation thereof from the United States and all territory subject to the jurisdiction thereof for beverage purposes," and followed in October 1919 by the passage of the Volstead Act, which established measures for its enforcement. Kahn contended two and a half years later: "Whatever we may think of prohibition, I believe the particular fanatical application of that principle as expressed in the Volstead Act goes much too far and is both practically ill-judged and morally a breeder of great harm."

But political allegiance superseded moral repugnance. Of the three presidents who served between the terms of the Democrats Woodrow Wilson and Franklin Roosevelt, all were Republicans and all were "drys" (or in the case of Warren G. Harding, a heavy tippler in private, at least a professed prohibitionist). Kahn, however, believed that the Republicans were better equipped than the Democrats to steer the nation to prosperity, and in September 1920, during Harding's campaign for the Republican nomination, he traveled by private railroad car to Marion, Ohio, where Harding lived. After a private talk inside the house and a press conference outside, the two men stood side by side on the Harding veranda, and each delivered a campaign oration.

"What impressed me most . . . ," said Kahn in a thoroughly misestimated characterization, "is the fine dignity of the man, his manifest sincerity, his clear and calm judgment, his high conception of public service and his determination to do or say nothing but what is sanctioned by his conscience and convictions.

"I was a follower of Colonel Roosevelt, and I believe I had the honor of his confidence. I would not and could not follow reactionary leadership. Senator Harding seeks progress. The greatest attainable wellbeing for all, not for any particular class under our rooftree, is his aim. But he knows that rash and reckless promises or phrases accomplish nothing and lead only to disappointments and to that increased discontent which follows disillusionment. He knows that the structure of wellbeing for all which he means to lead in re-erecting can only stand if built upon the solid foundation of truthfulness and sound, sane and tested doctrines of social justice and not upon socialistic or semi-socialistic appeal.

"It is evident that Senator Harding is a man who not only will not resent but who diligently seeks correct information and sound disinterested advice. It is equally evident that having gathered such advice his mental processes are his own and his decisions are clear-cut and firm. And anyone who thinks that in Senator Harding he will find a 'standpatter,' a man in sympathy with reactionary views, a man that can be swayed or controlled by any clique or combination, will make a great mistake."

It was an almost complete inventory of the qualities lacking in Harding, whose six senatorial years had been chiefly distinguished by his slavish conformity to the will of the party bigwigs. Kahn donated $5,000 to Harding's campaign and was appointed to the Executive Committee on Policies and Platforms. He drafted some of Harding's oratory, devised publicity stratagems, and helped guide the conduct of the campaign.

When Harding won the nomination, Kahn wrote in a letter dated June 17, 1920: "You represent and exemplify in your career that calm-minded, unspectacular, resolutely American type which, equally opposed to the selfish reactionary and to the utopian radical, believes in the time-honored and tested doctrines, spirit and traditions of the American constitutional system of government, the disregard of which within recent years is largely responsible for the troubles that beset us. I am convinced that in what you stand for you express the steady sentiment and the considered views of the great majority of Americans who are too busy with work and duties of the day to make their voices heard above the din of noisy agitators. I am entirely confident that as the people in the course of the campaign will come to know better your personality and views, they will recognize and welcome in you a worthy bearer of the standard under which they wish America to march, progress and prosper, and they will overwhelmingly ratify both the platform and the Chicago convention."

Upon Harding's election Kahn offered him an attractive fortnight of relaxation. ". . . if before your inauguration, or any time after, you would like to have and can spare the time to take a couple of weeks of good air and sunshine, golf and excellent fishing, I should be happy to put my little house at Palm Beach at the disposal of yourself and Mrs. Harding. It is a simple, comfortable place containing six master bedrooms, each with bathroom, and I don't know any better bathing beach anywhere. The golf links is very good and only about a mile and a half distant. My servants can be at the house whenever you like, and I can promise you pretty nearly as good fishing at Point Isabelle, no norther, a real southern sun, comfort and privacy inasmuch as there are no immediate neighbors. . . ."

Harding was unable to accept the invitation, but in the fall of 1921 he invited the Kahns to Washington, where the men played golf, Harding victorious. Kahn wrote afterward: "I am taking pleasure in sending you by express a heavy mashie, an exact duplicate of my own, which makes it a positive joy to get into the 'rough' for the sheer satisfaction of getting out of it. I trust that you will do me the favor of accepting it and that it will serve you as faithfully and effectively as its twin brother has served me for a number of years. . . .

"As to the golf match, I feel that it was morally a draw, and I shall hope that you may feel inclined some other time to renew the contest. I shall always be happy to follow a Presidential summons for this or any other purpose.

"I have instructed the management of the Metropolitan Opera to hold the date of November 26th [*Rigoletto* with Galli-Curci] open in the hope that you and Mrs. Harding will honor the Opera with your attendance on that evening by yourselves or in conjunction with the delegates to the Conference for the Limitation of Armaments. . . ."

The stench of corruption that emanated from Harding's administration, the Teapot Dome scandal with its revelations of conspiracy and bribery by Secretary of the Interior Albert Fall, may partially explain why Kahn never entered politics, though several offices were pressed upon him. He felt, moreover, that he could better serve his adopted country as a private citizen than as a politician.

With neither the austere Calvin Coolidge, who succeeded to the presidency when Harding died in office, nor with the stolid Herbert Hoover, did Kahn establish a relationship as close as he had with Harding. He held no official position under either president, but, true-blue Republican that he was, he had contributed $7,000 to Coolidge's bid for a second term and $25,000 to Hoover's candidacy. When, just before Hoover's election, an anonymous Democrat chided Kahn, a committed "wet," for supporting a "dry," Kahn enumerated his reasons to the press on October 25, after breakfasting with the future president:

"Mr. Hoover is the wisely constructive liberal and humanitarian now that he was in 1920 when he was hailed by leading spokesmen for the liberal cause. . . .

"The kind of prosperity which Mr. Hoover is so earnestly seeking to promote and perpetuate . . . is widely diffused prosperity ['a chicken in every pot'] . . .

"Mr. Hoover is cautious of speech, reticent of promise, averse to resounding professions. . . ."

Alluding to Governor Alfred E. Smith, the Catholic Democratic nominee, "I do not consider that bigotry is an issue in this campaign. To the extent that this ugly and un-American prejudice ever was an issue, as it admittedly was in the Madison Square Garden convention in 1924, it was settled in essence by Governor Smith's nomination. It has been indignantly repudiated by Mr. Hoover. . . .

"As for prohibition, I cannot see the logic of a Republican departing from his usual political affiliations because of that question. . . ."

Finally, the majority of voters to whom Kahn talked, whether "wets" or "drys," clearly indicated that they considered Hoover the better-qualified candidate.

Kahn's last venture into practical politics ended with an ironic twist almost as soon as it began. In October 1929, preparatory to the 1930 senatorial primaries, Republican senator George Higgins Moses of New Hampshire, chairman of the Republican Senatorial Campaign Committee, chose Kahn as the committee's treasurer. This aroused violent controversy within the party. The progressive wing, consisting chiefly of Western senators, opposed the appointment of a Wall Street banker on the grounds that it would signal a repudiation by the Hooverites of the progressives. Yet Kahn, though categorized as a conservative, harbored liberal views. Because contention threatened to split the party, he dropped out.

"My dear Senator," he wrote on October 28, 1929, ". . . I told you that I feared your kindly sentiment toward me, springing from a long friendship, was swaying your judgment, that I felt sure that I was not the right man for the position, that, moreover, I was overwhelmed with demands upon my time and energies and that I hoped very much you would not persist in your request.

"You argued to the contrary and, among other things, pointed to the fact that, while a Wall Street man, I was shown to be, as indeed I am, a liberal in politics. You repeated your invitation. . . .

"I thereupon stated that, though my views were unchanged, I felt that if we want effective party government, such as our political system requires, every citizen should be willing to make good his professions of allegiance by submitting to being drafted, within the limits of reason and possibility, and that if the leaders of the party to which I belong demanded of me a service which did not conflict with my other duties and responsibilities I was not at liberty to refuse, however reluctant I was to accept. . . .

"But the divided reception with which the report of the appointment . . . has met, however erroneous some of the interpretations placed thereon, appears to have confirmed the validity of the doubts which I ventured to express when you offered that position to me, and to justify me in concluding to abstain from occupying it. . . ."

23

From Conquest to Crash

The twenties witnessed some of Kahn's signal victories as well as defeats. It was in 1928 that Kahn, with masterly diplomacy, psychological insight, and personal charm, brought off the most productive stratagem of his career when he effected a conciliation between the two railroad tycoons, Leonor Loree of the Delaware & Hudson and William Atterbury of the Pennsylvania, thereby averting a conflict that would have created chaos in the industry. As a result of Kahn's manipulations, the Pennsy paid Loree more than $100 million for his holdings while retaining intact its own network of four systems, and Kuhn, Loeb banked an immense fortune in Pennsy stock as its management fee in the complicated negotiations that followed.

By 1914 the motion picture industry, having emerged from the nickelodeon era, was developing fast with Charlie Chaplin's shorts, D. W. Griffith's first full-length film, *Judith of Bethulia*, and popular serials like *The Perils of Pauline*, *The Million Dollar Mystery*, and *The Hazards of Helen*. Not precisely Kahn's kind of fare, but he foresaw in the movies an investor's El Dorado. Among the fruitful relationships he had established in the industry was one with Adolph Zukor, chairman of the board of Paramount Pictures. In 1919, at Kahn's prompting, Kuhn, Loeb handled Paramount's first financing, a $2 million stock issue, and from then until 1932 served as its principal banker, with Kahn on Paramount's board of directors. In 1926 Kuhn,

Loeb formed a syndicate that offered $10 million in first mortgage loan certificates of the Paramount Broadway Corporation, a wholly owned subsidiary of Paramount that built the Paramount Theatre. The following year the syndicate sold $16 million worth of bonds. When bankruptcy halted Paramount's progress in 1932, Kahn, who like his Kuhn, Loeb partners had invested heavily in the company, helped formulate plans for its rehabilitation that ultimately proved successful. The same year RKO-Pathé Inc. elected him vice president.

In February 1928 an announcement by the Broadway producer Arch Selwyn that he had bought the American rights to a British film entitled *Dawn* outraged Kahn, among others. Produced and directed by Herbert Wilcox and starring Sybil Thorndike, *Dawn* depicted the martyrdom of Edith Cavell. A British nurse who headed the nursing staff of the Berkendael Institute in Brussels, she did a great deal to raise the standards of her profession. When Germans occupied Belgium in World War I, she joined an underground group that helped Allied fugitives escape into neutral Holland. She was caught, court-martialed, and shot. The film ends with a close-up of her grave.

In England, *Dawn* created a violent controversy. Many prominent figures, such as the statesman and lawyer Lord Birkenhead, all objected to the film's release on the same grounds. Edith Cavell's last words had been "Patriotism is not enough. I must have no hatred or bitterness for anyone." Referring to those words, Birkenhead wrote: "Does anyone suppose that the woman who, at the very moment of her agony, could speak like this would permit her death to be commercialized, with the certain result that the bitter memories associated with it would be kept alive and fertilized so as to prevent the sweet restoration of friendship and good relationships between the nations of the world?"

Selwyn set the American premiere of *Dawn* for May 29 at the Times Square Theatre under the sponsorship of the Film Bureau, an agency for the promotion of cinema through various organizations. Kahn, a member of the bureau's advisory board, promptly tendered his resignation along with a letter echoing Birkenhead and reflecting the idealistic side of his own nature:

". . . Rightminded people everywhere are eager that nothing be done to keep awake or to revive, and that everything be done to assuage and efface, the bitter memories of the late war. They are eager that every endeavor be made to have the peoples of the world, and especially those who lately were in arms against one another, come together in a spirit of good-will and fairness and enlightened cooperation, looking away from the past to the present and the future.

"To use for a sheer commercial purpose (and there is not even a pretense that the purpose of showing the Cavell film is other than to make money) the pathetic story and the tragic end of a signally noble woman is to me an utterly repellent proceeding. It is desecrating, for mere financial gain, a memory which ought to be held sacred, but the appealing eloquence of which should be mute. . . .

"I hope that those proposing to produce that film in America may yet be prevailed upon to withdraw from that intention. Failing that, I trust that the same object may be achieved by the persuasive process of determined non-attendance on the part of the public."

The film opened on schedule. The reviews were, on the whole, favorable, though a number of them echoed Kahn's protest.

Kahn disdained ballyhoo as a vulgar means of attracting audiences to an art as elegant as opera. In the case of a teenage soprano from Kansas, however, he bent a little, and Gatti-Casazza with him, such were the box-office prospects. Marion Talley came from Kansas City in 1922, at the age of fifteen. Gatti found the precocious child's voice extraordinary enough to warrant extensive training and invited her to return for another audition in about three years.

The manager and the president of the Met cooperated closely, proposing new singers to each other, and generally exchanging views concerning the Met's productions, either face-to-face or by correspondence. On September 11, 1925, Gatti wrote to Kahn from Milan:

"I take the liberty of informing you about the new engagements I have made for the Metropolitan, and about the auditions of such artists as you recommended to me particularly in the letters you write me.

"The most important is that of Miss Marion Talley, of Kansas City, who sang for me an excellent audition. I have concluded with her a contract for three years. . . . I realize of course that it is much more difficult to be a prophet in theatrical affairs than in any others; however I hope that this time we have found a good ace who will make happy also all the nationalistic element. . . ." By which he meant those who protested that the Met passed over American singers in favor of foreigners.

The announcement that Marion Talley, now eighteen, would make her debut as the heroine of *Rigoletto* on February 17, 1926, touched off a publicity campaign such as P. T. Barnum might have conceived. Two hundred cheering Kansas City natives traveled to New York for the opening. Since Charles Talley, the soprano's father, was a telegraph operator, Gatti permitted the Associated Press to set up telegraph equipment backstage so that the proud parent could transmit to the world his impressions of his daughter's debut. Kahn contributed his bit to the hoopla by persuading Mayor Walker, a publicity magnet, to occupy his box. More than 4,000 people jammed the theater, and thousands more lingered around the entrances. Next day the *Evening World* headlined its report of the event: 10,000 BATTLE MOUNTED POLICE TO HEAR DEBUT OF 18-YEAR-OLD DIVA.

Talley's self-confidence was invulnerable. Shortly before her first Met night, she was entrusted to the great Marcella Sembrich, the retired soprano who taught at the Juilliard School, for some last-minute work. Madame Sembrich began outlining a program of exercises when Talley interrupted her to explain that she required only coaching in certain roles. The once world-famed prima donna showed her the door.

As long as public curiosity lasted, Talley laid golden eggs. A single matinee performance of *Lucia di Lammermoor* fetched almost $14,000 in the days when the price of seats ranged from $1.65 for family circle to $8.25 for orchestra. But critically, she won few bouquets. "Talley," wrote the distinguished operaphile Irving Kolodin, "showed no greater progress toward artistry than in her previous roles, setting herself carefully for the top notes, and otherwise imposing her curiously personal views upon the music."

Two days after her first *Rigoletto*, Kahn wrote philosophically to the Met's assistant manager, Edward Ziegler: "Even if Marion Talley should turn out, as the majority of the critics and some other benevolent people are good enough to forecast, a lemon, in due course of time, at least she brought us a few full houses and the opportunity to squelch for some time to come the absurd talk about the Metropolitan not being willing and desirous to give a fair chance to American artists."

In the same five-page letter that reported Talley's successful audition, Gatti mentioned, almost by the way and with less enthusiasm, the engagement of "the Italian basso Ezio Pinza. . . . He possesses an excellent voice, a good presence and a very large repertoire. He is credited with being the best basso at present in the Italian career [*sic*]. . . ." Also, "the Danish tenor Lauritz Melchior who will make his debut with us during the coming season. . . ."

"Unfortunately," Kahn in Florence had written to Gatti in Milan the previous spring, "I had no opportunity to convey your message to

Mussolini, as your cable arrived the day after I saw him. I had a long talk with him and was again profoundly impressed by the greatness and irresistible personality of that wonderful man. If only he would take a little better care of himself! The amount of work he does, and of energy he dispenses daily, is simply prodigious. He looked tired and worn, but his intimates assure me that by sheer will-power he has really overcome his recent illness. I do trust they are right and that he will be preserved for many years."

Kahn's greatest discovery for the Met occurred in 1927, though eight years elapsed before the marvel of it was fully recognized. He heard Kirsten Flagstad for the first time as Tosca in Oslo's National Theatre. She was then thirty-four and had been singing in Scandinavia for fourteen years. Kahn, overwhelmed, directed Eric Simon, the Met's German agent, to find out more about her. Flagstad did not trouble to answer Simon's letter. It was not an invitation to an audition, but merely a request for reviews, press notices, and other material relevant to her career. Since they were all written in Norwegian, she did not care to translate them into Simon's tongue. By 1933 she was on the verge of retirement when Gatti and Artur Bodanzky, prompted by Kahn, who had heard her again the year before at the Bayreuth Festival, asked her to meet them in St. Moritz for a private audition. A full-fledged audition followed at the Met, and on February 2, 1935, she made her debut as Sieglinde in *Die Walküre*. "Yesterday," wrote the *New York Herald Tribune*'s music critic, Lawrence Gilman, "was one of those comparatively rare occasions when the exigent Richard might have witnessed with happiness the embodiment of Sieglinde. For this was a beautiful and illusive re-creation, poignant and sensitive throughout, and crowned in its greater moments with an authentic exaltation." Until her last Met performance seventeen years later, Kirsten Flagstad shone as one of its most glorious assets.

For years Kahn had entreated Gatti to revive *Don Giovanni*. The Met's last presentation had occurred in 1908. Gatti had always argued against bringing it back because of the scarcity of singers whom he deemed capable of doing justice to Mozart's masterpiece. In the fall of 1929, however, he managed to assemble a cast likely to satisfy the most exacting taste, and on November 29 Kahn's wish was realized. Ezio Pinza incarnated the Don. Rosa Ponselle, too ill for the first performance, appeared as Donna Anna for the sixth. Elisabeth Rethberg sang Donna Elvira; Editha Fleischer, Zerlina; Beniamino Gigli, Don Ottavio; Pavel Ludikar, Leporello; Léon Rothier, the Commendatore; and Louis D'Angelo, Masetto. Tullio Serafin conducted.

Kahn was dead set against foreign operas translated into English, as sizable segments of Met customers felt they would prefer. "Every opera loses," he insisted, "and is bound to lose, by having the text, to which the composer set the music, twisted into the sound and rhythm of a different language. Especially since Wagner, the connection between the music and the tonal value of the original words is so close that the advantage of having the text understood—or more probably partially understood at best—is more than offset by the disadvantage of having the relation of accent and sound between the text and music arbitrarily set aside. To preserve it, or even approximate it, defies, in many instances, the art of the most skillful translator."

English, in its essence, does not accommodate itself to the silliness and sentimentalities of numerous operatic texts, he contended. Such texts would disrupt the mood of an American audience, whereas the inanities pass unnoticed in their original language. For example, Siegfried's exclamation as he lifts the shield from the slumbering Brünnhilde, usually a well-upholstered woman—"*Das ist kein Mann!*" —sung in English—"That's no man!"—would likelier rouse the listener to laughter than to romantic feelings.

Kahn recalled how, when some directors tried to persuade Caruso to sing Wagnerian tenor roles in the original German instead of his native Italian, the timbre of his voice, his style, changed. When he did sing in German opera houses, he sang in Italian, while the rest of the company stuck to German.

Kahn refuted the argument that opera in France, Germany, and Italy is sung in the language of those respective countries and therefore opera in the United States should be sung in English. Those foreign opera companies, he pointed out, could not afford the cost of presenting each opera in the language of the composer.

"It is the operagoers of Europe who should envy us, as, in fact, their best informed artistic leaders do. Over and over again I have heard visiting musicians from Europe comment enthusiastically upon the veritable revelation it was to them to hear, for instance, the standard Italian operas produced in Italian style and in the Italian language. . . .

"By all this I do not mean that I am opposed, indiscriminately, to the theory of translated opera. I am opposed to it as applied to the Metropolitan. Those who would impose it on the Metropolitan misjudge the function and the mission of that institution and fail to take into account, or be concerned about, the inevitable depreciation of its standard which the adoption of their views would bring about."

That tradition still prevails at the Met.

Yet Kahn wanted to democratize opera. "It is a solemn obligation of a semi-public institution, such as the Metropolitan Opera," President Kahn declared in a pamphlet distributed to subscribers in October 1925, "to provide amply and generously for opera lovers of modest means. I have had frequent occasion to observe how much music means to such devotees of the art. Indeed, I venture the assertion that it means a good deal more to the denizens of, say, Third Avenue than to those of Fifth Avenue."

From the beginning of his tenure as the Met's manager, Gatti-Casazza had frequently reiterated his objections to the structure, which he judged hopelessly inadequate for opera. Of the 4,000 seats, 1,000 of the less expensive—in the dress circle, balcony, and family circle—afforded scarcely any view of the stage because of the plethora of boxes, fifty-four of them, around the horseshoe configuration that placed those seats at right angles to the stage. The scenic mechanisms and the electrical equipment were obsolete, the storage area so cramped that the flats had to be left outdoors between acts and covered with tarpaulins if it rained. The yellow-brick exterior of the building was inappropriate. When Artur Bodanzky visited New York for the first time in 1914, he mistook it for a large stable.

Kahn had promised that a new Met would arise on a more suitable site, but the war intervened, a depression followed, and the choice of a better site proved limited. Moreover, the shareholders of the Metropolitan Opera and Real Estate Company, which owned the building, leasing it to the Metropolitan Opera Company, offered Kahn meager support. As owners of the boxes, they enjoyed a perfect view of the stage and thus had no wish to sell the property and erect a new edifice elsewhere in the interests of the less affluent. Kahn's primary goal was to accommodate the true opera lover rather than the shareholders to whom *Time* magazine compared the feudal barons who "clung to their castles and patents of nobility [just as] the elect of Manhattan's social register cling to the boxes of the Metropolitan."

When Kahn returned from a European trip on August 12, 1924, he assured the press that a new opera house was not simply desirable, but essential. The following year he acquired a block of property on Fifty-seventh Street between Eighth and Ninth avenues, upon which he proposed to construct the new Met. The cost was $3 million. From the Metropolitan Life Insurance Company he borrowed $1.9 million with which the Metropolitan Opera Company would begin construction. The seats would total 5,000, and even the cheapest would command a full view of the stage. The boxes would be reduced to a single parterre crescent of thirty-two, with none in the grand tier.

The entire enterprise depended upon the sale of the old building by the Metropolitan Opera and Real Estate Company, the proceeds to help finance the new building. An offer of $10 million had already been made. If it was not accepted, Kahn figured, he would simply treat his real estate purchase as an investment to be employed in some other fashion. To his chagrin, Fulton Cutting, chairman of the Metropolitan Opera and Real Estate Company board (of which Kahn's old foe, the late J. P. Morgan, had been a member), declared: "If the music lovers of New York wish a new home for opera, they are entitled to have one, and the trustees of the present property will certainly not oppose any obstacle or competition to such a project. They are not, however, of the opinion that the present building is antiquated or is undesirable. . . . It is desirable that the building should be replaced by one larger and more scientifically equipped. I presume the company of which Mr. Kahn is chairman [the Metropolitan Opera Company] will undertake the project."

He was right. The Metropolitan Opera Company members unanimously supported Kahn. So did a minority of the younger members of the Metropolitan Opera and Real Estate Company, most importantly Vincent Astor, E. Roland Harriman, and Edward Harkness. And so did the press and public, the latter expressing their approval with a flood of telegrams and letters.

But social feudalism prevailed. A faction within the Metropolitan Opera and Real Estate Company, headed by the imperious Mrs. Cornelius Vanderbilt, while conceding the need for certain internal improvements, rejected the Fifty-seventh Street site in 1928 and chose no other. The stockholders continued to own their boxes until the 1938–39 season, when the system was supplanted by seasonal leasing. The murky old monolith on Thirty-ninth Street remained the home of the Metropolitan Opera for almost thirty more years, when it moved to Lincoln Center.

The collapse of his plans for the Met was Otto Kahn's first major defeat. Another followed swiftly. Amid the speculative frenzy that convulsed Wall Street in 1928 and most of 1929 two clashing prophecies resounded through the land. Speaking before the annual National Business Conference in Wellesley, Massachusetts, on September 5, 1929, two days before the stock market averages zoomed to an all-time high, Roger Babson, a financial statistician, warned: "I repeat what I said at this time last year and the year before, that sooner or later a crash is coming which will take in the leading stocks and cause a decline from 60 to 80 points in the Dow-Jones Barometer." Factories would shut down and men would be thrown out of work. A severe depression would ensue.

Charles E. Mitchell, chairman of the National City Bank of New York, the country's largest bank, differed sharply. "The industrial condition of the United States is absolutely sound and our credit situation is in no way critical," said he on October 8.

His optimism, expressed three weeks before catastrophe struck, did not extend as far as Professor Irving Fisher's. On October 15, in a prediction memorable for its fatuity, the highly reputed Yale political economist assured the Purchasing Agents Association at its monthly dinner that stock prices had reached "what looks like a *permanently* [italics mine] high plateau."

Kahn could detect no black clouds ahead either, though he spoke somewhat more guardedly. According to a dispatch he had wired from Chicago to Dow, Jones and Company, on June 26, 1928, "Intrinsically, underlying conditions are good and America is still having a fair modicum of prosperity. I think the extremes and excesses of the bull market are ended and stock prices, in future, will more actually portray existing conditions and values and more closely attune the industrial and financial progress of the nation. . . ."

"And there's nothing in sight that would affect the fundamental currents of business to cause any change."

On Wednesday, October 30, 1929, the day after what historians have dubbed "Black Tuesday," *The New York Times* carried the front-page headline: STOCKS COLLAPSE IN 16,410,030-SHARE DAY . . .

24

Depression

Amid the panic and hysteria, the cries of speculators facing ruin, the fading hopes of a rally, Kahn maintained an imperturbable calm. Kuhn, Loeb's deposits shrank from $88.5 million in 1929 to $11.5 million in 1932. Other investment houses endured an even sharper decline, and some were totally destroyed. How many millions Kahn personally lost is unknowable. He was no longer a Croesus, yet not so reduced as to produce a marked change in his life-style. He still traveled incessantly on two continents —except for relatively brief periods during the early thirties when his old enemy, heart trouble, kept him abed.

His benevolences continued, though on a somewhat smaller scale. He could not save the Provincetown Playhouse, which closed its doors toward the end of 1929 when $60,000 in pledges failed to materialize. But he seldom refused requests from creative people for relatively small gifts or loans. His donees included the actress Miriam Hopkins, to whom he had loaned money before the second of her four marriages. "You are a most conscientious debtor," he wrote to her, "and I find my investment is perfectly safe in your keeping." Her husband, a writer named Austin Parker, took her to Barbizon, not far from Paris, for their honeymoon. The union stirred Kahn's romanticism. "To be young, to be in love, and to be in Barbizon," he exclaimed in a letter of congratulation. "What more could one wish?" In 1930 he loaned the actress $1,250, which she repaid after playing on Broadway in *Lysistrata* and starring in her first film, *Fast and Loose*.

To Emjo Basshe, a playwright who had been associated with the defunct Provincetown Playhouse, Kahn wrote, unasked, on November 12, 1930: "I enclose a check [$100] to help you over until your much overdue ship comes in at last. . . ." Two years earlier he had loaned $2,000 to Maurice Schwartz, the founder and star of the Yiddish Art Theatre, who managed to pay back only half the sum. "As to the balance of your indebtedness to me," Kahn assured him on August 13, 1930, "please do not let this matter be a source of worry to you. I know that you will pay when you can, and am perfectly willing to wait." Horace Liveright had borrowed $25,000 in 1927, which he repaid. After the crash he needed and received from Kahn another loan of a thousand dollars.

Two protégés of Sherwood Anderson owed a modest boost to Kahn. ". . . Not many of our painters have much straight sensual joy in life," the novelist wrote on January 26, 1929, from Marion, Virginia, where he published two newspapers, one Democratic, the other Republican, "—in fruits, hills, women's bodies, skies, rivers, etc. . . .

"I have within the last year found a young man [Charles Bockler] who has these qualities. He lives in New York and makes his living as a bookkeeper for a big banking house. . . . He is the son of a small town banker of North Dakota who went broke by a failure of the wheat crop out there some years ago.

"This young man is, I should say, about twenty-eight to thirty years of age. I met him and got acquainted with his work by accident. He goes to work in the bank at five o'clock in the afternoon, after the stock exchange closes, and works until midnight. In the mornings and afternoons he paints. His wife is a stenographer and works every day. . . .

"What I want to know is this—will you be one of five or six men to pay this young man three hundred dollars for a painting. . . ."

Three days later Kahn enclosed a check for $300 in a letter that began: "What a refreshing, stimulating, zestful combination you are! A writer, journalist, editor, painter (at least in spirit), critic, all around human, and, what is a particularly rare thing in America, your own distinctive self. . . ."

The following April, Bockler gave his first exhibition at Baltimore's Charcoal Club.

The second protégé was David Greear, "a little white-haired mountain white kid." Anderson had found him in the mountains, the son of a lumber-camp engineer. "The lumber business has gone bad," he wrote to Kahn on July 2, 1930. "They are farming now, on a little North Georgia hill farm. . . .

"[He] is one of the most talented little rats I ever saw. He is sharp as chain lightning. He had got hold of a cheap set of carving tools and alone, with no one to guide him, was doing wood carvings, crude, of course, but damned significant stuff.

"I've been watching the kid. He's only about fifteen. He works like a little Turk and his work constantly improves. . . .

"I'd like to give him a chance.

"The point is this—the schools down in those Georgia hills are rotten. The boy can't get beyond the lowest grammer [sic] grade . . . but I think he should be put through high school.

"He will need about $400 a year for four years. . . ."

On July 7 Kahn offered to send $400 for the first year, "hoping that the Fates and friends of yours, other than myself, will find ways and means to take care of the young man after that." On July 16 he sent Anderson a check.

How the "talented little rat" fared we do not know.

One of Kahn's largest contributions during the depression era was $2,000 to the American Jewish Joint Distribution Committee in its quest for funds to alleviate the sufferings of Eastern European Jews. In addition, donations ranging from a few dollars to a hundred dollars or so flowed to innumerable religious organizations, Christian and Jewish.

Despite the deepening depression, Kahn's optimism persisted. According to a report by the financial writer Merryle S. Rukeyser on July 23, 1930, he predicted, without attempting a timetable, complete economic recovery. The following year he was less sanguine. In a letter to Gatti-Casazza on August 5, 1931, he wrote: "Economic conditions here continue to be very depressed." Then he added a comment, astonishing coming from one who abhorred violence and believed unquestionably in the democratic process: "The world's statesmen (with the exception of Mussolini and, in his particular field, Stalin) as well as its financiers, have lamentably failed in effective leadership." Still an admirer of the Italian dictator and a seeming endorser of the Soviet tyrant, he was undoubtedly so impressed by the economic order they sought to impose upon their countries that he failed to recognize the enormities they perpetrated in the process.

By 1932 his optimism had returned. Stopping briefly in Jacksonville, Florida, en route to Palm Beach, Kahn assured an Associated Press reporter, on January 3, that the national economy would recover within six months. (He was off by a decade.) But he entered a cautionary note: "Someone has said, 'Confidence is suspicion asleep,' and we must keep it asleep."

Dismayed by Hoover's fecklessness in the eye of the storm, Kahn executed a political reversal that stunned his Wall Street colleagues. He voted for Franklin Delano Roosevelt. He voted for him, and on May 12, 1933, he conveyed to him his general objections to the Securities Act of 1933, then about to become the subject of a conference between the Senate and the House. "I make free to reiterate," he wrote, "on the strength of many years' experience in the investment business here and abroad and of some little knowledge of practical economics, that the securities bills, if enacted in the shape in which they left the Senate and the House, respectively, would inflict great damage upon the economic structure of the country, would retard enterprise and gravely interfere with the legitimate needs of trade and commerce."

Roosevelt answered: ". . . The difficulty about the opposition to the Securities Bill is that no one seems to be in the least specific in regard to what section or sections will hurt legitimate business. I know you will not mind my being frank with you."

Kahn needed no urging. On May 23 he wrote again, specifying his recommendations for amendments. He assured Roosevelt that he was not advancing objections *"pro domo,"* but for the general economy. "It [the Securities bill] imposes an unfair liability on each individual seller of all securities, Government bonds, commercial paper and common stocks, now outstanding or to be issued. Broadly speaking, the bill imposes requirements as to detailed information and responsibility upon officers, directors and underwriters which are unworkable and destructive of the free investment market which is absolutely essential for the free flow of capital funds needed by industry."

It was too late, however, to affect the outcome. Four days later Roosevelt signed into law the Securities Act of 1933. The following year, though, the Securities Act was amended to incorporate a number of suggestions advanced by Kahn. For example, from Kahn's memorandum to Roosevelt: damages that an investor could claim should be "limited to those arising as a direct consequence of the untrue statement or deceitful omission." The amended act relieved defendants of liability for damages that they could prove had no relation to their misconduct.

Another addition reflected Kahn's conviction that "only those underwriters should be liable who contract directly with the issuer or who hold themselves out as sponsors for the issue. The liability for the entire issue imposed on subunderwriters with small participations is so out of proportion that it will prevent such underwriting."

Kahn was also concerned lest a suit might be brought years later—that is, after the securities covered by the registration statement had been sold. The 1934 amendments to the 1933 Act reduced the periods of limitations during which an action could be brought for certain violations of the Act.

What influence Kahn's analyses may have exerted upon the legislators who in 1934 enacted these amendments to the Securities Act is no longer possible to determine.

25

Finale

The last of the German Kahns.

In 1933, soon after Hitler became chancellor, the first Nazi official act of anti-Semitism to affect the Kahns was the closing of the Bernhard Kahn Reading Room in Mannheim, founded by his widow in his memory and supported by his son Otto from its inception. Further subsidy from Otto Kahn was decreed unacceptable and the honorary supervisor, Paul Eppstein, dismissed.

On October 5, 1927, at 1100 Fifth Avenue, Otto Kahn had given a dinner in honor of his visiting German brother-in-law, Felix Deutsch, privy councillor of defense in the government of the Weimar Republic as well as director general of A.E.G. Sixty notables were invited, chiefly publishers and industrialists. It was the last time Otto saw the in-law to whom he had written during the war, execrating Prussianism. Felix was spared the lash of Hitler. He died of natural causes the following year at the age of seventy.

Felix's widow, Lili, was deprived of her citizenship under the Nazi anti-Jewish laws of July 14, 1933. With her daughter Gertrude and her daughter's husband, Gustav Brecher, she managed to flee to the Belgian seaport of Ostend, where, after German troops occupied the country, they were awaiting an opportunity to move south through France. Nothing more was ever heard of them.

In 1943 Nazi thugs brutalized the hapless Paul Kahn in Athens, permanently crippling him. He died of his injuries four years later.

After a long, fruitful career as pianist, composer, and teacher, Robert Kahn and his wife, Katharina, retreated to their summer house, Obdach, near Mecklenburg, in 1933. The name of the house derived from one of his songs, "Obdach gegen Sturm" (Shelter from the Storm). By 1937 the Robert Kahns' life under the Nazis had become intolerable, and they emigrated to England, settling in the town of Biddenden, Kent, where the musician died at eighty-six, after converting to the Church of England.

Kahn's health declined with his fortune. He suffered from high blood pressure, angina pectoris, and a lung infection. On October 26, 1931, having served the Metropolitan Opera for twenty-eight years, first as a dominant board member, then board chairman, and finally Met president, he resigned. He also relinquished his board membership and vice presidency of the Philharmonic. Soon after, he had a confidential talk with *The New York Times* music critic Olin Downes, which Downes recounted to Irving Kolodin as follows: "He said it was a good thing for him, and it was a good thing for the Metropolitan Opera Company that he had resigned his position with that organization. They were content to have him take much of the responsibility for the practical operations of the organization and to interest himself in the affairs of the company, as long as it gave them no trouble or additional burden. He said the primary cause, he believed, of their coolness to him was the fact he was a Jew, and that they were not wholly favorable to having a Jew as the chairman of their Board of Directors. As a result of this feeling, he continued, he had to work almost entirely alone, with very little cooperation from any but one or two of the members. If he had had cooperation and been given a greater amount of support than he felt he would be likely to receive, he would have experimented more boldly than the Metropolitan had experimented, with repertory and in various aspects of stage presentation. Under the circumstances, he felt that the only advisable course to pursue would be one which guaranteed popular support of the Metropolitan performances and a balanced budget."

Paul Cravath succeeded Kahn, but the latter continued to exercise an active and influential voice on the board. His last major coup, if a sneaky one, occurred not long before his resignation. William S. Paley, founder and president of the Columbia Broadcasting System, had conceived the idea of weekly opera broadcasts. He approached Kahn, who initially recoiled from the prospect of the sedate Met so cheapening itself.

Paley persisted. He invited Kahn, Edward Ziegler, and Gatti-Casazza to his office, having meanwhile deployed microphones around the opera stage, and transmitted the performance by closed circuit to

CBS. The trio sat silent and tense through the overture and into the first act. Suddenly Kahn jumped to his feet, crying, "I can't believe it. It's simply marvelous . . . and just imagine, hearing that wonderful music and those marvelous voices and we don't have to look at those ugly faces!"

Thus assured, Paley hastened to conclude the logistical details with Ziegler. Then, without warning, the Met, on Kahn's advice, signed up with the National Broadcasting Company, because Kahn considered it more prestigious than CBS. Paley never forgave him. "It was," he recalled, "a callous, dirty trick. . . ."

The first NBC opera broadcast, the Christmas matinee of 1931, was Humperdinck's *Hänsel und Gretel* with Editha Fleischer and Queena Mario in the title roles. The most recent Met broadcast, as I write this, Massenet's *Werther*, on April 16, 1988, was the 949th.

In a wistful mood Kahn sent Constantin Stanislavsky a letter dated May 18, 1932, congratulating him on what he mistook to be his seventieth birthday.* "The times through which the world has been passing, and in the midst of which it still struggles lamentably, have emphasized all too sharply that the only dependable and lasting values are those of the spirit. . . ."

For almost six weeks, in the fall of 1932, he was confined to his bed with a recalcitrant heart. "One thing I believe I can promise when I come to face the world again," he wrote to Herbert Bayard Swope, former editor of the *New York World*, on November 1: "I shall be a somewhat wiser man than heretofore, in the sense of being more clearly conscious of the relative worthwhileness of things. I am trying to practice philosophy and learn somewhat late in life the real meaning of 'vanitas vanitatum.' "

Three days later he wrote to Beaverbrook: "I should rather be in England than anywhere else in the world but I fear I shall have to wait till April is here."

By the new year he was able to resume some of his customary activities, though at a slower pace. He made two leisurely, restorative tours of Europe. In New York he missed few opening nights, and toward the spring was again behind his desk at Kuhn, Loeb. With high-grade bonds in their vaults, the company had survived the storm of 1929, but Kahn sustained such heavy capital losses in his personal investments that for the three years 1930, 1931, and 1932 he paid no

---

* Stanislavsky's seventieth birthday actually fell on January 18, 1933.

federal income tax. Before the crash he had sold to his daughter Maud five blocks of miscellaneous stocks. By 1930 their value had severely declined. At his request Maud returned them, thereby establishing a tax loss of $117,584.

The severest strain Kahn endured began on June 27, 1933, when he was summoned to testify before the Subcommittee of the Senate Committee on Banking and Currency. With the ferocious Ferdinand Pecora as counsel, the subcommittee was investigating the financial practices that had contributed to the crash and the ensuing depression, and seeking the groundwork for reforms. (Out of this and subsequent investigations developed the Securities and Exchange Commission.)

Because of Kahn's recent illness, a physician accompanied him to the Caucus Room in the Senate Office Building where the hearings took place. Kahn showed no signs of debility. Straight-backed as always, smiling and affable, sartorially impeccable, a rose for a boutonniere, his white mustache waxed to fine points, he looked younger than his sixty-six years. His testimony, candid and detailed, though couched in his usual florid style, not only revealed the workings of a potent international investment banking firm second only to the House of Morgan, but propounded measures to purge Wall Street of its worst practices.

"How would you describe the nature of the business conducted by the firm of Kuhn, Loeb and Company?" Pecora asked.

"The firm . . . buys and sells securities from and to its clients," Kahn smoothly replied. "It accepts deposits from its clients but not from the general public, and it is not in the business of soliciting deposits. . . . It is our function to advise our clients . . . upon financial affairs in general. . . ."

Pecora: "Does the clientele of your firm consist of any particular persons—that is, persons engaged in any particular kind of business?"

Kahn: "The clientele of our firm, Mr. Pecora, is primarily corporations engaged in different lines of business. We have few private clients. . . ."

Pecora: "With what kind of corporations?"

Kahn: "Railroad corporations and some industrial corporations . . . they would constitute the majority of our clientele. . . ."

Pecora: "What is the general method, or what has been the general method by which your firm has financed railroad operations?"

Kahn: "Well, I should say precisely the same method by which a lawyer approaches clients."

The sally caused laughter, especially among the lawyers present.

Pecora: "Well, lawyers are not supposed to approach clients."

Kahn: "I was coming to that, Mr. Pecora. Or the method by which a doctor approaches a patient who is sick. He does not go after him. Ethically and as a standard of the legal profession you are not permitted to go after him. And I do not suppose that a doctor would be permitted to go after a patient under the ethical standards of the medical profession. For instance, if someone told him that 'Mr. Smith in the next block is very sick with pneumonia, you better run in and try to find out if you can get him.' That would not be the way to do it. He gets his clients by reason of his reputation for ability and for successful cures and for sound advice given. And so in our case it has long been our policy and our effort to get our clients, not by chasing after them, not by praising our own wares, but by an attempt to establish a reputation which would make clients feel that if they have a problem of a financial nature, Dr. Kuhn, Loeb and Company is a pretty good doctor to go to."

Pecora: "Well, the contact having been established between doctor and patient, or in your case between banker and railroad, what is the next step in the operation of financing the railroad?"

Kahn: "A railroad . . . would come to us and would say: 'We have such and such a problem to solve, being a problem of a financial nature. We would like to get your advice as to the best kind of security to issue for that purpose—and, by the best kind of security I mean a security which on the one hand gives to the railroad the most useful instrument, not only for immediate purposes but for long-time purposes, and gives to the public the greatest possible protection without tying up the railroad unduly and beyond what is safe for it.' So, he says: 'Will you tell us what is the best kind of instrument for that purpose? Should it be a mortgage bond? Should it be a debenture? Should it be a convertible bond? Should it be preferred stock? Should it be an equity? We would like you to look into it and tell us. Here are facts and figures. Go through them. . . .'

"We have no show window. Our only attractiveness is our good name and our reputation for sound advice and integrity. If that is gone, our business is gone, however attractive our show window might be. We hold our position, and every leading banker holds his position, solely by reason of the confidence of the community in his skill, in his sponsorship, in his integrity, in his desire to be thorough and to advise correctly."

He denounced ruthless competition among bankers for foreign bond issues, and as an egregious example he recounted the behavior of a group of his colleagues between the years 1926 and 1928: ". . . to my own knowledge, fifteen American bankers sat in Belgrade, Yugoslavia, making bids and a dozen American bankers sat in a half dozen South and Central American States, or in Balkan States—. . . that kind of cutthroat competition, one outbidding the other foolishly, recklessly, to the detriment of the public, compelling him to force bonds upon the public at a price which is not determined by the value of that security so much as by his eagerness to get it—that kind of competition I hope is ended."

Senator Edward P. Costigan, Democrat from Colorado, interjected: "Was your firm represented in this competition?"

Kahn: "Never, Senator. Not once."

From 1925 to 1929 American investors bought $90 million worth of first mortgage bonds of the Mortgage Bank of Chile. Five issues unconditionally guaranteed by the Chilean government were underwritten by Kuhn, Loeb and other investment companies. When Pecora referred to the transaction, Kahn, rueful as well as proud, remarked, "You have touched a sore point," for the bonds were now quoted at about fourteen cents on the dollar. "It is the only issue which my firm has made since the war, the only foreign issue which is in default.

"We made it after what we believed to be a very careful and thorough examination. We had before us the record of a country whose constitutional history was almost free from revolutions and which, for many, many years had had a favorable balance of trade. . . . Everything that we could find out seemed to prove that this was a bond that we were justified in sponsoring."

Senator Alben W. Barkley, Democrat from Kentucky, wanted to know whether other bankers had attempted to steal Kuhn, Loeb's clients. Kahn knew of several. "I hope you will not press me," he said.

Pecora: "Has it succeeded? Has the effort succeeded in these instances?"

Kahn: "In some instances, yes. We are poorer for that effort."

Barkley: "Do you still regard them as reputable bankers?"

Kahn: "I regard them as reputable bankers. I would not have done what they did, but who am I to sit in judgment upon others? 'Let him who is without sin first cast the stone.' I guess I am guilty of other sins, too. But this particular thing I do not believe in."

He did not attempt to exonerate his fellow bankers from the

gambling lunacy of 1928–29 that led to catastrophe for millions and years of depression.

Pecora: "Do you think that bankers are in a position to apply influence or brakes to such mania?"

Kahn: "They should be."

While Kuhn, Loeb emerged from the Pecora investigation relatively unscathed, it did not entirely escape censure. The core of its offense was the Pennroad Corporation, a holding company organized in 1929 to acquire railroad properties before its competitors, notably J. P. Morgan and Company, could do so. Following Kahn's advice, Kuhn, Loeb did not sell Pennroad shares to the public, but to the Pennsylvania Railroad's 157,000 stockholders at $15 a share. Those investors, however, did not actually receive the shares, but were persuaded to accept instead "voting trust certificates." Such certificates indicated that though they owned the stock they allowed three trustees to retain it and to vote it for the owners. Thus, this trio, which remained in office for a decade, completey controlled Pennroad.

Kahn himself had played the principal role in devising the Pennroad maneuver, yet he came to denounce it as one that robbed the stockholders of control. The voting certificates, he told Pecora, were "inventions of the devil."

Kahn testified for the better part of three days. When he left the witness chair, as blithe and genial as when he first occupied it, the chairman of the committee, Senator Duncan U. Fletcher, Democrat from Florida, hastened to thank him for his "kind and generous" cooperation. Even Pecora, who had striven hard to uncover any wrongdoing by Kuhn, Loeb, proclaimed: ". . . our thanks to the witness and his firm for the cooperation they have uniformly accorded us from the beginning of our investigation into their activities."

26

"I Shall Die a Jew"

It was perhaps an increasing sense of mortality that brought Kahn at sixty-six closer to the Roman Catholic Church, and by 1933 he had determined to convert. He never did so. What prevented him were the horrors being visited by the Nazis upon his fellow Jews in Europe. They moved him to proclaim in a magazine interview: "I was born a Jew, I am a Jew and shall die a Jew." (The current quip in Jewish circles was "Otto Kahn has been bar mitzvah'd at last.")

On Christmas Day 1933 the gossip columnist Walter Winchell driveled in the *Daily Mirror* with his wonted lack of accuracy: "FLASH!—Otto H. Kahn is a Jew again! . . . The renowned banker, whose sons were married at St. Thomas's, where he is a member, fervently announced his return to his 'own people' last week at a private dinner by financiers of the Jewish Federation. . . . Mr. Kahn stated he would rather be 'a real Jew in a small way than the biggest man of any other thing.' "

Kahn, who had uttered no such statement, repressed his disgust and replied gently to Winchell on the twenty-ninth:

"A proverb (Latin or Greek) says that even Homer nods at times.

"May I point out, in all good temper and without any sense of grievance, that, in the reference which you made to me . . . the following 'noddings' occurred:

"1st. I have never ceased to be a Jew, though I never belonged, and do not now belong, to any Jewish congregation.

"2nd. I am not, and never was a member of St. Thomas's Church, or any other Christian Church.

"3rd. My sons were not married at St. Thomas's. (It is true that they are of the Christian faith, but they belong to no congregation.)

"4th. I attended no dinner 'given by financiers of the Jewish Federation' and made no statement of the nature attributed to me."

Winchell apologized.

What Kahn did state, as co-chairman, with the president of RCA David Sarnoff, of the Minute Campaign of the Jewish Federation, was:

"This is not the time or the occasion for the Jew to blow his own horn and to point to the immortal achievements of his race and to the outstanding services which it has rendered in every field thrown open to its genius. The enemies of our race are doing that by the very infamy and atrocity of their warfare; they are challenging the conscience of the world which no man and no nation can do with impunity for any length of time. The very centuries are rising up to testify on behalf of our deathless race. History has shown that, however fierce and cruel intolerance, it always meets its battle of the Marne.

"But this *is* the time for us all to take increased devotion to the Jewish race from the very sorrows which have now befallen it, one of the most tragic chapters in its long history of sorrows (a chapter unbelievable in our day and generation, but alas! all too hideously true). In the face of bitter and ruthless provocation, this is the time, indeed, for every one of us to heed the call of the blood which courses in his veins, and loyally and proudly to stand up and be counted.

"And this meeting *is* the occasion to call for a conspicuous and resounding manifestation of Jewish cohesion and charity on behalf of the great cause of Federation."

The premiere, on February 10, 1934, of Howard Hanson's *Merry Mount*, the libretto adapted by Richard Stokes from a story by Nathaniel Hawthorne, reflected for the last time one of Kahn's most cherished dreams—to promote American opera. He had commissioned *Merry Mount* years earlier before Hanson wrote a note. During the twenty-eight years Kahn wielded power at the Met, ten other native works were staged, none of them a notable success.*

* * *

* Frederick Converse's *Pipe of Desire* (1910); Horatio W. Parker's *Mona* (1912); Walter Damrosch's *Cyrano de Bergerac* (1913); Reginald de Koven's *The Canterbury Pilgrims* (1917); Charles Wakefield Cadman's *Shanewis* (1917); Joseph Breil's *The Legend* (1919); John Adams Hugo's *The Temple Dancer* (1919); Henry Kimball Hadley's *Cleopatra's Night* (1920); Deems Taylor's *The King's Henchman* (1927) and *Peter Ibbetson* (1931).

On Thursday, March 29, 1934, at his Kuhn, Loeb desk, Kahn dictated his last letter. It was addressed to the editor of *The Jewish Who's Who*, John Simons, who had circulated a report on the suitability of South West Africa as a resettlement colony for Jews. Kahn assured him that he would study it with interest.

His principal nonbanking operation that day was preparing a speech he planned to deliver in the evening when presiding at a dinner for a group of visiting British dignitaries. Before completing the draft he joined a young partner, Benjamin Buttenwieser, for lunch in the company's fourth-floor private dining room. Buttenwieser, who joined the firm in 1918 (and after World War II resigned to take up the post of United States assistant high commissioner for Germany), enjoyed a congenial friendship with the older man. One day, in 1929, following his engagement to Helen Lehman, daughter of Arthur Lehman, third-born of the illustrious banking Lehman Brothers, Kahn told him: "You go down the street [to 22 William Street, the Lehman offices] and tell your future in-laws I want ten thousand shares of the common stock being offered at $104. If not, the engagement is off." Buttenwieser gladly complied. Two days later the stock soared to $134. Then came the crash.

Near the end of the lunch together, while sipping coffee, Kahn fell forward. Buttenwieser caught him, and Kahn died in his arms.

The partners sent for an ambulance as well as Kahn's personal physician, Dr. Harold Hyman, who presently informed the press: "Mr. Kahn had had general arteriosclerosis for some years. With that, he had high blood pressure and had suffered attacks of angina pectoris. He was suddenly seized today with what was probably an acute occlusion of the coronary artery and died instantly."

Buttenwieser typewrote a short statement for the press, repeating the cause of death and adding: "I hope I never have to give out such sad news again."

A crowd gathered around the renowned banking house, and the flag over the William Street entrance was lowered to half-mast. At midafternoon a coffin was carried out of the building, loaded into a hearse, and driven uptown to 1100 Fifth Avenue. A few minutes later J. P. Morgan the younger and two of his partners walked over from their headquarters at 23 Wall Street, entered the Kuhn, Loeb building, stood there in silence for five minutes, and silently departed.

Addie Kahn and her son Roger were waiting by the main entrance to the Fifth Avenue house. At sight of the coffin Addie burst into tears and wept so long and so bitterly that she could not discuss funeral arrangements.

When composed, she decided that the funeral services should be conducted according to the rites of Reform Judaism, and she so notified Rabbi Samuel Goldenson of Temple Emanu-El, a Reform synagogue. (Orthodox Judaism requires burial within twenty-four hours of death, whereas Reform Judaism imposes no such limitation.) For three days Kahn lay in the vast reception room, shadowed by old paintings, while friends and colleagues filed past the bier.

On March 30—Good Friday—the Met staged *Parsifal*. During the intermission preceding the third act Mayor Fiorello LaGuardia appeared before the curtain. "May we pause for just one moment," he said, "to pay a silent tribute to the memory of a great New Yorker whose name is linked with this institution and who has done so much to make grand opera in New York possible."

At Carnegie Hall the next day Toscanini conducted the New York Philharmonic Symphony Orchestra in Beethoven's *Eroica* symphony. A program note indicated that the slow second movement, *Marche funèbre: adagio assai*, should be regarded as a tribute to Otto Kahn for his support as vice president and trustee of the organization. By request the audience remained silent for several minutes after the performance.

Monday, April 2, a hearse, followed by a motorcade, conveyed the dead man to Cold Spring Harbor. Inside the immense imitation French château, Rabbi Goldenson read a brief prayer service, attended only by members of the family and a few close friends. A cortege then accompanied the coffin to Memorial Cemetery, which was nondenominational, though owned by St. John's Church. The body was the first to be interred in the Kahn family plot.

Kahn left $3,970,869 in liquid assets and approximately $15 million in real estate. His will divided his shrunken fortune equally among his four children. Addie received nothing since she was wealthy in her own right as Abraham Wolff's heiress. The real estate, along with the paintings and other valuables, were soon disposed of. The Fifth Avenue house became the Convent of the Sacred Heart.

Oheka passed through some curious incarnations. In 1939, empty and dilapidated by neglect and vandalism, it was acquired for a nominal sum by the New York City Sanitation Department as a recreational retreat for its 15,000 "white wings." It was renamed Sanita, and the opening-day festivities were catered by Horn & Hardart. The tony neighbors were less than enchanted by the sight of garbagemen disporting themselves all over the estate, and the local authorities, charging a violation of zoning laws, shut the place down. Next came the War Shipping Administration, which leased Oheka as a training center for merchant marine radio operators. They were succeeded after World War II by a boys' military academy, which bulldozed the once lush gardens, put up Quonset huts, and sent armored tanks lumbering up and down driveways formerly reserved for the Kahns' Cadillacs and Rolls-Royces. The Eastern Military Academy lasted some thirty years before it went bankrupt, and Oheka once again fell into shabby desuetude, the haunt of vandals, arsonists, and pot-smokers.

The latest lord of Oheka is a flamboyant Long Island real estate developer named Gary Melius. He bought the estate for $1.5 million and spent some $12 million reconstructing it. Under the company name of Castle Ventures Ltd., he proposed to create within the edifice thirty-seven condominiums, priced from $750,000 to $1.1 million. Though he claimed to have received 300 offers, the reconstruction came to a halt in 1986. He planned to occupy the second floor himself with his wife and four children, seeking meanwhile some profitable purpose for the remainder of the building and the grounds. At last accounts he was offering to sell Oheka for $52 million.

Addie Kahn survived her husband by fifteen years. She succeeded him on the board of the Met, as her daughter Margaret would succeed her. She was partly instrumental in bringing Rudolf Bing to the Met as general manager. She remained an intimate friend of Bernard Berenson to her last day, occasionally chaffing him as he chaffed her. She continued to sojourn frequently at I Tatti, and to travel with him, to the fury of Nicky Mariano, who once observed: "I can't see why she brings seventy-five dresses. They all look the same."

Addie owned a pair of the new infrared binoculars that enabled her to see in the dark. One summer in Venice, Berenson and some companions, including Addie, Nicky, and Frederick Hartt, an art historian, took a launch to visit the cathedral on the island of Torcello. Hartt recalled: "There was Addie, well in her seventies, snuggling up to B. B. . . . saying, 'Shall I adjust these glasses for you?' and he was answering, 'My eyes are the same as yours. We have so much in common, don't we, darling?' Nicky was in a rage."

In his diary for July 2, 1947, Berenson wrote: "Addie Kahn, now staying here [at I Tatti], is pro-Soviet and pro-Arab. How account for the first is a problem, for she resents every infringement of her right to do as she pleases with her own, and would not readily merge with a national pool her immense income. We avoid discussion, the more so as her tether is short and one quickly reaches the stake to which she is tied."

Like her husband, Addie Kahn died of a heart attack. She was staying at Claridge's Hotel in London on May 15, 1949, finishing a letter to Berenson, when stricken. Her body was flown to New York, and on the twenty-fourth, following a brief ceremony in the chapel of Memorial Cemetery at Cold Spring Harbor, cremated, and the ashes buried in the family plot beside Otto Kahn. As arranged by the older son, Gilbert, an Episcopalian minister, the Reverend Lyman Bleecker, officiated.

On December 28, 1951, a year and a half after the Kahn heirs sold at private auction for $90,000 Rembrandt's *Portrait of a Young Student* and donated the proceeds to the Metropolitan Opera, a bronze plaque was embedded in the south wall of the parterre floor (it was later moved to Founders Hall on the lower level of the new building at Lincoln Center):

> IN GRATEFUL MEMORY OF MR. & MRS. OTTO H. KAHN AND IN RECOGNITION OF THEIR LIFELONG INTEREST IN THE METROPOLITAN OPERA COMPANY.
>
> THROUGH THEIR GENEROSITY THE NEW PRODUCTION OF DON CARLO IN THE SEASON 1950–1951 AND COSÌ FAN TUTTE 1951–1952 WERE MADE POSSIBLE.

Source Notes

The following abbreviations have been used:

COHC   Columbia University Oral History Collection
KP   Kahn Papers in the William Seymour Theatre Collection, Princeton University
MOA   Metropolitan Opera Archives
NYT   *The New York Times*

1. The Strategist

PAGE
5 "the Lorenzo de Medici of his day . . .": Strauss, p. 71.

2. The Kahns of Mannheim

6 "excellent and very strong. . . .": Letter of November 9, 1777.
7 "I did not yet know . . .": Goethe, p. 440.
9 "*Wo man singt* . . .": Matz, *Opera News*, March 23, 1959.
10 "Isn't she beautiful!": Matz, *Many Lives*, p. 9.
11 "An intelligent man . . .": Rolston.
11 "It had the natural and irreparable effect . . .": Letter to *The Reflex*, January 1928.
12 "Those of us sitting in a line . . .": Address before Harvard Business School, November 13, 1924.

SOURCE NOTES

12 "It was a useful, salutary training . . .": Forbes, p. 216.
12 "I hate the arrogance of wealth . . .": *New York World-Telegram*, March 31, 1934.
13 "Brilliant. Formidable. . . .": Juxon, p. 16.

3. America

15 ". . . I think that a majority of the men . . .": *NYT*, April 15, 1893.
19 "We employ no salesmen . . .": *Newsweek*, July 8, 1933.
20 "You are made for America": Adler, vol. 1, p. 9.
20 "I know you haven't any clear conception . . .": Quoted by Birmingham, p. 165.
21 "As conditions now stand . . .": American Jewish Archives.
22 IF THEY DON'T PAY . . .: Buttenwieser, COHC, vol. 2, p. 280.

4. A "Two-Dollar Broker"

23 "A draggled creature . . .": Eckenrode and Edmunds, p. 56.
23 "two streaks of iron rust . . .": Birmingham, p. 169.
24 "It's that little fellow Harriman . . .": Kennan, vol. 1, p. 123.
24 "Mr. Harriman, my associates and I . . .": Ibid., pp. 123–25.
26 "Engine taking water, sir . . .": Eckenrode and Edmunds, p. 54.
27 "A promising chap . . .": *New York American*, January 2, 1928.
27 "I must atone for my wealth. . . .": *Mirrors of Wall Street*, p. 170.
28 "showed people what God could have done . . .": Rolston.
28 "Thank God . . .": KP.

5. Banking and the "Art Job"

29 "You just go ahead . . .": Matz, *Many Lives*, p. 55.
32 "Mr. Kahn, I understand . . .": Buttenwieser, COHC, vol. 2, pp. 266–69.
33 ". . . the outgoing mail . . .": Strauss, p. 82.
33 ". . . I remember one of the things . . .": Ascher, COHC, p. 106.
33 "No, no, not you— . . .": Ibid., p. 107.
33 "Call up Max. . . .": Ibid., p. 112.
34 "Reorganizations embody a certain element . . .": Forbes, p. 218.

6. Cedar Court

36 "You are instructed . . .": Taber and Taber.
37 "Give him anything he wants!": Author's interview with source who requested anonymity.
37 "Ask her yourself . . .": Ibid.

40 "You will have to learn to adjust your way of living . . .": *House Tour*, p. 42.
40 "Meet me at six-fifteen . . .": Mrs. Charles Gleaves, interview with author.
41 "It's not the swift work that wears you out . . .": *The New Jerseyan*, January 19, 1914.
41 "Please telephone to Morristown . . .": KP, August 21, 1917.

7. Harriman Triumphant

45 "It shows a cynicism . . .": Roosevelt, vol. 17, pp. 434–35.
45 "The real trouble with Harriman . . .": Bishop, vol. 2, p. 42.
45 "That some trouble has been caused . . .": Ibid., p. 43.
45 "The Harriman Extermination League . . .": "Edward Henry Harriman: The Last Figure of an Epoch," in Kahn, *Of Many Things*, p. 141.
46 "Whether long continued . . .": Ibid., p. 142.
47 "I owe the public nothing.": Matz, *Many Lives*, p. 32.
47 "Where is this thing going to stop? . . .": I.C.C., Proc. Spec. Ex., pp. 802–803, quoted in Trottman, pp. 333–34.
48 "There is more before us . . .": "Edward Henry Harriman," in Kahn, *Of Many Things*, p. 140.
49 "Not infrequently . . .": Ibid., p. 112.
49 "He once said to me . . .: 'All the opportunity . . .' ": Ibid., p. 114.
49 "His genius . . .": Ibid., p. 114.
49 ". . . The way to the heights . . .": Ibid., p. 115.
49 "He had measured strength . . .": Ibid., p. 116.
49 "His word was equally good . . .": Ibid., p. 133.
50 "His career was the embodiment . . .": Ibid., p. 150.
50 "Harriman will be remembered . . .": *Living Age*, October 11, 1909.
50 "Mr. Kahn has his face set toward the light.": J. H. Thomas, *Home and Abroad*, Summer 1930, p. 127.
50 "If my actions were called for . . .": "A Few Reminiscences of Conversations with the Late Colonel Roosevelt," in Kahn, *Of Many Things*, p. 184.
50 ". . . He saw that business had grown . . .": "Roosevelt and Business," in Kahn, *Of Many Things*, pp. 317–18.

8. The Diamond Horseshoe

52 "If she invited you . . .": Quoted in Birmingham, p. 304.
53 "a very distinguished lady . . .": Gatti-Casazza, p. 143.
53 "Look here, Gatti . . .": Ibid., p. 144.
54 "I thank you, Mr. Kahn . . .": Ibid., p. 146.
54 "But of course I will have no difficulty . . .": Ibid., p. 148.
55 ". . . in the best sense . . .": *New York Tribune*, November 17, 1908.

55 "As the director's wife . . .": Alda, p. 173.
56 "The auditorium . . .": Gatti-Casazza, pp. 153–54.
57 "It is no secret . . .": *New York Sun,* January 3, 1915.
57 "I don't think there is one singer . . .": Kobler, *American Heritage,* February–March 1984.
58 I AM INFINITELY SHOCKED . . .: KP.
59 ". . . I don't know of a single instance . . .": *Brooklyn Eagle,* October 25, 1925.
59 "Last spring you paid me the honor . . .": KP.
60 "I'd give my right arm . . .": *Boston Globe,* November 18, 1924.
61 "But I do hope . . .": *London Evening News,* June 5, 1925.

9. Ballet

64 "The lives of the vast majority . . .": Kahn, *Of Many Things,* pp. 26–27.
66 "O Mr. Nijinsky . . .": Quoted in Buckle, *Nijinsky,* p. 358.
67 ". . . I am thoroughly convinced . . .": KP.
68 "I quite understand . . .": KP.
69 "When we realize . . .": Quoted in Matz, *Many Lives,* p. 113.
69 "When I arrived . . .": Monteux, pp. 102–103.

10. Kahn vs. Hammerstein

71 "Mr. Hammerstein, you are a genius. . . .": *Philadelphia Inquirer,* November 18, 1908, quoted in Cone.
72 ". . . Your frank comments . . .": *Saturday Review,* May 30, 1964.
74 "In the spring of 1913 . . .": KP.
75 ". . . I beg to state . . .": KP.
75 "See here you. . . .": KP.

11. England Beckons

77 "[She] came yesterday . . .": Courtesy of Margaret Ryan.
77 "I had a strange time in England . . .": Courtesy of Prof. Ernst Schulin.
79 "I never knew what Kahn was . . .": George Whitney, COHC, p. 50.
79 MANY THANKS . . . : KP.
79 ". . . I may have leave . . .": KP.
80 . . . HAVE PRACTICALLY CONCLUDED . . .: KP.
80 ". . . I am looking forward . . .": KP.
82 "the Stock Exchange was widely known . . .": Brooks, p. 54.
82 "the greedy bankers of Wall Street": Thomas and Morgan-Witts, p. 41.
82 "The newspaper articles . . .": KP.
82 CHANGE YOUR PLANS . . . : KP.
82 ". . . I need not say . . .": KP.

83 "I would much rather be burdened . . .": Matz, *Many Lives*, p. 161.
84 "Otto H. Kahn, it is confidently expected . . .": *NYT*, February 23, 1913.
84 "I discovered . . .": Forbes, p. 222.

12. War

86 "My last letter . . .": Courtesy of Margaret Ryan.
87 "I was very greatly worried . . .": Ibid.
88 "Italy by waiting . . .": Matz, *Many Lives*, p. 167.
89 "I have always loved France . . .": Ibid., p. 167.
89 "Rathenau's sexual character . . .": Felix, p. 54.
91 "Possibly you may be interested . . .": KP.
91 ". . . I fear I must confess . . .": KP.
91 "We should be somewhat careful . . .": Adler, vol. 2, p. 254.
91 "May I say to you . . .": Ibid., p. 255.
91 ". . . The Romanoff dynasty . . .": Ibid., p. 256.
91 Letter to Lillian Wald: Ibid., p. 257.
92 "Lili has told me . . .": Courtesy of Prof. Ernst Schulin.
92 "What in the world? . . .": Ibid.
93 ". . . I am sorry to hear . . .": Ibid.
93 Excerpts from Paul Kahn's letters: Ibid.
95 "Prior to the war . . .": *NYT*, April 29, 1917.
97 "to rise . . .": Kahn, *Right Above Race*, p. 65.
98 "It is the purpose . . .": Ibid., pp. 65–66.
98 ". . . Speaking as one born . . .": Ibid., pp. 68–69.
98 "From each successive visit . . .": Ibid., p. 80.
100 "I wear the vilification . . .": Matz, *Many Lives*, p. 183.
100 "Against unscrupulous promotion . . .": Kahn, *Reflections of a Financier*, pp. 250–51.
101 ". . . some of its rites . . .": Ibid., p. 236.
101 "For art is democracy . . .": Ibid., pp. 371–83.
102 ". . . What you have said . . .": KP.
102 ". . . Praise has value . . .": KP.

13. European Mission

104 "It is absolutely right . . .": *NYT*, May 28, 1917.
105 "I regard the labor union movement . . .": *The New York Humanitarian*, March 1918.
106 "I enclose a little essay . . .": *L'Eclair*, Paris, June 8, 1918.
107 "If we find ways . . .": *NYT*, July 29, 1918.
109 "Nothing that we fought for . . .": KP.

14. Oheka

112 "all our . . . schemes . . .": Quoted by Robert King from Olmsted papers in Library of Congress.
112 "I discussed once . . .": Ibid.
112 "We have made up our minds . . .": Ibid.
113 "Being a Kahn pensioner . . .": Quoted by Mrs. Gilbert Kahn in interview with author.
113 "Well, wake him up. . . .": *New Yorker*, January 16, 1926.
116 "He would not move the parkway route . . .": Caro, pp. 277–78.
116 "I shudder to think . . .": Delano, COHC, pp. 31–32.

15. St. Peter's, St. Bartholomew's, St. John's

120 "Marshall, isn't it beautiful? . . .": Payne, p. 83.
121 "Gentlemen, all my life . . .": *House Tour*.
121 "And the third? . . .": Ibid.
122 "When I received . . .": KP.
122 "I am wondering . . .": Ibid.
122 "I did not have the occasion . . .": Ibid.
123 "Permit me to say . . .": Ibid.
123 "I send you enclosed . . .": Ibid.
124 "There were several . . .": *NYT*, June 16, 1920.
124 "We are showing on the screen . . .": KP.
125 "The fact is . . .": Ibid.
126 "Miss Williams has retired . . .": *NYT*, February 9, 1931.

16. Adventures in Theater

127 "Reinhardt's greatest spectacle . . .": Reinhardt, pp. 342–43.
128 "Max Reinhardt, come over to us! . . .": Ibid., p. 215.
128 "The people of all sections . . .": "Some Observations on Art in America," in Kahn, *Reflections of a Financier*, pp. 387–88, 391–92.
130 "As little as possible . . .": Langner, p. 120.
131 "When I first met them . . .": KP.
132 "I have extended . . .": KP, December 24, 1924.
133 "God shows what he thinks of wealth . . .": "Search-Light," *New Yorker*, February 20, 1926.
134 "The Moscow Players need no language . . .": *New York Globe*, January 17, 1923.
134 ". . . Americanism is not so frail . . .": *NYT*, December 27, 1922.
135 "The seventh anniversary . . .": KP.

17. Paul Robeson

136 All Robeson letters: KP.
137 "a damnable thing . . .": Gilliam, p. 33.

18. The Miracle

141 He notified his secretary . . . : KP, November 6, 1929.
141 "Clever and godfatherly . . .": Cooper, p. 287.
141 "a man I was attached to . . .": Ibid., p. 287.
141 "the funniest . . .": Quoted in Ziegler, p. 129.
141 "Bukovinian world citizen . . .": Reinhardt, p. 57.
142 "A 1000 thanks . . .": KP.
142 "Ah, Kätchen . . .": Ziegler, p. 129.
142 "Dearest Boss . . .": KP.
144 "My most dear Diana . . .": KP.

19. Of Parties, Premieres, and Grand Tours

147 "We have an interval . . .": May 26, 1924, in Kahn, *Of Many Things*, p. 25.
147 "Mix a degree of idealism . . .": June 8, 1923, ibid., p. 35.
147 "When an honorary committee . . .": Quoted in Matz, *Many Lives*, p. 224.
148 PEACE HATH VICTORIES . . .: KP, December 12, 1922.
148 I CAN BUT THANK YOU . . .: KP.
149 "My memory of our stay . . .": Davidson, p. 197.
149 "Hold it, boss . . .": Ibid., p. 198.
151 "Mr. Kahn was a strange . . .": Interview with author.
152 "When women are about . . .": March 3, 1927, in Bennett, *Letters*, vol. 3.
152 "Otto, the host . . .": Preface, Bennett, *Mediterranean Scenes*, p. v.
152 "We're passing Ithaca! . . .": Ibid., p. vii.
152 "we swept through many thoroughfares . . .": Ibid., p. ii.
153 "I have never in all my life . . .": Ibid., p. iii.
153 "The governments of all the countries . . .": Bennett, *Letters to His Nephew*, p. 201.
154 MAX KAHN, COUSIN OF OTTO KAHN: *Time*, May 16, 1966.
155 "Kahn must have inadvertently hung . . .": Teichmann, p. 135.
156 "Is he absolutely honest? . . .": Mrs. Dorothy Schiff, interview with author.
156 "Tell me, Mr. Otto . . .": KP.
156 "Can I order from the menu . . .": Matz, *Many Lives*, p. 235.

157 "Otto Kahn has been mentioned . . .": Quoted in ibid., p. 5.
157 "To dear Otto . . .": Marx and Clayton, pp. 180–81.
157 "My boat, the Oheka . . .": KP.
157 "Are any of them married to . . .": KP.
157 "If it be not gluttonous . . .": KP.
158 "Otto Kahn was my ideal American millionaire . . .": Nichols, *All I Could Never Be*, pp. 111–12.
159 "Two thousand five hundred . . .": Nichols, *Star-Spangled Manner*, pp. 171–72.

20. Patronage

160 ". . . For the last six weeks . . .": *Letters of Hart Crane and His Family*, ed. Thomas S. W. Lewis, pp. 445–46.
160 ". . . My first collected poems . . .": *Letters of Hart Crane*, ed. Brom Weber, pp. 222–24.
161 "Re Hart Crane . . .": KP.
161 "I have just had an interview . . .": Weber, p. 310, and Lewis, p. 610.
162 "as important a poem . . .": Horton, p. 267.
162 ". . . I wish to take this occasion . . .": KP.
162 "You ought to go abroad for a while. . . .": Alexander King, p. 15.
162 "That was Otto Kahn . . .": Ibid., p. 16.
163 "Green, I have been following . . .": Green, COHC, pp. 126–27.
163 "It is indeed a source . . .": KP, March 27, 1930.
164 ". . . if the purpose . . .": KP.
165 "My request is the following 21. Women . . .": KP.
167 "Rose Cumming never even met . . .": *NYT*, June 7, 1979.
168 "The Opera itself is too alluring": Moore, p. 89.
168 "You know, this is one of the few things . . .": Ibid., p. 95.
168 "I feel the romance of Venice . . .": Ibid., p. 95.
168 "Your voice has lost color . . .": Ibid., p. 99.
168 "There has been a remarkable improvement . . .": Ibid., p. 99.
169 JUST HEARD GRACE MOORE . . . : MOA.
169 WILL KEEP GRACE MOORE IN MIND . . . : MOA.
169 "First: Grace Moore. . . .": MOA.
169 ". . . She sang for me . . .": MOA.
170 ". . . the unvarnished truth . . .": Moore, p. 178.
170 "Unlike a great many women . . .": Ibid., p. 179.
170 "Dear Boss, I am sending this little note . . .": KP.
171 "My dear Grace . . .": KP.
172 "To the best of my recollection . . .": *NYT*, October 16, 1932.
172 "I . . . made favorable comment . . .": *NYT*, October 25, 1932.
172 "Madame Lindgren . . .": *New York Sun*, September 29, 1931.
173 "It was my own trouble . . .": *New York Post*, February 3, 1927.

Source Notes [221]

173 "I don't shake hands . . .": Mariash, interview with author.
173 "At the request of Mr. Kahn . . .": *New York Sun*, September 30, 1931.
174 "I don't want this kind of thing . . .": Mariash, interview with author.
174 "I shall hold as a matter of law . . .": *NYT*, October 2, 1931.

22. *Mussolini, Harding, and Hoover*

175 "The worker is neither a machine . . .": *Baltimore Record*, July 3, 1919.
176 "I give my money gladly . . .": *Time*, February 24, 1930.
176 "the butler was able to withstand . . .": Matz, *Many Lives*, p. 140.
176 "You are Socialists . . .": *New York World-Telegram*, March 30, 1930.
176 "The greatest statesman . . .": International News Service, May 30, 1925.
176 "Contrary to all that has been written . . .": Ibid.
178 "I have received several letters . . .": *NYT*, May 28, 1917.
178 "To those who take the view . . .": *Detroit Free Press*, August 21, 1920.
178 "I am in favor . . .": *NYT*, February 10, 1922.
179 "We have the pleasure . . .": KP.
180 "I am taking you at your word . . .": KP.
181 "Whatever we may think . . .": Address before Transportation Club, April 22, 1922.
181 "What impressed me most . . .": *NYT*, September 24, 1920.
182 "You represent and exemplify . . .": KP.
182 ". . . if before your inauguration . . .": KP.
182 "I am taking pleasure in sending you . . .": KP, October 13, 1921.
183 "Mr. Hoover is the wisely constructive liberal . . .": *NYT*, October 26, 1928.
184 "My dear Senator . . .": *NYT*, October 30, 1929.

23. *From Conquest to Crash*

186 "Does anyone suppose . . .": Museum of Modern Art Film Archives.
186 ". . . Rightminded people everywhere . . .": *NYT*, May 12, 1928.
187 "I take the liberty of informing you . . .": MOA.
188 "Talley showed no greater progress . . .": Kolodin (1936), p. 33
188 "Even if Marion Talley . . .": KP, February 19, 1926.
188 "Unfortunately, I had no opportunity . . .": MOA, April 29, 1925.
190 "Every opera loses . . .": *NYT*, December 30, 1928.
191 "It is a solemn obligation . . .": Kahn, *Of Many Things*, p. 64.
191 "clung to their castles . . .": *Time*, November 25, 1925.
192 "If the music lovers of New York . . .": *NYT*, January 14, 1926.
193 "I repeat what I said . . .": *NYT*, September 6, 1929.
193 "The industrial condition . . .": *NYT*, October 9, 1929.
193 "what looks like a permanently high plateau": *NYT*, October 16, 1929.

24. Depression

193 "Intrinsically, underlying conditions . . .": *Wall Street Journal*, June 26, 1928.
193 "And there's nothing in sight . . .": *New York American*, March 23, 1928.

24. Depression

194 "You are a most conscientious debtor . . .": KP, July 23, 1928.
194 "To be young . . .": KP.
195 "I enclose a check . . .": KP.
195 "As to the balance . . .": KP.
195 ". . . Not many of our painters . . .": Anderson, pp. 185–86.
195 "What a refreshing . . .": KP.
195 "The lumber business . . .": KP.
196 "hoping that the Fates . . .": KP.
196 Rukeyser story in Pittsburgh *Sun-Telegraph*.
196 "Economic conditions . . .": KP.
197 "I make free to reiterate . . .": KP.
197 ". . . The difficulty about the opposition . . .": KP, letter of May 22, 1933.
197 "It imposes an unfair liability . . .": KP.

25. Finale

200 "He said it was a good thing . . .": Kolodin (1966), p. 257.
201 "I can't believe it . . .": Paley, p. 72.
201 "The times through which . . .": KP.
201 "One thing I believe I can promise . . .": KP.
201 "I should rather be in England . . .": KP.
202 "How would you describe . . .": *Stock Exchange Practices*, pp. 958–61.
204 ". . . to my own knowledge . . .": Ibid., p. 964.
204 "Was your firm . . .": Ibid., p. 965.
204 "I hope you will not press me . . .": Ibid., p. 969.
205 "Do you think that bankers . . .": Ibid., p. 1008.
205 ". . . our thanks to the witness . . .": Ibid., p. 1326.

26. "I Shall Die a Jew"

206 "I was born a Jew . . .": *Time*, April 9, 1934.
206 "A proverb . . .": KP.
207 "This is not the time . . .": KP, December 1933.
208 "You go down the street . . .": Buttenwieser, interview with author.
208 "Mr. Kahn had had general arteriosclerosis . . .": *NYT*, March 30, 1934.
208 "I hope I never . . .": Ibid.
210 "I can't see . . .": Secrest, p. 389.
210 "There was Addie . . .": Ibid.
211 "Addie Kahn, now staying here . . .": Berenson, p. 24.

Bibliography

Books

Adler, Cyrus. *Jacob H. Schiff.* 2 vols. Garden City, N.Y.: Doubleday, Doran, 1928.
Alda, Frances. *Men, Women and Tenors.* Boston: Houghton Mifflin, 1937.
Allen, Frederick Lewis. *The Lords of Creation.* New York: Harper & Brothers, 1935.
Anderson, Sherwood. *Letters.* Selected and edited with an introduction by Howard Mumford Jones in association with Walter B. Rideout. Boston: Little, Brown, 1953.
Assouline, Pierre. *Gaston Gallimard.* Paris: Balland, 1984.
Baker, Richard. *Mozart.* New York: Thames & Hudson, 1982.
Bennett, Arnold. *The Journals of Arnold Bennett.* 3 vols. Edited by Newman Flower. London: Cassell, 1932–33.
———. *Letters of Arnold Bennett.* 3 vols. Edited by James Hepburn. London: Oxford University Press, 1970.
———. *Letters to His Nephew.* New York and London: Harper & Brothers, 1935.
———. *Mediterranean Scenes.* Limited edition of 25 copies. London: Cassell, 1928.
Berenson, Bernard. *Sunset and Twilight: From the Diaries of 1947–1958.* New York: Harcourt, Brace & World, 1963.
Bernays, Edward L. *Biography of an Idea.* New York: Simon & Schuster, 1965.
Biancolli, Louis. *The Flagstad Manuscript.* New York: G. P. Putnam's Sons, 1952.
Birmingham, Stephen. *"Our Crowd."* New York: Harper & Row, 1967.
Bishop, Joseph Bucklin. *Theodore Roosevelt and His Time.* Vol. 2. New York: Charles Scribner's Sons, 1920.

Boardman, Gerald. *The Oxford Companion to American Theatre.* New York: Oxford University Press, 1984.
Brooks, John. *Once in Golconda: A True Drama of Wall Street 1920–1938.* New York: Harper & Row, 1969.
Brown, Henry Collins. *In the Golden Nineties.* Hastings-on-Hudson, N.Y.: Valentine's Manual, 1928.
Buckle, Richard. *Diaghilev.* New York: Atheneum, 1979.
———. *Nijinsky.* London: Weidenfeld & Nicolson, 1971.
Caro, Robert A. *The Power Broker: Robert Moses and the Fall of New York.* New York: Alfred A. Knopf, 1974.
Carosso, Vincent P. *Investment Banking in America.* Cambridge: Harvard University Press, 1970.
Carr, Francis. *Mozart and Constanze.* New York: Franklin Watts, 1983.
Cone, John Frederick. *Oscar Hammerstein's Manhattan Opera Company.* Norman: University of Oklahoma Press, 1966.
Connell, Brian. *Manifest Destiny: A Study in Five Profiles of the Rise and Influence of the Mountbatten Family.* London: Cassell, 1953.
Cooper, Diana. *Autobiography.* New York: Carroll & Graf, 1985.
Corey, Lewis. *The House of Morgan.* New York: G. Howard Watt, 1930.
Crane, Hart. *The Letters of Hart Crane, 1916–1932.* Edited by Brom Weber. New York: Hermitage House, 1952.
———. *Letters of Hart Crane and His Family.* Edited by Thomas S. W. Lewis. New York: Columbia University Press, 1974.
Davidson, Jo. *Between Sittings: An Informal Autobiography.* New York: Dial Press, 1951.
Deutsch, Helen, and Stella Hanau. *The Provincetown: A Story of the Theatre.* New York: Russell & Russell, 1931.
Dobkowski, Michael N. *The Tarnished Dream: The Basis of American Anti-Semitism.* Westport, Conn.: Greenwood Press, 1979.
Durham, Weldon B., ed. *American Theatre Companies, 1888–1930.* Westport, Conn.: Greenwood Press, 1987.
Eckenrode, Henry James, and Pocahontas Wight Edmunds. *E. H. Harriman.* New York: Greenberg, 1933.
Ewen, David. *George Gershwin.* New York: Ungar, 1986.
———. *The New Encyclopedia of the Opera.* New York: Hill & Wang, 1971.
Farrar, Rowena Rutherford. *Grace Moore and Her Many Worlds.* East Brunswick, N.J.: Cornwall Books, 1982.
Felix, David. *Walter Rathenau and the Weimar Republic: The Politics of Reparations.* Baltimore: Johns Hopkins University Press, 1971.
Forbes, B. C. *The Men Who Are Making America.* New York: B. C. Forbes Publishing Co., 1926.
Freedley, George, and John A. Reeves. *A History of the Theatre.* New York: Crown, 1968.

Galbraith, John Kenneth. *The Great Crash, 1929.* 2d ed. Boston: Houghton Mifflin, 1961.
Gartenberg, Egon. *Mahler: The Man and His Music.* New York: Schirmer Books, 1978.
Gatti-Casazza, Giulio. *Memories of the Opera.* New York: Charles Scribner's Sons, 1941.
Geduld, Harry M., and Ronald Gottesman, eds. *Sergei Eisenstein and Upton Sinclair: The Making and Unmaking of "Que Viva Mexico!"* Bloomington: Indiana University Press, 1970.
Gelb, Arthur, and Barbara Gelb. *O'Neill.* New York: Dell, 1962.
Gershwin, Ira. *Lyrics on Several Occasions.* New York: Alfred A. Knopf, 1959.
Gilliam, Dorothy Butler. *Paul Robeson: All-American.* Washington, D.C.: The New Republic Book Co., 1976.
Goethe, Johann Wolfgang von. *Poetry and Truth from My Own Life.* Translated by R. O Moon. Washington, D.C.: Public Affairs Press, 1949.
Goldstein, Malcolm. *The Political Stage: American Drama and Theater of the Great Depression.* New York: Oxford University Press, 1974.
Gottlieb, Polly Rose. *The Nine Lives of Billy Rose.* New York: Crown, 1968.
Greenfield, Howard. *Caruso.* New York: G. P. Putnam's Sons, 1983.
Heiseler, Bernt von. *Schiller.* Translated and annotated by John Bednall. Philadelphia: Dufour, 1963.
Heymann, C. David. *Poor Little Rich Girl: The Life and Legend of Barbara Hutton.* New York: Random House, 1983.
Holborn, Hajo. *A History of Modern Germany, 1840–1945.* New York: Alfred A. Knopf, 1969.
Horton, Philip. *Hart Crane.* New York: W. W. Norton, 1937.
Hough, Richard. *Edwina, Countess Mountbatten of Burma.* New York: William Morrow, 1983.
———. *Mountbatten.* New York: Random House, 1980.
Jablonski, Edward. *Gershwin.* New York: Doubleday, 1987.
Jackson, Stanley. *Caruso.* New York: Stein & Day, 1972.
———. *J. P. Morgan.* New York: Stein & Day, 1983.
Josephson, Matthew. *The Money Lords.* New York: Weybright & Talley, 1972.
———. *The Robber Barons.* New York: Harcourt, Brace & World, 1962. (Reprint of 1934 edition.)
Juxon, John. *Lewis and Lewis: The Life and Times of a Victorian Solicitor.* New York: Ticknor & Fields, 1984.
Kahn, Otto. *Edward H. Harriman: An Address Delivered before the Finance Forum in New York on January 25, 1911.* (Privately printed.)
———. *Of Many Things.* New York: Boni & Liveright, 1926.
———. *Our Economic and Other Problems.* New York: George H. Doran, 1920.
———. *Reflections of a Financier.* London: Hodder & Stoughton, 1921.
———. *Right Above Race.* New York: The Century Co., 1918.

Kaschewski, Marjorie. *The Quiet Millionaires: The Morris County That Was.* Morristown, N.J.: Morristown Daily Record, 1970.
Kennan, George. *E. H. Harriman.* 2 vols. Boston: Houghton Mifflin, 1922.
Kerensky, Oleg. *Anna Pavlova.* New York: E. P. Dutton, 1973.
Kessler, Count Harry. *Walter Rathenau: His Life and Work.* London: Gerald Howe, 1929.
King, Alexander. *Mine Enemy Grows Older.* New York: Simon & Schuster, 1959.
King, Moses. *King's Handbook of New York City, 1893.* Boston: Moses King, 1893.
King, Robert R. *Raising a Fallen Treasure: The Otto H. Kahn Home, Huntington, Long Island.* Middleville, N.Y., 1985. (Privately printed.)
Kolodin, Irving. *The Metropolitan Opera, 1883–1935.* New York: Oxford University Press, 1936.
———. *The Metropolitan Opera, 1883–1966.* New York: Alfred A. Knopf, 1966.
Kuhn, Loeb & Co. *A Century of Investment Banking.* 1967. (Privately printed.)
———. *Investment Banking through Four Generations.* 1955. (Privately printed.)
Langner, Lawrence. *The Magic Curtain.* New York: E. P. Dutton, 1951.
Mahler, Alma. *Memories and Letters.* Enlarged edition, revised and edited with an introduction by Donald Mitchell. Translated by Basil Creighton. London: John Murray, 1969.
Marx, Samuel, and Jan Clayton. *Rodgers and Hart: Bewitched, Bothered, and Bedeviled.* New York: G. P. Putnam's Sons, 1976.
Matthews, Denis. *Arturo Toscanini.* Tunbridge Wells, Kent, England: Midas Books, 1982.
Matz, Mary Jane. *The Many Lives of Otto Kahn.* New York: Macmillan, 1963.
Mayer, Martin. *The Met: One Hundred Years of Grand Opera.* New York: Simon & Schuster, 1983.
McArthur, Edwin. *Flagstad: A Personal Memoir.* New York: Alfred A. Knopf, 1965.
The Mirrors of Wall Street. New York: G. P. Putnam's Sons, 1933.
Money, Keith. *Anna Pavlova.* New York: Alfred A. Knopf, 1982.
Monteux, Doris. *It's All in the Music: The Life and Work of Pierre Monteux.* New York: Farrar, Straus & Giroux, 1965.
Moore, Grace. *You're Only Human Once.* Garden City, N.Y.: Doubleday, Doran, 1944.
Mozart, Wolfgang Amadeus. *The Letters of Mozart and His Family.* Edited and annotated by Emily Anderson. New York: W. W. Norton, 1985.
Nichols, Beverley. *All I Could Never Be.* New York: E. P. Dutton, 1952.
———. *The Star-Spangled Manner.* Garden City, N.Y.: Doubleday, Doran, 1928.
Ottaway, Hugh. *Mozart.* Detroit: Wayne State University Press, 1980.

Page, Will A. *Behind the Curtains of the Broadway Beauty Trust.* New York: Edward A. Miller, 1927.
Paley, William S. *As It Happened.* Garden City, N.Y.: Doubleday, 1979.
Pecora, Ferdinand. *Wall Street Under Oath.* New York: Simon & Schuster, 1939.
Raynor, Henry. *Mozart.* London: Macmillan, 1978.
Reinhardt, Gottfried. *The Genius: A Memoir of Max Reinhardt.* New York: Alfred A. Knopf, 1979.
Robinson, Francis. *Celebration: The Metropolitan Opera.* Garden City, N.Y.: Doubleday, 1979.
Roosevelt, Theodore. *American Problems.* Vol. 17 of *The Works of Theodore Roosevelt.* New York: Charles Scribner's Sons, 1926.
Sachs, Harvey. *Toscanini.* Philadelphia and New York: J. B. Lippincott, 1978.
Sadie, Stanley. *Mozart.* New York: W. W. Norton, 1980.
Samuels, Ernest. *Bernard Berenson: The Making of a Legend.* Cambridge: The Belknap Press of Harvard University Press, 1987.
Sayler, Oliver M. *Inside the Moscow Art Theatre.* New York: Johnson Reprint Corp., 1970.
———, ed. *Max Reinhardt and His Theatre.* New York: Benjamin Blom, 1968.
Schevill, James. *Sherwood Anderson: His Life and Work.* Denver: University of Denver Press, 1951.
Schulin, Ernst. *Walter Rathenau.* Göttingen, Zürich, and Frankfurt: Musterschmidt, 1979.
Secrest, Meryle. *Being Bernard Berenson.* New York: Holt, Rinehart & Winston, 1979.
Shanet, Howard. *Philharmonic: A History of New York's Orchestra.* Garden City, N.Y.: Doubleday, 1975.
Sheaffer, Louis. *O'Neill: Son and Artist.* Boston: Little, Brown, 1973.
Sheehan, Vincent. *Oscar Hammerstein I: The Life and Exploits of an Impresario.* New York: Simon & Schuster, 1956.
Sobel, Robert. *Panic on Wall Street.* New York: Macmillan, 1968.
Sokolova, Lydia. *Dancing for Diaghilev: The Memoirs of Lydia Sokolova.* Edited by Richard Buckle. New York: Macmillan, 1961.
Sombart, Werner. *The Jews in Modern Capitalism.* London: T. F. Unwin, 1913.
Stock Exchange Practices: Hearings before the Committee on Banking and Currency, United States Senate, 73rd Congress, 1933.
Strauss, Lewis L. *Men and Decisions.* Garden City, N.Y.: Doubleday, 1962.
Swaine, Robert T. *The Cravath Firm and Its Predecessors, 1819–1948.* 2 vols. New York: Privately printed at Ad Press, Ltd., 1948.
Taber, Thomas Townsend, and Thomas Townsend Taber III. *The Delaware, Lackawanna & Western Railroad in the Twentieth Century, 1899–1960,* Part 1. Muncy, Pa.: Thomas T. Taber III, 1980.
Taylor, A. J. P. *Beaverbrook.* New York: Simon & Schuster, 1972.

Teichmann, Howard. *Smart Aleck: The Wit, World, and Life of Alexander Woollcott*. New York: William Morrow, 1976.
Thayer, William Roscoe. *Theodore Roosevelt: An Intimate Biography*. Boston and New York: Houghton Mifflin, 1919.
Thimme, Hans. *Weltkrieg ohne Waffen: Die Propaganda der Westmachte gegen Deutschland, ihre Wirkung und ihre Abwehr*. Stuttgart and Berlin: Cotata, 1932.
Thomas, Gordon, and Max Morgan-Witts. *The Day the Bubble Burst: A Social History of the Wall Street Crash of 1929*. Garden City, N.Y.: Doubleday, 1979.
Trottman, Nelson. *History of the Union Pacific*. New York: Augustus M. Kelley, 1966.
Tuggle, Robert. *The Golden Age of Opera*. New York: Holt, Rinehart & Winston, 1983.
Unterecker, John. *Voyager: A Life of Hart Crane*. New York: Farrar, Straus & Giroux, 1969.
Van Rensselaer, Mrs. John King, with Frederic Van de Water. *The Social Ladder*. New York: Henry Holt, 1924.
Ziegler, Philip. *Diana Cooper*. New York: Alfred A. Knopf, 1982.
———. *Mountbatten*. New York: Alfred A. Knopf, 1985.

Articles

Benedict, Libbian. "Otto H. Kahn—Maecenas." *The Reflex*, November 1927.
Cruikshank, Herbert Knight. "The Great Kahn." *Theatre Magazine*, November 1929.
Dartt, Helen. "Special Train." *PLA Report*. Post Library Association (C. W. Post College), vol. 10, 1988.
Flynn, John T. "Other People's Money." *New Republic*, July 12, 1933.
Gilbert, Douglas. "The Impressions of an Unprejudiced Newspaper Man." *New York Telegram*. Reprinted by the Tribune Printing Co., January 1, 1931.
Hendrick, Burton J. "The Jewish Invasion of America." *McClure's*, March 1913.
Kahn, Otto H. "Europe as It Is Today." *The Forum*, September 1922.
———. "The Failure of the League." *The Nation*," November 3, 1920.
———. "George Gershwin and American Youth: An Appreciation." *Musical Courier*, January 22, 1929.
———. "Labor and Liberty." *The New York City Humanitarian*, March 1918.
———. "The Market of American Securities." *The Forum*, April–May 1921.
———. "A Plea and a Plan for Tax Revision." *The Forum*, April–May 1923.
———. "Prosperity and Taxation." *The Forum*, June 1922.
———. "Some Suggestions on Tax Revision." *The Forum*, November–December 1920.

Kobler, John. "Bravo Caruso!" *American Heritage*, February–March 1984.
Laugwitz, Burkhard. "Robert Kahn, ein vergessener Mannheimer komponist, mit unveröffentlichten Erinnerungen von Kahn an Johannes Brahms." *Mannheimer Hefte*, no. 1, 1986. (Translated for the author by Louis Miller.)
Marshall, Edward. Untitled article. Edward Marshall Syndicate, 1920.
Matz, Mary Jane. "Maecenas in Tails." *Opera News*, March 23, 1959.
McCormick, William B. "The Otto H. Kahn Collection." *International Studio*, January 1925.
Moody, John, and George Kibbe Turner. "Masters of Capital in America." *McClure's*, January 1911.
"Mr. Kahn & Mr. Gatti." *Time*, November 2, 1925.
"Otto Kahn before the Senate Banking Committee." *Literary Digest*, July 8, 1933.
Payne, George Henry. "Otto H. Kahn: A Study of a Progressive Financier." In *The Fourth Estate and Radio, and Other Addresses*. Boston: The Microphone Press, 1936.
Roberts, Priscilla M. "A Conflict of Loyalties: Kuhn, Loeb and Company and the First World War, 1914–1917." In *Studies in the American Jewish Experience*, vol. 2. Lanham, Md.: University Press of America and American Jewish Archives, 1985.
Rolston, Sophie. "Morris County's Historic Railroads." *Morris County*, Spring 1985.
Salpeter, Harry. "Otto the Magnificent." *The Outlook*, July 4, 1928.
"Search-Light" (Waldo Frank). "In Tune with the Finite" (*New Yorker* profile). *The New Yorker*, February 20, 1926.
Seldes, Gilbert. "Hammerstein the Extravagant." *Harper's*, July 1932.
Thomas, J. H. "Otto Kahn" (written September 22, 1920). *Home and Abroad*, Summer 1930.
Wechsberg, Joseph. "The General Manager." *The New Yorker*, September 17, 1966.
Weiss, Ermaline. "The Mini-Empire of Otto H. Kahn." *Morris County*, Spring 1984.

Miscellaneous

House Tour of the Otto Kahn Mansion (1100 Fifth Avenue, now the Convent of the Sacred Heart), January 29, 1984. (Mimeographed brochure.)
Roberts, Priscilla. "Kuhn, Loeb & Co., the International Bank, and European Affairs, 1914–1933." (Outline for a dissertation.)
Schulin, Ernst. Speech on Walther Rathenau, Schweinfurt, West Germany, 1985.

Oral Histories from the Oral History Collection of Columbia University

Ascher, Charles. *Reminiscences*, 1979.
Buttenwieser, Benjamin J. *Reminiscences*, 1979.
Delano, William Adams. *Reminiscences*, 1950.
Green, Paul. Interview by Billy E. Barnes, March 5, 1975, Southern Oral History Program Collection, Southern Historical Collection, University of North Carolina at Chapel Hill.
Whitney, George. *Reminiscences*, 1963.

Permissions Acknowledgments

Grateful acknowledgment is made to the following for permission to quote from copyrighted material and unpublished letters:

Margaret Ryan (Mrs. John Barry Ryan) for letters and papers of her father, Otto Kahn, in the William Seymour Theatre Collection, Princeton University and in the Metropolitan Opera Archives; passages from published books and articles by Otto Kahn; and passages from *The Many Lives of Otto Kahn* by Mary Jane Matz, copyright © 1963 by Margaret D. Ryan.

American Jewish Archives, Cincinnati, Ohio, for letter from Jacob Schiff to Ernest Cassel, April 26, 1896, in Jacob Schiff Papers.

Benjamin Buttenwieser for excerpts from his reminiscences in the Oral History Collection of Columbia University.

Oral History Research Office, Columbia University, for excerpts from reminiscences of Charles Archer, William Delano, George Whitney (all copyright by Trustees of Columbia University), and Paul Green (copyright by University of North Carolina).

Columbia University Press for excerpts from *Letters of Hart Crane and His Family*, ed. Thomas S. W. Lewis.

Excerpt from *It's All in the Music* by Doris Monteux. Copyright © 1965 by Doris G. Monteux. Reprinted by permission of Farrar, Straus and Giroux, Inc.

Eric Glass Ltd. on behalf of Estate of Beverley Nichols for excerpts from *All I Could Never Be* and *The Star-Spangled Manner* by Beverley Nichols.

William Hammerstein for letters of Oscar Hammerstein.

David Mann for letters of Hart Crane and Grace Hart Crane.

Samuel Marx for anecdote in *Rodgers and Hart* by Samuel Marx and Jan Clayton.

Richard L. Moore III for letter of Grace Moore to Otto Kahn.

The New York Times for various quotes; and for account of Otto Kahn's daughter's wedding, June 16, 1920, copyright 1920 by The New York Times Company. Reprinted by permission.

The New Yorker for passage from "The Talk of the Town," January 16, 1926. Reprinted by permission; copyright 1926, © 1958 The New Yorker Magazine, Inc. Excerpts from "In Tune with the Finite" by Search-Light (Waldo Frank), February 20, 1926. Reprinted by permission; copyright 1926, © 1958 The New Yorker Magazine, Inc.

John Julius Norwich for letters of his mother, Lady Diana Cooper.

Harold Ober Associates on behalf of Sherwood Anderson Literary Estate for letters of Sherwood Anderson.

Lina Prokofiev for letters of Sergei Prokofiev.

Paul Robeson, Jr., for letters of Paul and Eslanda Robeson.

Prof. Ernst Schulin for letters of Paul Kahn.

Excerpts from *Memories of the Opera* by Giulio Gatti-Casazza copyright 1941 by Leon Schaeffer, Ancillary Executor; copyright renewed © 1969 by Estate of Gatti-Casazza. Reprinted with the permission of Charles Scribner's Sons, an imprint of Macmillan Publishing Company.

Watkins/Loomis Agency on behalf of Estate of Edith Wharton for letter of Edith Wharton to Otto Kahn.

A. P. Watt Ltd. on behalf of Madame V. Eldin for excerpts from Preface to *Mediterranean Scenes* by Arnold Bennett.

Index

Aarons, Alex, 61
Adams, Franklin P., 146, 156
Africaine, L' (Meyerbeer), 58
Aida (Verdi), 55
Aitken, Sir William Maxwell (Lord Beaverbrook), 78–82, 84, 85, 106, 201
Akins, Zoe, 154
Albert, King of Belgians, 106–107
Alda, Frances, 53, 55, 65
Alfonso XIII, King of Spain, 106
Algonquin Round Table, 146, 154, 157
Allgemeine Elektrizitäts-Gesellschaft (A.E.G.), 10, 89, 199
All God's Chillun Got Wings (O'Neill), 132, 137
American Defense Society, 134
American International Corp., 34
American in Paris, An (Gershwin), 155
Amsterdamsche Bank, 87
Anderson, Sherwood, 195–96
Anisfeld, Boris, 59
Antheil, George, 60
Armstrong, Hamilton Fish, 124
Ascher, Charles, 33
Ashley, Wilfred William, 22
Astor, Mary, 151
Astor, Vincent, 192
Astor, Mrs. William Waldorf, 52
Atterbury, William Wallace, 3, 5, 185

Babson, Roger, 193
Bach, Johann Christian, 6
Baker, Newton, 108
Bakhmetieff, George, 67, 68
Ballet Mécanique (Antheil), 60
Ballets Russes, 63–68
Baltimore & Ohio Railroad, 4, 34
Banque Bénard, 148
Banque de Commerce de l'Azoff-Don, 91
Banque de Paris et des Pays Bas, 87
Banton, Joab H., 137
Baragwanath, Jack, 157, 158
Baring, Guy, 81
Baring Brothers, 87
Barkley, Alben W., 204
Barrientos, Maria, 53
Barrymore, Maurice, 17
Barton, Ralph, 154
Baruch, Bernard, 124
Basshe, Emjo, 194–95
Battistini, Mattia, 58
Bear, The (Chekhov), 130
Beaumont, Comte Marc de, 148, 149
Beaverbrook, Lord. *See* Sir William Maxwell Aitken
Beebe, Charles, 114
Beecham, Sir Thomas, 108
Beethoven, Ludwig van, 209
Before Breakfast (O'Neill), 132
Bel Geddes, Norman, 140
Bellini, Giovanni, 42

[233]

Bellini, Vincenzo, 70
Belmont, August, 79, 124
Bénard, Georges, 148
Benchley, Robert, 156
Benedict, Libbian, 79n
Benedict XV, Pope, 121
Bennett, Arnold, 152–53
Benois, Alexandre, 63
Benz, Karl, 7
Berenson, Bernard, 43, 210–11
Berlin, Irving, 60
Berry Brothers & Co., 179
Bethell, Maj. Gen. Hugh, 123
Be Yourself! (film), 154
Bing, Rudolf, 210
Bingham, Theodore Alfred, 81
Birkenhead, Lord, 186
Birmingham, Stephen, 89
Black Sun Press, 161
Bleecker, Lyman, 211
Blue Boy (Gainsborough), 151
Bockler, Charles, 195
Bodanzky, Artur, 124, 168, 189, 191
Bohème, La (Puccini), 30, 168, 169
Boito, Arrigo, 58
Bolshoi Ballet, 69
Bonar Law, Andrew, 78–80, 83
Bonci, Alessandro, 70
Boni & Liveright, 99
Boris Godunov (Mussorgsky), 58
Botticelli, Sandro, 42, 86
Bound East for Cardiff (O'Neill), 132
Boyce, Neith, 132
Brandeis, Louis D., 91
Breil, Joseph, 207n
Brewster, Eugene V., 35
Briand, Aristide, 106
Brice, Fanny, 154
Bridge, The (Crane), 161, 162
Brisbane, Arthur, 180
Brooks, John, 82
Broun, Heywood, 137
Brown, Lawrence, 137, 138
Bugatti, Giuseppe, 114
Burlington Railroad, 27
Burne-Jones, Edward, 10, 13
Buttenwieser, Benjamin, 208

Cadman, Charles Wakefield, 207n
Campanini, Cleofonte, 59, 75
Campbell, Mrs. Patrick, 77, 136
Camus, Albert, 132
Cantacuzene, Princess Julia, 124
Canterbury Pilgrims, The (de Koven), 207n
Carl Rosa Co., 108
Carmen (Bizet), 17, 71
Carmi, Maria, 140
Carnegie, Andrew, 117
Caro, Robert A., 115–16
Carpaccio, Vittore, 42
Carter, Amon G., 151
Caruso, Enrico, 30, 55, 57–58, 70, 108, 190
Cassel, Sir Ernest, 21, 22, 91
Castle, Irene, 154
Cavalieri, Lina, 18
Cavell, Edith, 186, 187
Central Pacific Railroad, 23
Chabrier, Emmanuel, 63
Chaliapin, Feodor, 58
Change Your Style (Cook), 132
Chaplin, Charlie, 185
Charley's Aunt (Thomas), 17
Charpentier, Gustave, 31
Chekhov, Anton, 130, 134
Cherry Orchard, The (Chekhov), 134
Chicago Opera, 58, 59, 172
Chicago & St. Louis Railroad, 4
Christie's, 42
Claussen, Julia, 173
Clemenceau, Georges, 147–48
Cleopatra's Night (Hadley), 207n
Cleve, Joos van, 42
Cleveland, Grover, 15
Cocteau, Jean, 132
Cohen, Harriet, 152
Colby, Mrs. Bainbridge, 124
Columbia Broadcasting System, 200–201
Comstock, F. Ray, 133
Confrey, Zez, 156
Congress, U.S., 23, 101
Connelly, Marc, 163
Conried, Heinrich, 17, 18, 30–31, 52–54, 56, 72

Constancy (Boyce), 132
Constantine, King of Greece, 93
Contemporaries (Steele), 132
Converse, Frederick, 207n
Cook, Jig, 132
Coolidge, Calvin, 183
Cooper, Lady Diana, 140–45
Cooper, John Julius, 142–45
Copeau, Jacques, 130–33
Coppélia (Delibes), 63
Coq d'Or, Le (Rimsky-Korsakov), 108
Cornell, Katharine, 130, 157
Costigan, Edward P., 204
Covarrubias, Miguel, 154
Crane, Hart, 160–62
Cravath, Paul, 74, 75, 78, 111, 124, 200
Cristoforo Colombo (Franchetti), 54
Crosby, Caresse, 161
Crowninshield, Frank, 150, 151
Cumming, Rose, 167
Cushing, Leonard, 150
Cutting, Fulton, 192
Cyrano de Bergerac (Damrosch), 207n

Damrosch, Walter, 16, 207n
D'Angelo, Louis, 190
Dartt, Helen, 150–52
Dartt, James, 123, 141, 150, 161, 165
Davidson, Jo, 148–49, 152
Dawn (film), 186–87
Death Day (film), 164
Debs, Eugene V., 15, 45
Debussy, Claude, 31
De Koven, Reginald, 207n
Delano, William Adams, 111, 116
Delaware, Lackawanna and Western Railroad, 35
Delaware & Hudson Railroad, 3, 185
Delibes, Léo, 53
De Mille, Cecil B., 159
Dempsey, Jack, 126
Denver & Rio Grande Railroad, 32
Desire under the Elms (O'Neill), 132
Destinn, Emmy, 55
Deutsch, Felix, 10, 11, 28, 78, 89–90, 95, 199

Deutsch, Lili Kahn, 10, 28, 77–78, 89, 92, 95, 199
Deutsche Bank, 13, 14
Devereux, Robert, Earl of Essex, 77
Diaghilev, Serge, 63–67, 69
Dippel, Andreas, 72
Disraeli, Benjamin, 83
Don Giovanni (Mozart), 30, 58, 189
Donizetti, Gaetano, 30
Dorsey, Tommy, 62
Dougherty, Paul, 152
Downes, Olin, 200
Downey, Morton, 62
Druhan, Charles J., 173, 174
Drummond, Mrs. Maldwin, 83
Du Bois, W. E. B., 137
Duffy, Francis Patrick, 121, 125
Duncan, Augustin, 136
Duveen, Joseph, 42, 86

Eames, Emma, 16, 30
Eaton, Walter Pritchard, 31
Eberstadt, Ferdinand, 8
Eberstadt, Maria Johanna, 8
Eddy, Jesse Leeds, 35
Edward VII, King of England, 13, 22
Eisenstein, Sergei, 163–64
Eisenstein in Mexico (film), 164
Elektra (Strauss), 71–73
Elisabeth, Comtesse Greffuhle, 66
Elisir d'Amore, L' (Donizetti), 30
Elizabeth I, Queen of England, 77
Emancipation Act (1871), 11
Emperor Jones, The (O'Neill), 132, 137–39
Enchanted Princess, The (ballet), 65
Episcopal Actors' Guild, 164
Eppstein, Paul, 199
Equitable Trust Co., 125, 150
Erie Railroad, 26
Erskine, John, 60
Eugene Onegin (Tchaikovsky), 57

Fall, Albert, 183
Family Group (Hals), 42
Fanciulla del West, La (Puccini), 57
Farrar, Geraldine, 55
Fast and Loose (film), 194

Faust (Verdi), 16, 17, 51, 69
Felix, David, 89
Ferguson, Elsie, 155
Field, Marshall, Jr., 83
Fiesco (Schiller), 7
Fiesta (Gold), 132
Film Bureau, 186
Firebird, The (Stravinsky), 65
Fisher, Irving, 193
Flagstad, Kirsten, 189
Flaming Angel, The (Prokofiev), 59, 60
Fleischer, Editha, 189, 201
Fletcher, Duncan U., 205
Flotow, Friedrich von, 70
Fog (O'Neill), 132
Fokine, Mikhail, 63
Forbes, Bertie Charles, 12
Ford, Henry, 82
Forza del Destino, La (Verdi), 169
Franchetti, Alberto, 54
Frank, Waldo, 154, 161
Franz Josef, Emperor, 66
Frelinghuysen, Peter, 35
Fremstad, Olive, 31
Frères Karamazov, Les (Copeau), 131
Frewin, Leslie, 133*n*
Frohman, Charles, 17

Gadski, Johanna, 30
Gainsborough, Thomas, 151
Galli, Rosina, 53, 65
Galli-Curci, Amelita, 108, 183
Gallimard, Gaston, 131–32
Gambler, The (Prokofiev), 59
Garden, Mary, 18, 73, 139, 168
Gatti-Casazza, Giulio, 5, 53–60, 64–65, 69, 72, 89, 108, 168, 169, 187–89, 191, 196, 200
George V, King of England, 77
Gerard, James W., 124
Gershwin, George, 60–61, 129, 155
Gershwin, Ira, 60–61, 126
Gest, Morris, 133, 134, 140, 142
Geva, Tamara, 157
Ghosts (Ibsen), 130
Gigli, Beniamino, 189
Gilbert, Charles P. H., 117
Gilbert, William S., 13

Gilman, Lawrence, 189
Gilpin, Charles, 137
Giorgione, 168
Giovanni Gallurese (Montemezzi), 168
Giselle (Adam), 63
Giuliano de Medici (Botticelli), 42, 86
Glaenzer, Jules, 155
Glaspell, Susan, 132
Glaoui, El Hadj Thami, 149
Gleaves, Mrs. Charles, 40
Glorifying the American Girl (film), 159
Goelet, Robert, 30
Goethe, Johann Wolfgang von, 6–7
Gold, Michael, 132, 176
Goldenson, Samuel, 209
Goldman Sachs and Co., 82
Gorky, Maxim, 134
Gould, Jay, 23
Goyescas (Granados), 57
Granados, Enrique, 57
Grau, Maurice, 30
Gray, David, 150, 151
Great Northern Railroad, 47
Greco, El, 92
Greear, David, 195–96
Green, Paul, 162–63
Green Pastures (Connelly), 163
Griffith, D. W., 185
Grumman Corp., 115, 126
Guinan, Texas, 159
Gypsy Baron, The (operetta), 18

Hadley, Henry Kimball, 207*n*
Hals, Frans, 42
Hammerstein, Arthur, 73
Hammerstein, Oscar, 17–18, 57, 70–76
Hampden, Walter, 130, 152
Hanauer, Jerome, 3, 5, 87
Handbook of New York City, 1893 (King), 17
Hänsel und Gretel (Humperdinck), 127, 201
Hanson, Howard, 207
Harding, Warren G., 181–83
Hardy, Thomas, 155
Harkness, Edward, 117, 192
Harriman, E. Roland, 192

Index

Harriman, Edward Henry, 24–27, 29, 32, 34, 44–50, 80, 97, 128, 146
Harriman, William Averell, 24
Hartt, Frederick, 210
Harvey, Col. George Brinton McClellan, 178
Hauptmann, Gerhart, 10
Hawthorne, Nathaniel, 207
Hayes, Helen, 158
Haywood, William D. ("Big Bill"), 45
Hearst, William Randolph, 137
Hecht, Ben, 157
Heine, Heinrich, 41
Heinrich Lanz Co., 7
Heinsheimer, Louis, 20n
Heliker, Sara Jane, 125
Henderson, W. J., 57
Hendricks, Burton J., 81
Henry VIII (Shakespeare), 17
Hertford, Francis Charles, Marguess of, 83
Hesse, André, 149
Hewlett, Walter, 120
Heyward, DuBose, 61
Hibben, John Grier, 125
Hicks, Granville, 161
Hidalgo, Elvira de, 63
Hill, James, 27, 44
Hitler, Adolf, 179, 199
Hodges, John, 83–84
Hofmannsthal, Hugo von, 71
Homer, Louise, 55
Hoover, Herbert, 183, 184, 197
Hopkins, Miriam, 194
Howland, Charles P., 122
Huber, Fritz, 7
Hugo, John Adams, 207n
Humperdinck, Engelbert, 57, 127, 201
Huntington, Henry Edwards, 151
Hutton, Barbara, 96n
Hyde, James Hazen, 29, 31
Hyman, Harold, 208

Ibsen, Henrik, 130
Illinois Central Railroad, 24–25, 47, 48
In Abraham's Bosom (Green), 162
Interiors (Maeterlinck), 130
Interstate Commerce Commission, 4, 45–48
In the Zone (O'Neill), 130
Irving, Henry, 17

Jefferson, Joseph, 17
Jeritza, Maria, 166–67, 170
Joergensen, Johannes, 41
Joffre, Marshal Joseph Jacques Césaire, 104
Johnstone, Justine, 157
Joint Distribution Committee, 196
Jonas, Paul, 28
Jonny Spielt Auf (Křenek), 60, 61
Josephson, Matthew, 101
Joshua, Ella, 22
Judith of Bethulia (film), 185
Juilliard School of Music, 60

Kabale und Liebe (Schiller), 7
Kahn, Addie Wolff, 20–21, 27, 63, 71, 86, 117, 152, 157
  art and, 42–43
  children of, 37–38, 40
  death of, 211
  England and, 78, 85, 95
  Long Island estate of, 112–13, 116
  Morristown house of, 20–21, 36
  and Otto's affairs, 166, 167
  at Otto's death, 208–209
  religion and, 78–79, 120, 121, 164
  Robeson and, 139
  town house of, 117–19
  as widow, 210–11
Kahn, Bernhard, 8–9, 11, 28, 40
Kahn, Clara Maria, 10, 28
Kahn, Emil, 8, 9, 40
Kahn, Emma Eberstadt, 8–10, 28
Kahn, Felix Paul, 10, 40
Kahn, Franz Michael, 10
Kahn, Franziska, 8
Kahn, Gilbert, 37, 78, 81, 111, 117, 125, 211
Kahn, Hedwig, 10, 40
Kahn, Hermann, 8, 9
Kahn, Leopold, 8, 9

INDEX

Kahn, Margaret, 37–41, 77, 78, 86, 87, 123, 125, 148n, 210
Kahn, Maud, 37, 43, 78, 103, 104, 123–24, 202
Kahn, Michael Benedikt, 8, 9
Kahn, Otto
   appearance of, 4–5, 13, 41
   arrives in New York, 15–18
   art collection of, 42
   ballet and, 63–69
   birth of, 11
   childhood of, 9, 11
   death of, 208–11
   death of parents, 28
   Depression and, 193–97, 201–202
   English politics and, 78–85
   family life of, 37–43
   Fifth Avenue town house of, 117–19
   first job, 11–12
   fortune of, 27
   Hammerstein and, 70–76
   Harriman and, 26, 27, 29, 32, 44–50
   illness of, 133, 200, 201
   jazz and, 60–62
   at Kuhn, Loeb, 3–5, 20–23, 32–34, 80, 84, 108, 114, 117, 133, 146, 153, 185, 201, 208
   in London, 13–14, 77–78
   Long Island estate of, 111–16
   marriage of, 20–21
   marriages of children of, 123–26
   and Metropolitan Opera, 5, 29–31, 51–61, 80, 89, 108, 114, 117, 133, 146, 152, 167–69, 187–92, 200–201, 207, 211
   military service of, 12
   Morristown house of, 20–21, 27–28, 35–36
   motion picture industry and, 185–87
   as patron, 160–65
   philanthropy of, 9, 96, 122
   politics and, 175–84
   as public figure, 153–59
   religion and, 78–79, 120–23, 153, 164, 206–207
   Robeson and, 136–39
   Senate testimony of, 202–205
   siblings of, 10
   as theater backer, 128–35, 140–42
   Theodore Roosevelt and, 44, 50
   travels of, 146–53
   women and, 36–37, 141–45, 166–74
   during World War I, 86–110
Kahn, Paul, 10–11, 77–78, 92–95, 199
Kahn, Robert, 10, 11, 199–200
Kahn, Roger Wolfe, 37, 61–62, 78, 114–15, 125, 126, 156, 208
Kahn, Sidney, 123
Kamenka, Boris, 91
Karl Theodor, Elector of the Palatinate, 6–7
Karsavina, Tamara, 63, 65
Kaufman, George S., 157
Kaufman, Mrs. George S., 158
Kelly, John, 121, 125
Kennedy, John F., 24
Kern, Jerome, 60
Kessler, Count Harry, 89
King, Alexander, 162
King, Moses, 17
King, Robert, 112
King's Henchman, The (Taylor), 207n
Kirstein, Lincoln, 69
Koenigskinder (Humperdinck), 57
Kolodin, Irving, 51, 188, 200
Kommer, Rudolf, 141, 142, 151
Krehbiel, Henry, 31, 55
Křenek, Ernst, 60
Krull, Anny, 73
Kuhn, Abraham, 18–20
Kuhn, Loeb & Co., 3, 21, 31–33, 36, 58, 66, 82, 84, 108, 111, 114, 115, 117, 125, 130, 144, 146, 148, 153, 162, 163, 167, 208
   history of, 18–20
   Paramount and, 185–86
   railroads and, 4–5, 23–27, 34, 46, 48, 80, 133
   stock market crash and, 194, 201–205
   during World War I, 87, 88, 91, 97
Ku Klux Klan, 137

Index [239]

Lady, Be Good! (Gershwin), 61, 129
LaGuardia, Fiorello, 209
Lakmé (Delibes), 53
Lane, Franklin K., 47
Langner, Lawrence, 130
Langtry, Lillie, 13, 17
Lansing, Robert, 66
Lardner, Ring, 159
Lazzari, Virgilio, 58
League of Nations, 108–109, 147
Lee, Ivy, 99
Legend, The (Breil), 207n
Lehigh Valley Railroad, 4
Lehman, Helen, 208
Lehman Brothers, 82, 208
Lehmann, Lillie, 17, 30
Lenin, V. I., 91
Lewis, Elizabeth Eberstadt, 8, 13
Lewis, Sir George Henry, 13, 123
Lillie, Beatrice, 158
Lindbergh, Charles, 155
Lindgren, Lydia, 172–74
Liveright, Horace, 161, 162, 195
Lloyd George, David, 84, 106
Loasby, Arthur, 150
Loeb, James, 20n
Loeb, Solomon, 18–20
Long Island Railroad, 111
Loree, Leonor, 3, 5, 185
Louise (Charpentier), 18, 168, 169
Love of Three Oranges, The (Prokofiev), 59
Lower Depths, The (Gorky), 134
Lucia di Lammermoor (Donizetti), 188
Lucio Silla (Bach), 6
Lyautey, Maréchal Louis Hubert Gonsalve, 148
Lysistrata (Aristophanes), 194

M. Kahn & Sons' Bank, 9
McAllister, Ward, 52
MacArthur, Charles, 157, 158
McClintic, Guthrie, 157
McCormack, John, 73, 108
Macdonald, Ballard, 154
Mackay, Clarence, 30, 111
McKenna, Kenneth, 33
McKinley, William, 16, 44

McMein, Neysa, 157
Madama Butterfly (Puccini), 55
Maeterlinck, Maurice, 130
Magda (Sudermann), 17
Magic Flute, The (Mozart), 30
Mahler, Gustav, 54
Mainz Hussars, 12
Man in Armor (Carpaccio), 42
Manhattan Opera Co., 57, 70–73
Manon (Massenet), 168
Mansfield, Richard, 17
Mantegna, Andrea, 42
Manton, Martin, 32
Manuscript Society, 16
Mariano, Nicky, 43, 210
Mariash, Irving, 172–74
Mario, Queena, 201
Marriage of Figaro, The (Mozart), 30
Marriott, Capt. John Charles Oakes, 123
Marta (Flotow), 70
Marx Brothers, 156
Massenet, Jules, 31, 63, 201
Matchiabelli, Prince, 140
Matisse, Henri, 139
Matz, Mary Jane, 18, 89
Mazarin, Mariette, 73
Mefistofele (Boito), 58
Melba, Nellie, 18, 30
Melchior, Lauritz, 188
Melius, Gary, 210
Merchant of Venice, The (Shakespeare), 17
Merry Mount (Hanson), 207
Metro-Goldwyn-Mayer, 170
Metropolitan Museum of Art, 42, 117
Metropolitan Opera, 9, 16, 29, 36, 40, 42n, 51–61, 80, 114, 117, 133, 146, 152, 172, 173, 177, 183, 189, 209–11
  American works at, 207
  ballet at, 63–69, 129
  broadcasts of, 200–201
  Caruso at, 30, 55, 57–58, 70, 108, 190
  Conried and, 30–31, 52–56
  Hammerstein and, 17, 70–76
  Jeritza at, 66

INDEX

Metropolitan Opera (*cont.*)
  Moore at, 167–69, 171
  opposition to translated opera at, 190–91
  proposed new opera house for, 5, 191–92
  Talley at, 187–88
  during World War I, 89
Meyerbeer, Giacomo, 58
Midnight Sun, The (ballet), 65
Mielziner, Leo, Jr., 33
Mignon (Thomas), 17, 169
Miracle, The (spectacle), 127–28, 140–42
Missouri Pacific Railroad, 34
Mitchell, Charles E., 193
Modjeska, 17
Molière, 130
Mona (Parker), 207*n*
Montemezzi, Italo, 168
Monteux, Pierre, 68, 69, 108
Moore, Grace, 167–71
Moore, Marianne, 161
Mordkine, Mikhail, 63, 129
Morgan, J. P., 3, 16, 18, 23–24, 27, 31, 42, 44, 47, 52, 72, 79, 88, 111, 178, 192
Morgan, J. P., & Co., 177, 202, 205
Morgenthau, Henry, 31
Morini, Rosalinda, 171–72
Mortgage Bank of Chile, 204
Moscow Art Theatre, 133–35
Moses, George Higgins, 184
Moses, Robert, 115–16
Mountbatten, Edwina, 22
Moyer, Charles, 45
Mozart, Wolfgang Amadeus, 6, 30, 108, 189
Mrs. Warren's Profession (Shaw), 130
Much Ado About Nothing (Shakespeare), 17
Music Box Revue, 167
Mussolini, Benito, 176–78, 189, 196
Musurgia, 16

Napoleon, 41
Naret-Koning, Johan, 10
Nast, Condé, 150

National Broadcasting Co., 201
National City Bank, 27, 193
Nelson, Edith May, 126
Nemirovich-Danchenko, Vladimir, 134
New York, Chicago & St. Louis Railroad, 4
New York Central Railroad, 4
New York City Ballet, 69
New York Philharmonic Orchestra, 16, 54, 147, 200, 209
Nichols, Beverly, 158
Niesen, Gertrude, 62
Nijinsky, Romola, 64
Nijinsky, Vaslav, 63–68
Noguès, Jean, 73
Nordica, Lillian, 30
Northern Pacific Railroad, 26–27, 47
Northern Securities, 44

Olgin, Moissaye J., 135
Olmsted Brothers, 112
O'Neill, Eugene, 130, 132, 136, 137, 155, 160, 161
One Night of Love (film), 170
Oppenheim, E. Phillips, 180
Oratorio Society, 16
Otello (Verdi), 55

Paderewski, Ignace Jan, 13
Page, Will A., 141–42
Paley, William S., 200–201
Palmer, Corliss, 35
Paramount Pictures, 147, 151, 159, 163, 185–86
Paris Bourse, 34
Parker, Austin, 194
Parker, Dorothy, 133*n*, 157
Parker, Horatio W., 207*n*
Parravicini, Angelo, 55
Parsifal (Wagner), 31, 209
Pasco, Anselm di, 122
Pater, Walter, 147
Patterson, Thomas MacDonald, 45
Pavillon d'Armide, Le (Tcherepnine), 63
Pavlova, Anna, 63, 64, 129
Pearson, Sir Arthur, 96

Index [241]

Pease, Maj. Frank, 163
Pecora, Ferdinand, 202–205
Peixotto, Percy, 148
Pelléas et Mélisande (Debussy), 18
Pelletier, Wilfred, 168
Pennroad Corp., 205
Pennsylvania Railroad, 4, 34, 185, 205
Perera, Valentin, 170
Perrin, Dwight, 113
Pershing, Gen. John, 100, 106
Peter Ibbetson (Taylor), 207n
Peters, Rollo, 130
Petrushka (Stravinsky), 67
Pinchot, Rosamund, 140–41
Pinza, Ezio, 188, 189
Pipe of Desire (Converse), 207n
Plançon, Pol, 30
Poil de Carotte (Renard), 131
Poindexter, Miles, 109
Pollack, Raymond, 10
Pollock, Ellen, 10
Ponselle, Rosa, 169, 189
Poole, Alice, 37
Popper de Podhurgen, Baron Leopold, 166
Porgy and Bess (Gershwin), 61
Porter, Cole, 158
Portrait of a Young Student (Rembrandt), 42, 211
Princess Nicotine (operetta), 17
Prokofiev, Sergei, 59–60
Proust, Marcel, 66, 132
Provincetown Playhouse, 132–33, 137, 194
Prussian Academy of Arts, 11
Puccini, Giacomo, 30, 57, 153
Pullman Car Co., 15
Punton, John, 115
Puritani, I (Bellini), 70
Purves, Austin, 114

Querze, Raoul, 172, 173
Que Viva Mexico! (film), 164
Quo Vadis? (Noguès), 73

Rathenau, Walter, 10, 89
Räuber, Die (Schiller), 7

Reading, Lord, 88, 106
Reinhardt, Gottfried, 141
Reinhardt, Max, 127–28, 140–42
Rembrandt, 42, 211
Renard, Jules, 131
Rest on the Flight to Egypt (Bellini), 42
Reszke, Edouard de, 16, 30
Reszke, Jean de, 16, 30
Rethberg, Elisabeth, 189
Revenue Act (1918), 105
Rigoletto (Verdi), 30, 55, 183, 187, 188
Rimsky-Korsakov, Nikolai, 108
Ring des Nibelungen, Der (Wagner), 30, 57
Rip Van Winkle (play), 17
Ritz Brothers, 156
RKO-Pathé Inc., 186
Robeson, Eslanda, 136n, 138, 139
Robeson, Paul, 136–39
Rockefeller, John D., 99
Rockefeller, William, 44
Roméo et Juliette (Gounod), 168
Romney, George, 42
Root, Elihu, 16
Roosevelt, Franklin Delano, 35, 181, 197
Roosevelt, Theodore, 16, 44–47, 50, 71, 97, 106, 181
Rose, Billy, 126, 154
Rosenkavalier, Der (Strauss), 57
Ross, Harold, 157
Rothermere, Lord, 96n
Rothier, Leon, 189
Rothschilds, 87, 97
Rough Riders, The (film), 151
Royal Opera, 73
Rukeyser, Merryle S., 196
Russell, Henry, 55
Russell, Lillian, 17
Russian Revolution, 91
Russo-Japanese War, 87
Ryan, John Barry, 125
Ryan, Thomas Fortune, 125

St. Jerome (Mantegna), 42
St. John on Patmos (van Cleve), 42
Sala, Mario, 55
Salemme, Antonio, 138

INDEX

Salome (Strauss), 31, 71–73
Salome (Wilde), 130
Salvini, Tommaso, 17
Santa Fe Railroad, 47
Sargent, John Singer, 13
Sarnoff, David, 207
Sartre, Jean-Paul, 132
Sauerbronn, Baron Karl Drais von, 7
Scala, La, 53–55, 65
Scheherazade (Rimsky-Korsakov), 65, 67
Schiff, Jacob, 19–25, 29, 32, 46, 87–88, 91, 97, 100, 108
Schiff, Mortimer, 3, 4, 21, 87, 88, 91, 108, 111, 124
Schiller, Friedrich von, 7
School for Scandal (Sheridan), 17
Schumann, Clara, 10
Schumann-Heink, Ernestine, 30
Schuster, Max, 147
Schwartz, Maurice, 195
Scotti, Antonio, 30, 55
Scull, David, 45
Seagull, The (Chekhov), 130
Securities Act (1933), 196–97
Securities and Exchange Commission, 202
Seidl, Anton, 16
Seligman, Jesse, 16
Seligman, Theodore, 15–16
Seligmann, Sara Zelie, 8
Selwyn, Arch, 186
Sembrich, Marcella, 30, 188
Senate, U.S., 109
  Committee on Banking and Currency, 202–205
Serafin, Tullio, 190
Seume, Johann Gottfried, 9
Sévigné, Madame de, 41
Sganarelle (Molière), 130
Shakespeare, William, 17
Shanewis (Cadman), 207*n*
Shaw, Artie, 62
Shaw, George Bernard, 10, 130
Sheridan, Richard Brinsley, 17
Sherman, James Schoolcraft, 44
Sherman Antitrust Act, 44, 46

Sienkiewicz, Henryk, 73
Simon, Eric, 189
Simon, Richard, 147
Simons, John, 208
Sinclair, Mary, 164
Sinclair, Upton, 164
Slade, W. J., 97
Smith, Alfred E., 183–84
Smith, Sydney, 133*n*
Sniper, The (O'Neill), 132
Southern Pacific Railroad, 46, 48
Spectre de la Rose, Le (ballet), 67
Speyer, Sir Edgar, 14
Speyer & Co., 14, 16, 18
Stalin, Joseph, 196
Stanford, Leland, 23
Stanislavsky, Constantin, 134, 201
Steele, Richard, 133*n*
Steele, Wilbur Daniel, 132
Stenhouse, J. Armstrong, 117, 118
Steuer, Max, 174
Stillman, James, 27
Stokes, Richard, 207
Stone, Charles, 34
Stover, Polly Ann, 125
Straight, Mrs. Willard, 137
Strange Interlude (O'Neill), 154
Strauss, Lewis, 4, 33
Strauss, Richard, 31, 57, 71–73
Stroock, Sol, 173
Sudermann, Hermann, 17
Sullivan, Sir Arthur, 13
Sulzberger, Rudolf, 172
Supreme Court, U.S., 44, 48
Suppressed (Cook and Glaspell), 132
Sweet and Low (revue), 126
Swift, Jonathan, 133*n*
Swope, Herbert Bayard, 201
Swope, Mrs. Herbert Bayard, 155
Sykes, Martin, 38, 41
Symphony Society, 16

Taboo (Wiborg), 136
Takahashi, Baron Korekiyo, 87
Talley, Marion, 187–88
Tate, Allen, 161
Taylor, Deems, 207*n*

Index

Taylor, Adm. Ernest August, 150
Tchaikovsky, Peter Ilyich, 16, 57
Tcherepnine, Nicolas, 63
Teapot Dome scandal, 183
Temistocles (Bach), 6
Tempest, The (Giorgione), 168
Temple Dancer, The (Hugo), 207n
Ten Commandments, The (film), 159
Terry, Ellen, 13, 17
Tetrazzini, Luisa, 18, 73
Thackeray, William Makepeace, 83
Theatre Guild, 130–31
Théâtre du Vieux Colombier, 130, 131
Thorndike, Sybil, 186
Thornhill, Claude, 62
Three Children of Captain Little (Romney), 42
Three Sisters, The (Chekhov), 134
Thunder Over Mexico (film), 164
Thwaites, Lt. Col. Norman, 150
Tocqueville, Alexis de, 41
Tolstoy, Leo, 134
Tosca (Puccini), 30, 153, 166, 189
Toscanini, Arturo, 53–55, 88, 209
Traverse, La (Villeroy), 131
Tristan und Isolde (Wagner), 12, 54
Trovatore, Il (Verdi), 17
Truth and Securities Law, 101
Tsar Fyodor (Tolstoy), 134
Turner, George Kibbe, 81

Unequal Match, An (play), 17
Union League Club, 15–16
Union Pacific Railroad, 23–26, 45–48
United Artists, 154
Untermyer, Samuel, 32

Vanderbilt, Mrs. Alfred, Jr., 117
Vanderbilt, Alfred G., 30
Vanderbilt, Mrs. Cornelius, 192
Vanderbilt, George Washington, 113
Vanderbilt, Mrs. William, Jr., 124
Vanderbilt, William K., 75
Van Vechten, Carl, 137, 138
Velasquez, Diego de, 159
Venizelos, Eleutherios, 93–95
Venuti, Joe, 62

Verdi, Giuseppe, 55
Versailles Treaty, 109, 121, 179
Victor Emmanuel III, King of Italy, 106, 177
Victoria, Queen of England, 13
Villeroy, Auguste, 131
Vollmoeller, Karl, 127, 140
Volpi, Count Giuseppe, 177
Volstead Act (1919), 181

Wabash Railroad, 4, 34
Wagner, Richard, 31, 57, 89, 108, 190
Wald, Lillian, 91
Walker, Jimmy, 159, 188
Walküre, Die (Wagner), 189
Wanger, Walter, 157
Warburg, Felix, 3, 5, 20n, 87, 117, 124
Warburg, Max, 87
Warburg, Paul M., 13, 87
Warren, Harry, 126
Washington Square Players, 129–30, 132
Weir, Andrew, 107
Weiss, Ermaline, 79n
Welles, Orson, 113
Wellman, William, 151
Wertheim, Clara Wolff, 21
Werther (Massenet), 63, 201
Western Maryland Railroad, 4
Wharton, Edith, 102
Whelan, Anne, 125
Whistler, James McNeill, 13
White Buildings (Crane), 160
Whitney, George, 79
Whitney, Harry Payne, 111
Whitney, Mrs. Harry Payne, 63
Wiborg, Mary Hoyt, 136
Wilcox, Herbert, 186
Wilde, Oscar, 13, 17, 130, 133
Wilder, Marshall, 120–21
Wilhelm, Kaiser, 100
Williams, Hannah, 126
Wilson, Woodrow, 91, 97, 100, 105, 107–108, 181
Winchell, Walter, 206–207

Wings (film), 151
Wiseman, Sir William, 167, 171
Wolff, Abraham, 20, 21, 61, 209
Woman of No Importance, A (Wilde), 17
Woollcott, Alexander, 137, 155, 157, 158
Workers' Lab Theatre, 176
World War I, 34, 86–110
Wycherly, Margaret, 136

Yiddish Art Theatre, 164–65, 195
Young, Roland, 130

Zangwill, Israel, 91
Ziegfeld, Florenz, 37, 159
Ziegler, Edward, 40, 66, 168, 188, 200, 201
Zirato, Bruno, 58
Zukor, Adolph, 185